The Great Secret of Mind

The Great Secret of Mind

SPECIAL INSTRUCTIONS ON THE NONDUALITY OF DZOGCHEN

A translation of the Tibetan
Sems kyi gsang ba mngon du phyung ba

Tulku Pema Rigtsal

Translated and edited by Keith Dowman

SNOW LION
BOSTON AND LONDON
2012

Snow Lion
An imprint of Shambhala Publications, Inc.
Horticultural Hall
300 Massachusetts Avenue
Boston, Massachusetts 02115
www.shambhala.com

9 8 7 6 5 4 3 2

Printed in the United States of America
♾ This edition is printed on acid-free paper that meets the American National Standards Institute z39.48 Standard.
♻ This book is printed on 30% postconsumer recycled paper.
For more information please visit www.shambhala.com.

Distributed in the United States by Penguin Random House LLC
and in Canada by Random House of Canada Ltd

Designed and typeset by Gopa & Ted2, Inc.

Library of Congress Cataloging-in-Publication Data

Padma-rig-rtsal, Sprul-sku, 1963–
[Sems kyi gsaṅ ba mṅon du phyuṅ ba. English]
The great secret of mind: special instructions on the nonduality of Dzogchen: a translation of the Tibetan Sems kyi gsang ba mngon du phyung ba / Tulku Pema Rigtsal; translated and edited by Keith Dowman.
pages cm
Translated from Tibetan.
Includes bibliographical references.
ISBN 978-1-55939-401-7 (alk. paper)
1. Rdzogs-chen. I. Dowman, Keith, translator, editor. II. Title.
BQ7662.4.P33913 2012
294.3'422—dc23
2012010125

Contents

Foreword by Tulku Thondup Rinpoche xi
About the Author by Dungse Thinley Norbu Rinpoche xv
Translator's Note xvii
Preface xix
Translator's Introduction xxiii
Introduction 1

The Great Secret of Mind

1. The View 15
   1.1 The nature of the physical world 15
   1.2 The difference between "insider" and "outsider" meditation 19
   1.3 The fallacy of materialism: how the actuality contradicts our assumption that our happiness and sadness depend upon material things 20
   1.4 The unreality of material things 21
   1.5 All things are figments of the mind 25
   1.6 How this body emerges from the karmically conditioned mind, and how we may anticipate the next life 26
   1.7 Distinguishing between impure outer appearances and the pure nature of reality 29
   1.8 All phenomena are unreal: all is just a delusive display of mind 33
   1.9 The method of eliminating belief in concrete reality, the cause of suffering 37
   1.10 The ways of establishing the unreal world as magical illusion in the different levels of approach 40

1.11 People ignorant of the illusory nature of their own unreal mind spin around in confusion 45

1.12 Pure presence itself is buddha 47

1.13 Illustrating the similarity of the world and magical illusion 51

1.14 The conviction that all is unreal accords with the sutras 53

1.15 An introduction to the secret of mind 56

1.16 The dualistic nature of the intellect illustrated in the question-answer method of the sutras 60

1.17 Reasonable proof that buddha-nature exists in our mindstream 65

1.18 When the natural perfection of mind is realized, there is no need to apply an appropriate antidote to each karmic impulse 71

1.19 Reconciliation of the view that the world is an empty, unreal, subjective delusion with the scientific view that it is composed of atoms 72

1.20 Sickness and physical pain are relieved by making a habit of recognizing pure empty presence 75

1.21 Mind is the root of all experience 80

1.22 Knowing the whole world as figments of mind, undisturbed at the time of death, we are released in the bardo 81

1.23 The creative and fulfillment phases are complete and perfect in the space of basic empty presence 84

1.24 Why all beings are continuously bound in samsara 86

1.25 Delusion dissolves when we look at the essence of mind 89

1.26 The advantage of perceiving all things as mere conceptual labels 94

1.27 When pure presence is spontaneously recognized, its veils naturally dissolve 95

1.28 Creativity is necessarily released in pure presence 100

1.29 Samsara never existed except as mere creative visions 102

1.30 In unconditioned pure presence, all buddha-potential is spontaneously manifest 104

1.31 When we abide in unchangeable mind, there is enormous instant advantage 106

1.32 Uncontrolled emotion effects severe ecological damage 108

1.33 The Dzogchen process necessarily and naturally preserves the environment 109
1.34 Illustrating that all things arise out of the basis of mind 113
1.35 With a full understanding of the inseparability of appearances and emptiness, vision is naturally suffused by infinite purity 115
1.36 A finger pointing directly at pure presence 116
1.37 Reasons for the necessity to seek a rigzin-lama to introduce pure presence 120
1.38 The potential of pure being and primal awareness is already manifest in basic pure presence 126
1.39 Dispelling doubt about the unconditioned potentiality of pure presence 127
1.40 How to make the five poisons into the path itself 131
1.41 Until discursive thought dissolves in spaciousness, karmic repercussions must be considered 136
1.42 The benefits of hearing Dzogchen precepts 137

2. Meditation as the Path 141
2.1 First, conviction in the view is essential 141
2.2 The reason for meditation 142
2.3 Disposition of meditation 143
2.4 Without meditation, even trivial events create severe suffering 147
2.5 Meditation removes the attachment that is the root of suffering 150
2.6 The cause of manifest suffering is hope and fear 152
2.7 A short explanation of how to sustain the primal awareness of intrinsic presence 155
2.8 The place of meditation 155
2.9 The disposition of the body 157
2.10 How to sustain pure presence in brief 158
2.11 How to sustain pure presence in general 158
2.12 The five faults that hinder concentration 159
2.13 The eight volitional antidotes to the five faults 160
2.14 In unitary shamata and vipasyana, the nine mental states and the five mystical experiences are correlated 161
2.15 The simple, quintessential disposition 165

2.16 The method of practicing the essential pure presence in sessions 166
2.17 The place of deviation into mystical experience 169
2.18 The distinction between mind and pure presence 176
2.19 The rigzin-lama's personal instruction inspires meditation 177

3. Conduct 181

3.1 An explanation of conduct 181
3.2 The sin of ignorance of the continuity of reflexively liberating thought 182
3.3 The preeminence of the mode of simultaneous arising and releasing of thought 183
3.4 Meditation experience arises naturally in the mindstream 185
3.5 When conduct consists of simultaneous arising and releasing, it is free of karma and its effects 186
3.6 A categorical assertion that Dzogchen transcends cause and effect 189
3.7 So long as dualistic perception obtains, heed karma and its effects 190
3.8 The evidence of the accomplishment of unchangeable self-beneficial pure presence is equanimity in the face of the eight worldly obsessions 195
3.9 The evidence of the accomplishment of unchangeable altruistic pure presence is spontaneous compassion and reliance on the laws of karma and their results 195
3.10 Practitioners of the lower approaches are bound by strenuous effort 198
3.11 Conduct is characterized by the three modes of release 198
3.12 The perspectives of both sutra and tantra agree in rejecting gross emotivity 200
3.13 Infusing conduct with the six perfections 202
3.14 Addiction to wealth leads to suffering 205
3.15 Everyone, high and low, has been a slave to attachment 206
3.16 The stupidity of suicide 209
3.17 With detachment, the mere possession of wealth and fame does no harm 211
3.18 Others are served best by an unselfish mind 213

3.19 When we know objects of attachment as delusion, the five sensory pleasures do us no harm 215
3.20 Those with pure presence are labeled "buddha," while the ignorant are "sentient beings" 217
3.21 Three special features of intrinsic awareness 218
3.22 Discursive thought necessarily dissolves into basic pure presence 219
3.23 Detachment from samsara, nirvana, and the path between them is the crux 221
3.24 "Hand-holding" instruction, in short 223

4. The Attainment 227
4.1 The spontaneous manifestation of buddha-potential in basic pure presence 227
4.2 Knowing the great perfection: buddha in one lifetime! 229
4.3 Contemporary stories of physical dissolution and liberation in a rainbow body 232

5. The Four Bardos 235
5.1 For those of middling acumen: instruction about liberation in the bardo 235
5.2 The bardo of life 236
5.3 The bardo of the process of dying 238
5.4 The actual practice in the bardo of the death process 240
5.5 Consciousness sublimation is among the five nonmeditation methods of attaining buddha 244
5.6 The bardo of reality 245
5.7 The bardo of becoming 247

Author's Colophon 253
Selected Glossary 255
Works Cited 257

Foreword by Tulku Thondup Rinpoche

> The nature of the mind is the ultimate sphere, like space.
> The nature of space is the meaning of the innate nature of the mind.
> In truth they are not separate: oneness is the Great Perfection.
> Please, you must realize it at this very moment.
>
> —LONGCHEN RABJAM

AWAKENING OF intrinsic awareness (*rig pa*), the innate nature of the mind as it is, is the realization of the ultimate nature of everything and the attainment of buddhahood. That is the great secret of the mind.

Each person is composed of body and mind. The body is precious, but like a hotel, it is a temporary abode of the mind—a collection of gross elements destined to dissolve into the earth.

Mind is a stream of consciousness produced and functioning by grasping at mental objects as if they had a truly existing "self" or entity (*bdag 'dzin*) with the passion of emotions—creating positive and negative deeds (*karma*) and causing joyful and painful reactions. Mind, not the body, is the identity of who we are as an ordinary person.

According to esoteric Buddhist teaching, such as Dzogpa Chenpo (*rdzogs pa chen po*; *mahasandhi*) or Dzogchen, the Great Perfection, mind has two aspects: the conceptual or relative mind (*sems*) and intrinsic awareness, the true nature of mind (*sems nyid*), which is buddhahood. Intrinsic awareness is the ever-present unity of the ultimate sphere (*dbyings*) and primordial wisdom (*ye shes*) as one taste.

Through training in meditation, we purify the two obscurations—emotional afflictions (*nyon sgrib*) and intellectual duality (*shes sgrib*)—of the mind, and we perfect the twofold accumulation (*tshogs*)—meritorious deeds (*bsod nams*) and realization of wisdom (*ye shes*).

As the result of such meditations, we realize the intrinsic awareness of the mind, the essence of which is openness (or emptiness—*stong pa nyid*) and the nature of which is clarity (*gsal ba*) and compassionate power that is ceaseless and all-pervasive. Then, naturally, we attain the threefold buddha-body: the perfection of twofold purity is the ultimate body (*chos sku*) of buddhahood. The ever-present pure forms (*sku*) of the five classes (*rigs*) of buddhas and the pure-lands (*zhing khams*) with fivefold wisdom (*ye shes*) and five certainties (*nges pa*) are the enjoyment body (*longs sku*). The emanation of infinite appearances to serve ordinary beings is the manifestation body (*sprul sku*). Kunkhyen Longchen Rabjam says,

> Having perfected the skillful means [merit] and wisdom,
> You accomplish buddha-bodies, wisdoms, and actions.[1]

All beings possess such buddha-nature in their innate nature. For most of us, though, it remains secret, as we have not even a clue as to its presence because it has been fully covered by the emotional and intellectual clouds of the mind that are rooted in dualistic grasping.

Attainment of buddhahood is not about getting somewhere else through some external means. It is about awakening the innate nature of our own mind itself, as it is, and transcending the conceptual mind. Rigzin Jigme Lingpa writes,

> Realization of the intrinsic awareness that transcends the mind
> Is the unique teaching of Dzogpa Chenpo.[2]

The Third Dodrupchen writes, "In Dzogpa Chenpo, you meditate solely on the intrinsic awareness of the mind, using it as the path training. It does not employ thoughts (*rtog pa*) since thoughts are mind (*sems*). Having made the distinction of intrinsic awareness from mind, you just contemplate on it."[3]

1. Drime Odzer, *Rdzogs pa chen po sems nyid ngal gso* (India: Dodrupchen Rinpoche), folio 51b/5.
2. Jigme Lingpa, *Yon tan rin po che'i mdzod dga' ba'i char* (India: Dodrupchen Rinpoche, 1985), folio 42b/4.
3. Jigme Tenpe Nyima, *Rdzogs chen skor*, in *Dodrupchen Sungbum* (Dodrupchen Rinpoche edition), vol. Cha., folio 7b/2.

In this lineage, not only have many meditators realized the true intrinsic awareness, buddhahood, but they have also physically transformed their gross bodies into subtle light bodies or fully dissolved them without leaving any remains behind at the time of death as the sign of their merging into the union of the ultimate sphere and primordial wisdom.

Dzogchen is the swiftest path and easiest goal to attain. Paradoxically, however, it is also the hardest for many of us to realize, as we are completely trapped in the habits of elaborate dualistic concepts and emotional afflictions, with no idea how to ease them and awaken the ultimate openness (emptiness) of our own minds. That is why Kyabje Dudjom Rinpoche once gave me this most simple and profound teaching, "The greatest difficulty of Dzogpa Chenpo meditation is that it is too easy for many to comprehend!"

In order to make the journey on this path and realize the true intrinsic nature of the mind as it is, it is essential to be under the careful guidance of a truly awakened master. Because of our strong habits of dualistic perception, without guidance we would easily fall into the traps of dualistic perception in various gross or subtle layers of the mind, without our recognizing them, while our meditation is in progress.

The inner secrets of the mind taught in Dzogchen that have been whispered among the fully awakened masters for centuries in the sacred sanctuaries of the Himalaya have been revealed clearly and thoroughly in this book by the highly accomplished teacher Tulku Pema Rigtsal Rinpoche. Keith Dowman, with his brilliant gift of letters, has rendered this text into English with great care.

Tulku Rinpoche, who comes from the lineage of Degyal Rinpoche of the Dudjom Lingpa tradition, received this teaching from the greatest Dzogchen masters of the twentieth century. In particular, he was taught and trained in the high remote mountains of Eastern Tibet by two most brilliant scholars and ascetic hermits, Khenpo Dawai Wozer of Rahor and Khenpo Choying Khyabdal of Horshul, of the Longchen Nyintig lineage as their heart-son for years.

The fundamental teaching of Mahayana Buddhism in general and of Dzogchen in particular—the profound philosophical views, precise meditation techniques, and the ultimate goals of attainment—are elucidated in this book in the clearest possible way, with citations and anecdotes for scholars and novices alike. For anyone who is open to learning the sacred secret of the mind that we all treasure, this is an eye-opening book to read.

Tulku Thondup Rinpoche
The Buddhayana Foundation, USA

About the Author
by Dungse Thinley Norbu Rinpoche

TULKU PEMA RIGTSAL RINPOCHE was born in 1963 to his wise father, the second Degyel Rinpoche, Pema Jigme Namgyel, and his mother, Kyama Tsering. At the age of three, he was recognized by His Holiness Kyabje Dudjom Rinpoche as the reincarnation of Chimme Rinpoche, the head lama of Ngari Pureng She Pheling Monastery, which is Riwo Gedenpa. Chimme Rinpoche was one of the best qualified disciples of the first Degyel Rinpoche and was recognized as one of the successive rebirths of the great Indian saint Pha Dampa Sangye. Until the age of nineteen, Tulku Pema Rigtsal studied Tibetan reading, handwriting, composition, and so forth, and the sadhana practices of the Dudjom Tersar (New Treasure Teachings), under his father, Degyel Rinpoche.

For more than a decade after turning nineteen, Pema Rigtsal Rinpoche, accompanied by Khenchen Dawai Wozer, received the teachings from Khenchen Choying Khyabdal Rinpoche. While studying under Khechen Choying Khyabdal Rinpoche, he studied and contemplated the *Zhungchen Chusum* and the teachings of Rongzompa, Longchenpa, Mipham Rinpoche, Jigme Lingpa, and Ngari Panchen.

In 1985, in Phurba Chen, in Humla Yolwang, in the far northwest of Nepal, he established Namkha Khyung Dzong monastery, building its exterior structure and inner supports (altars, libraries, and so on) for worship. About 150 monks now reside there. Besides continuously teaching sutra and tantra, the *Zhungchen Chusum* in particular, with a special emphasis on the wisdom views of Mipham Rinpoche, he also stayed in retreat to read the *Kangyur* and *Nyingma Gyubum*. He has completed a closed three-year and a six-month retreat as well.

In general, he gives teachings on the Tersar Preliminary Practices, the *Kunsang Lamai Zhalung*, *Bodhicharyavatara*, and the *Richo*, *Nangjang Neluk Rangjung*, and other Dudjom Tersar teachings, to the people of Humla and those from the Ngari part of Tibet, and especially to those among them who are sincere in their practice. He continues to teach and spread the profound teaching of this tradition.

He has mainly received empowerment, transmission, and teachings from his root gurus such as Kyabje Dudjom Rinpoche, Kyabje Dilgo Khyentse Rinpoche, Kyabje Dodrup Rinpoche, Kyabje Penor Rinpoche, and Khenchen Dawai Wozer. He also mentions my name among his lamas; I am thankful to him for very generously including me on this list.

So, in his present situation and circumstances, Pema Rigtsal Rinpoche does not lack the noble qualities of learning and sincerity. In my own experience of him, however, the presence of such noble qualities depends upon the absence of the demon of pride.

May sublime vidyadharas and all those with the eye of wisdom constantly watch over him with compassion. I pray with whatever prayers I know that the great waves of benefit that he generates for Buddha's teaching in general, and particularly the study and practice of the Kama and Terma teachings of the Nyingma and Tersar traditions, from his ancestors up to his holy father, increase, like rivers in summertime, and that he has a long life.

Translator's Note

A WORD ABOUT the manner of this translation: In the first place, Tulku Pema Rigtsal wrote this treatise for the East Asian students who requested it. Second, it is written with his Tibetan and Nepali monk-students in mind. Third, he had Tibetan youth in mind, youth educated in modern institutions who have been alienated by the heavy, conservative nature of the tradition in the exile community and may be brought back to sympathy with it by a more modern presentation of the dharma. Fourth, it has been written for Western Buddhists who may be attracted to Dzogchen by its current high media profile and for Western students of Dzogchen. In order to accommodate this mixed readership, we decided that the intended meaning pointing at the nature of mind should take precedent at every conceivable juncture over the grammatical and linguistic peculiarities of the Tibetan. The translation has thus become a paraphrastic rendition of the original. Furthermore, editing the text while translating it, we have sometimes amended it by addition or subtraction in order to clarify and elucidate the vital meanings for the benefit of one set of readers or another.

I extend my gratitude to Tulku Pema Rigtsal Rinpoche for the opportunity to translate and edit this book and to write an introduction to it. I would like to add my thanks to his for the fine and generous editing contribution of Michael Friedman and Michael Wakoff, the Snow Lion in-house editor.

Keith Dowman
The Great Stupa of Boudhanath
Kathmandu, Nepal
March 1, 2010

Preface

IN THIS SCIENTIFIC AGE, in all parts of the world, East and West, technology is improving our external environment. But hand in hand with technological development arise conflict, disease, and degeneration of the environment. Likewise, the many new types of weapons of war pose a great threat to both the world and its inhabitants. As a result, we all suffer intensely in a way that was unimaginable five hundred years ago. The suffering brought about by new illnesses and fear of modern weapons overwhelms the pleasure arising from technological advance, and everyone in this world, from the rich to the poor, suffers equally in this regard. Someone who experiences complete and perfect well-being, mentally and physically, is extremely rare. Further, if we consider that, no matter how great an abundance of possessions people have, many still kill themselves, and that every day still more and more people threaten others under the pretext of acting on behalf of culture or religion, it becomes clear that materialism cannot make this world a happy and pleasant place.

If we wish to enjoy a pleasant and happy life, first of all, we need the cause of happiness, which is loving-kindness and compassion. For example, in order for a household to be happy, it is vital that there be love and affection between husband and wife. In the same way, such sentiments are needed between friends, between cultures, and between countries. In short, once there are two people together wishing for happiness and well-being, loving-kindness and compassion must arise, each toward the other. Moreover, they need a pure intention, free of both expectation of reward and selfish attitudes. This is very important. If that is lacking, our loving-kindness and compassion are biased and partial, and when we encounter negative circumstances, we are conflicted, and again we suffer. It is as the

Tibetan proverb says, "When our compassion wears out, anger becomes the enemy."

Genuine loving-kindness and compassion that are free of selfish intentions and expectation of reward are like wonderful medicines that can benefit the whole of society. Until impartial loving-kindness and compassion are present, no matter how strong an affection may dwell in a kind person's heart right now, and no matter how strong the bond between different countries, such sentiments can never last. The hope that something will accrue in return may produce disappointment that stirs up resentment, and once again conflict will arise. The root of the problem is selfishness. If we can be free of such selfishness and take on loving-kindness and compassion, like fragrant scent on top of gold, then society as a whole may improve.

In this book, *The Great Secret of Mind*, I have tried to explain how to abandon selfish attitudes and give rise to uncontrived loving-kindness and compassion by means of the technique of the Great Perfection. From the general perspective of dharma practitioners, it is a way to accomplish buddhahood in their next lifetime and enjoy ultimate happiness. Not only that, but even for those who do not accept the likelihood of future lives, it is clear that, in each of us, as in society at large, the five poisons—ignorance, attachment, aversion, pride, and jealousy—cause suffering; clear also that anger and jealousy not only cause conflict between countries and discord between couples but may even lead people to the drastic measure of murder and suicide. It is my hope that this book will act as a means of relief and solace for all of these people.

I have written this book mainly for those of the younger generation who have an interest in dharma. Moreover, the monastery where I live, in the Humla district in west Nepal, is not far from Mount Kailash, and I often meet young trekkers from East and West who are on their way there. I have met many who, even though they have no belief in buddha-dharma, are curious about it, and when I discuss it with them and answer their questions, most of them seem to appreciate it. Not only that, but several times I have received messages from people telling me that the dharma I explained to them has been of great benefit in their lives. For these reasons, with these young people in mind, I have often thought it would be beneficial if I were to write a book. Further, my Taiwanese students, such as Shen Yee Ling and others, told me repeatedly that it would be very helpful if I would gather all the dharma teaching I had given until now and put it into a book.

To mention only the key people who helped during the composition of this book and its translation into English, first of all, I would like to thank both Tulku Kundrol Nyima and the monk Yonten for tidying up the text the first time round. I would also like to thank the monk Kyabne, who helped me search for reference texts and so forth while I was writing it, and Tsultrim, who later typed the Tibetan text into the computer and proofread it several times.

I would like to thank my translator and editor, Keith Dowman, who gave so much time and effort to translating the text into English, preparing the English edition, and writing a critical introduction; Tenzin Dorje, who assisted him and freely gave so much of his time; Sonam Lhundrub, who helped explain many crucial points during the translation process; my student Nyima Gyeltsen, who helped clarify different points to the translator while I was in a one-year retreat; Michael Friedman for the final editing of the English translation; and my younger brother Sangye Gyatso, who has overseen the entire project and also assisted with interpreting into English. To all of those who have helped, I would like to thank you from the depths of my heart.

Translator's Introduction

IT SHOULD BE STRESSED at the outset that the author of *The Great Secret of Mind*, Tulku Pema Rigtsal Dorje, is a fully ordained Buddhist monk. Not only is he a bhikshu, he is also the abbot of a large, functioning monastery integrated into the social fabric of the Himalayan society that it serves. He has in his charge 150 young and not-so-young monks who look to him for guidance on the Dzogchen path within the frame of the Nyingma school's religious training. He is also the guiding light of a group of tantric yogins and *ngakpas* who received Dzogchen instruction from his father, a highly respected tantric yogin from a Khampa family that had settled in the Mount Kailash area and built a monastery there (Namkha Khyung Dzong) in the early part of the twentieth century. Further, Pema Rigtsal is steeped in the Tersar tradition of Dudjom Rinpoche Jigtral Yeshe Dorje, another of his root gurus, who was very much concerned with the integration of the monastic and the tantric ethos, and thus emphasized the teaching of the three disciplines—monastic, bodhisattvic, and tantric—as unified and noncontradictory. But it is as a Buddhist monk whose discipline is derived from the Buddha's *vinaya* and *abhidharma* that Pema Rigtsal teaches Dzogchen.

Tulku Pema Rigtsal's background is important for a number of reasons. First, he is one of the last Tibetan tulkus to receive the benefit of a full traditional training without the interference of Chinese Communist authorities or the distraction of popular Western culture. He is one of only a handful of tulkus who run monasteries in the traditional manner, while ministering to the local community that created them. The Western Nepali-Tibetan borderlands in Humla provide that opportunity. Pema Rigtsal received a comprehensive academic training from several highly regarded khenpo scholars in Nepal, Sikkim, Bhutan, India, and also Tibet. This not only gave him grounding in the tradition of the Mahayana sutras but also, in India, opened up a window on the modern, western world. To counterbalance that sutric education and to plunge himself deeply into the strictly Tibetan cultural aspect of Vajrayana, he spent seven years in Tibet, five of them at the Dzogchen Gompa in Kham. In that way, he is a tulku who combines the qualities of a Buddhist pandita-academic, comfortable in monasteries, with those of a yogin-meditator who knows the rigors of retreat in a snowline hermitage. He has utilized the fruit of this education to teach buddha-dharma, in general, and Dzogchen, in particular, in Southeast and East Asia. He has thereby confronted the quandaries of Vajrayana praxis in the modern world and has arrived at various important conclusions regarding them. Finally, he is a Buddhist monk practicing Dzogchen, and that identity has brought the paradoxical complexities of sutra vis à vis Dzogchen into clear focus.

This book may appear at first sight, therefore, to be a textbook of graduated, progressive Dzogchen. With its accent on sutric Mahayana Buddhism, it may seem to be written for monks of the Nyingma school. But if we were to sieve out the pure Dzogchen precepts that are contained herein, we would hold in our hands the keys of radical Dzogchen, the pure Dzogchen of the old tantras. The structure of the text whereby the secret Dzogchen instruction forms a patchwork together with moralistic homilies and instruction on meditation technique imitates the manner in which recognition of the nature of mind may arise within the framework of the practices of Vajrayana Buddhism. Essentially, then, the message is, "Catch the ultimate meaning if you can, but otherwise settle down to a life of immersion in the tantric cultural traditions of old Tibet until your time is right, or until the synchronicitous moment adventitiously occurs." As Rongzompa says in *Applying the Mahayana Method*,

> For those who are unable to remain in the natural state that is the great perfection, we teach the graduated, progressive mode of striving.

And as Pema Rigtsal himself maintains:

> We will be released by the realization that everything is the intrinsic creativity of pure presence. When we fail in this

> understanding, holding object and subject as two, we wander in samsara where we need to depend upon antidotes and gradual progress on a path of cultivating the good and rejecting the bad.
>
> Until we recognize creativity itself as the magical illusion of pure presence, until we have gained confidence, optimized our creativity, and attained release, we must train on a gradual path.
>
> So long as we are plagued by dualistic concepts, like the viewer of a painting who sees in three dimensions what the artist had painted in two, we must distinguish between view and meditation. For this reason, the yogins and yoginis should strive in their meditation in a secluded place.[4]

Another way of saying it is that until the factors of enlightenment arise synchronistically and adventitiously in the mind, there is nothing better to do than sit and meditate. The merit accumulated may facilitate communication with one's fellow creatures and the environment because contrived meditation for the most part produces greater facility on the monastic or bodhisattvic path. More specifically, the meditative techniques of *shamata* (calm abiding) and *vipasyana* (insight meditation) are most usefully practiced in the absence of realization of the view, or in the case of some kind of permanent regression from the view. When the lama is preaching the value of the graduated path, insisting upon the importance of shamata as the method of taking us up the ladder of Dzogchen through the stages of Cutting Through (*trekcho*) and Direct Crossing (*togel*), rather than providing a method of realization, he is preaching the value of monastic Vajrayana culture. If shamata were effective in the recognition of the nature of mind, the world would be full of Dzogchen masters. Pema Rigtsal writes,

> But in actuality, the intrinsic awareness of Dzogchen is not produced or initiated by causes and conditions, for the potential of pure being and primal awareness is intrinsically present and manifests spontaneously.

4. All extracts in this introduction not otherwise attributed are from Pema Rigtsal's *The Great Secret of Mind*, contained in this volume.

> Apply effort to cultivate the sutric approach to buddha but allow not even a whit of aspiration to arise regarding the pure presence of *rigpa*.

The culture of monasticism, preferred by the Tibetans since the second propagation of the dharma in Tibet, may be a superior way of life in comparison with liberal market capitalism, but it does not specifically facilitate experiential understanding of the nature of mind or spontaneous release in the timeless moment of the here and now more than does any other culture. Insofar as the Tibetan monasteries drew in all types of minds from all social classes, those minds were all expected to enter the tunnel of learning that began with the sutras and ended with Vajrayana praxis. That curriculum contained no element that on its own could supply the wherewithal of Garab Dorje's first precept—recognition of the nature of mind. Buddhist (and also Bon) monasticism had greatly overshadowed and suppressed the old shamanism that did in fact contain no small measure of experiential and initiatory skillful means.

In order that all applicants diligently settle down to a monastically based life of study, reflection, and contemplation, they must possess an inner conviction that the progressive path of the Vajrayana does indeed lead to consummate Dzogchen; skillful introduction to goals and techniques provides and supports that conviction. Pema Rigtsal explains:

> Whether we wish to meditate through inseparable shamata and vipasyana in the ultimate Dzogchen manner, or whether we seek the five supersensory powers and temporary happiness in the realms of the gods or men, first, in order to become fit for the task, we need to cultivate the mind, just as we need to cultivate a field to prepare it for crops. If we train in shamata at the beginning, we prepare for the pure presence of Dzogchen.
>
> To reveal that vision we need to have confidence in meditation. If we lack such confidence, we will not be able to remove the veil of dualistic delusion. What we call "meditation" is nothing but a confident view, keeping pure presence fixed leisurely within that view. When we have gained confidence in meditation, all the phenomena of samsara, nirvana, and the path

> from one to the other arise as forms of emptiness, apparent yet nonexistent. Those forms are the path, and traversing it there is neither hatred for an enemy nor love for a friend, neither hope for nirvana nor fear of samsara. Moreover, when our potential for such meditation is realized, both samsara and nirvana are bound together in the one cosmic seed, free of all conceptual elaboration, and whatever we have specified, focused on, imagined, referenced, or elaborated will gradually vanish, like mist dissipating in the sky.

But in this work, insofar as Vajrayana and Dzogchen are considered side by side, in the same breath, as it were, the author lets the cat out of the bag when it is made clear that direct experience of the nature of mind cannot be induced while under a cloud of dualistic thinking on any of the nine approaches, which include Cutting Through and Direct Crossing:

> Applying ourselves to a process with the impure delusions of the vision of ordinary beings, or with the pure or impure vision of yogins or yoginis, as the case may be, or even with the Buddha's pure vision, there is no way to avoid the distinctions inherent in the rejection of some sensory appearances, the acceptance of antidotes, the graduation of stages and paths, and the difference between karmic cause and effect.

And in *The Heart-Essence of Vimalamitra*, Longchenpa says,

> Buddha will never be attained on the paths of the nine graduated approaches by engaging in their view, meditation, and conduct. Why not? Because in the views of the nine approaches, there is only intellectual conjecture that is sometimes convincing and sometimes not, but which can never induce the naked essence.

In this context, Pema Rigtsal explains,

> This pure presence is primordially free of conceptual elaboration and is the contemplation of the minds of all the buddhas. Putting any effort into purifying it or adulterating it by concepts

> tends to conceal its nature and is counterproductive. We need to abandon all effort, along with deductive reasoning and speculative concepts.

Shamata meditation technique is not exempt from this blanket rejection of all contrived meditation methods:

> During formal contemplation, gross happiness and sadness will not arise, but when we get up from shamata, the joy or the pain will come as before. Just as we contain a heap of dust by sitting down slowly on it, but upon our getting up, the dust arises in clouds, in the concentrated absorption of child's play, gross thoughts are stopped for a while, and we seem to experience happiness, but when we arise from the concentration, we find that more gross thoughts intrude than before.

Shamata, concentrated absorption, does not induce recognition of the nature of mind, but it can provide a relative calm in which to appreciate the profound refinements of cultural Vajrayana. Indeed no cause or condition can make manifest the realization of pure awareness as the ground from which all causal phenomena arise. However, it is the defining belief of this latter-day Dzogchen lineage that the rigzin-lama is the doorway into the natural state of mind, the timeless moment of the here and now:

> To find the natural state of mind that is the great perfection, there is no other way than through a lama. Furthermore, we need to depend upon such a one with faith, pure vision, and devotion.

The rigzin-lama is he in whom the inexpressible nature of mind effloresces as a constant illusory display of clear light. Or rather it is he whom we recognize as buddha:

> If we recognize our lama as buddha, then we will receive the blessings of buddha; if we recognize our lama as a yogin, then we will receive the blessings of a yogin; and if we see our lama as an ordinary human being, then we will receive no blessing at all.

In this way those of "middling acumen," those who do not realize the nature of mind immediately it is pointed out to them, those who immerse themselves in the religio-cultural modes of the tradition, attain the understanding of the spaciousness of pure presence where the dichotomy of relative and absolute no longer occurs. As Rongzompa says in *Applying the Mahayana Method*,

> For those who are unable to remain in the natural state that is the great perfection, we teach the mode of striving. Even though they practice that graduated, progressive mode, their view is still based in Dzogchen. Since the great bliss of the luminous mind is the root of all experience, it has the power to cure every sickness that afflicts us.

> Those who cannot abide in effortless Dzogchen are taught the path of endeavor that requires exertion. In the Dzogchen view, they will also succeed.

In this way, a life of meditation praxis is open to all, on any of the nine levels of approach, each involving a different lifestyle. On the sutric path, Buddhist culture induces some happiness in this lifetime and prepares those of middling acumen for death and the advent of the bardos, in which buddhahood may indeed be attained, and failing that, a better rebirth. Making no clear distinction between the psychological and the cultural, the nine levels of the Vajrayana path vary according to the manner of cultural conditioning. The dharma agenda in the Nyingma scheme of things, therefore, is to provide socially beneficial cultural activity for people across a range of differing aspirations and personality types. The specific modes offered are monastic, householder, and renunciate. The activity in these varying lifestyles, through time, may modify our karma, change our habits, and thereby induce a better rebirth, but it will not in itself take us an iota closer to Dzogchen. If and when these monks, bodhisattvas, and yogins and yoginis on the graduated path become aware of the nature of mind in the Dzogchen view and fall into the state of nonmeditation, they do not drop the lifestyle that is consistent with their Buddhist vows. Consonant with the atiyoga precept "without acceptance or rejection," they continue on the graduated path of the sutras without changing anything at all. But in a mind suffused by Dzogchen view and meditation, the precept of nonaction necessarily engages, and although, from the outsider's point of view, a monk or bodhisattva may still seem to be striving on the graduated path, internally the Dzogchen ethos has come to be the apex of his or her outlook, presiding over any other approach.

What this boils down to in practice for the Tibetans is that if their initiatory experience has not provided them with the Dzogchen view and its corollary of nonmeditation, then they must be satisfied with the daily round of their religious culture. Their religious practice may consist of the ascetic hermetic lifestyle of yogins practicing the creative stage or the fulfillment stage. Or it may consist of the lifestyle of neophytes practicing ngondro preparatory practices in a semiretreat situation; of lay tantrika ngakpas performing endless rituals designed to attain buddha or, more likely, to benefit themselves and others on a material plane; of householders committed to their family and professional duties and deeply engaged in their devotions and good works; or of sutric meditators who live a pure lifestyle, ordained or not, engaged essentially in constant shamata or vipasyana meditation. In old Tibet it could have been any of these styles of religious occupation, all denominated as gradual methods leading to enlightenment. In the Dzogchen view, however, they are merely forms of religious culture to be bathed in the illumination that the Dzogchen view provides.

For all these religious people, Dzogchen is approached from outside and below as a goal only to be invoked in prayer, a carrot extended beyond the donkey's nose to make him run. In H.H. the Dalai Lama's famous exposition of Dzogchen at Lerab Ling in France, for instance, he spoke mainly *round about* Dzogchen, describing it from the platform of the graduated path. Naturally enough, from that point of view, he stressed the cultural aspect of Dzogchen, the Vajrayana basis and groundwork, the context of lama worship and devotion, rather than providing the essential precepts of the view and meditation. Perhaps this emphasis on the maturation of the student's mind is derived from the necessity in the Tibetan monastic environment to cultivate the untrained minds of Tibetan nomads and farmers by means, for example, of the Madhyamaka dialectic. But reasoning does not lead to the recognition of the nondual nature of mind. As Patrul Rinpoche makes very clear in his *The Three Incisive Precepts*, the Dzogchen method is grounded in experience. Those who cannot recognize what is immediately in front of their nose here and now can, perhaps, recognize the clear light in the bardo of reality. Otherwise, in both this life and the next, they should immerse themselves in the religious culture of Vajrayana, in study of the sutras and Buddhist logic on the progressive path of spiritual materialism. In this way the Dalai Lama is here in line with the mainstream of Dzogchen teachers in the latter days in stressing the relativist, space-time aspect of Dzogchen rather than its mystical nondual core.

The proponents of this sutric Dzogchen design their lives according to the graduated path described by the Mahayana sutras, fill it with the ethos of the bodhisattva vow, and strive on the difficult path of self-sacrifice. They may take the logical step of ordination and practice tantric ritual in order to speed up the process of attainment of their altruistic goals. In that arena the processes of karmic causality are dominant and all-consuming, and the slow process of purification of karmic conditioning—or rather the reconditioning of the mind—proceeds over many lifetimes or for eons. In the valleys of Tibet, therefore, Buddhist religious activity was the form demonstrated by Dzogchen yogins and yoginis, particularly before the Chinese invasion, when Tibet's political structure was theocratic. In the Himalayan borderlands—in Dolpo for example—farming or yak herding may be the principal activity of the Dzogchen yogin. In the exiled refugee community, he or she may be a doctor or a priest, a trader or a farmer, an artisan or shopkeeper.

The three-in-one ideal that Dudjom Rinpoche has taught, particularly in his commentary on *Ascertaining the Three Vows* by Ngari Panchen, is predicated upon the assumption that the yogin has been inducted into the three levels of Tibetan Vajrayana praxis. These three consist of the sutric ordination that comes with a disciplinary codex, the bodhisattva vow of the perfection of wisdom, and the tantric samayas that imply the predominance of primal awareness. These three sets of vows may be related to outer, inner, and secret levels of practice. The monastic training is the outer; the flexible, superior moral training is the inner; and in secret the tantric samaya vows are sustained. These three levels are integrated into a single lifestyle and religious persona that we can identify in the Nyingma yogin whether dressed as a monk, layman, or ngakpa. The activity of this society of religious practitioners constitutes the *culture* of the Nyingma school, and the praxis of this culture is independent and continues whether or not it is illumined by the Dzogchen view. If it is indeed infused by the Dzogchen view, then it becomes the karmic form presented by the spontaneity of the view. The culture becomes the karma that is infused with light and awareness and eventually is exhausted in the rainbow body or body of light. If the Dzogchen view as an existential reality has not yet suffused that culture, then, as mentioned above, the individual cultivates the cultural form with the certainty of progressing along the path of the bodhisattva and refining the karma that may lead to a higher rebirth.

It seems evident and of huge importance to the vitality and continuation of the essence of the Tibetan tradition—Dzogchen atiyoga—that it should not become mixed up with culturally specific qualities and modes. If Dzogchen remains a factor of Vajrayana while Vajrayana remains a bundle of quasi-shamanic Central Asian concepts and quasi-Hindu tantric rituals and concepts, it continues to be unattractive and irrelevant to the contemporary global mainstream of science and technology. Some lamas of the tradition, particularly Dudjom Rinpoche and Dungse Thinley Norbu Rinpoche, showing the qualities of flexibility and incisive responsiveness that demonstrate their mastery, adapted the traditional forms of teaching and exposition to the needs of their Western disciples. With the difficult recognition that Westerners were not to be monks or religious practitioners in the Himalayan mold, the realization dawned that Western spiritual culture (and particularly the hippie culture that greeted the refugee lamas in India) needed only a minute shift of aspiration to allow the magic of the Dzogchen view to work. These masters saw no need for Western cultural forms to be radically changed and transmogrified into some kind of Tibetan clone-culture, but rather, by a simple redirection toward the ideal of Dzogchen, those in whom the natural state of being was incipiently blossoming could be infused by its illuminating spaciousness and awareness.

Westerners gazing closely at Tibetan monasticism, while retaining deep respect—even to a fault—tend to perceive it as a kindergarten stage. The cultural function of the monasteries has changed in the refugee society (although not much in Tulku Pema Rigtsal's gompa), becoming the means whereby the traditional culture is conserved and sustained particularly through the education of boys who have no initial intention of becoming monks but who cannot afford, or do not possess, the means of attaining a Western-style education in a modern institution. But the epithet "kindergarten" not only denominates the function of educating and socializing children, but also the training of the few monks, whose karma is suited to a lifetime of study, recollection, and meditation, in the Mahayana sutras, in Buddhist logic, in spiritual aspiration, in physical and moral training, and in the priestly functions, such as sanctifying rites of passage.

It is unfortunate that certain ancient Buddhist monastic and atavistic Tibetan attitudes are conserved in the monasteries. Faint traces of these attitudes peer through Pema Rigtsal's anecdotes in his text. Buddhist societies have always upheld the superiority of the monastic ideal and its necessity, and monks of course are the first to support such a view. Denigration of the lay option and the "sadhu" mode follow automatically. The superior and slightly disparaging attitude toward women—including nuns—is sometimes painfully felt, by feminists in particular. Materialism and its financial status-structured hierarchy is presented—and disdained—as a particularly Western affliction, while it should be evident by now that Asia, in general, and Tibetans, in particular, are plagued with gross materialistic attitudes. Such attitudes are held in the first place due to naïve adulation of the high technology developed in the West and only recently available in Asia, and in the second because wealth and conspicuous consumption are seen to indicate the favor of the gods—and therefore merit and virtue—among the wealthy.

So, finally, *The Great Secret of Mind* contains secret Dzogchen precepts hidden among excerpts from a manual of sutric Buddhism together with some gems of tantric instruction. Some readers will understand the sutric path of monasticism in which Tulku Pema Rigtsal is situated as the cultural context, and Dzogchen Ati as the mystical experience unfolding within it, unmarked by monasticism. To put it another way, consonant with Mahayana dogma, the temporal sutric path provides the form and the Dzogchen view-cum-meditation the emptiness. The sutric path, determined by karma, provides the time-space context, which in timeless awareness of the here and now becomes the pure presence of Dzogchen. The lesson in this for the post-Renaissance, post-Reformation West, where religious and lay cultures have been confounded for several hundred years, and in the developed Far Eastern societies into which those attitudes have been transposed, is that Dzogchen yogins and yoginis are completely anonymous, free of any attribute by which they could be recognized. Their activity cannot be defined. Their behavior cannot be described. Their conduct does not accord with any agenda. They wear no badge, or hat, by which they can be labeled or compartmentalized. If their karma is not exhausted in a rainbow body, their activity will appear from the outside to be consonant with their personal karma. If the spontaneity that is naturally induced by the recognition of the alpha-purity of all experience demonstrates an egoless awareness of the dynamic necessity of the totality, cushioned by the vibration of a bodhisattva, it will probably be appreciated only subliminally by those who witness it.

The last word is from Pema Rigtsal:

> In reality, therefore, all phenomena are merely mental labels, and in reality not even the smallest thing exists to be cultivated or rejected. Yogins and yoginis who have this view pay no attention to their own level of accomplishment regarding either attachment to the objective, material aspect of nominal experience or to the degree of any emotional attachment. Such yogins and yoginis make no distinction between high and low views, nor do they pay heed to the speed of accomplishment on the path.

Keith Dowman
Kathmandu
March 2010

Introduction

THE MAIN content of this book is the meaning of Ati Dzogchen, the peak of all Buddhist views and systems of belief. I have explained the view according to my own understanding, using words that are easy to follow, and entwining them with life stories. In this way, I have done my best to make Dzogchen as clear and accessible as possible. Moreover, I have explained the view, meditation, and conduct of Dzogchen in accord with the attitudes of the present age. I hope that this presentation will help those who are studying and enquiring into the dharma in a very broad and unbiased way to increase their understanding of Dzogchen in a way unlike any before. On top of that, I have the great hope that it will teach people how to easily integrate the daily activities of eating, lying down, moving around, and sitting into the practice and how to bring temporary happiness and suffering into the ambit of Dzogchen. This is also the special quality of the meaning explained in this book.

Every single one of us wants happiness and abhors suffering. What use, therefore, is fleeting and constantly changing, defiled happiness? When one has the aspiration to obtain ultimate, permanent happiness, it is extremely important to gain a foothold on the path to liberation in this life, particularly by practicing the profound path of Dzogchen. Other than that, as explained above, those wishing to enjoy a happy and pleasant life must cultivate the causes for that—loving-kindness and compassion—and the genuine source of those two things is Dzogchen.

Furthermore, at present many millions of people are suffering from depression, HIV, and other more severe diseases. Depression (or disturbed mind-energy), for example, is having a highly injurious effect on the overall well-being, development, and harmony of society as a whole. Depression, together with high blood-pressure and liver complaints, and so on, are, in short, all illnesses connected with mind. Mainly due to the affliction of mind by disturbing emotions, we compete among ourselves; and, due to the increase in the population—not only in cities but also in villages—people's living spaces have become very restricted, and the drinking water, air, and so on, have become polluted. As a result many people's mind-energy has become disturbed.

Actually, illnesses and suffering due to substances in the environment afflict us only to a certain, limited extent, but because the minds of sentient beings can scarcely bear even small external negative conditions, small initial irritations can snowball into a huge amount of additional suffering and can sometimes become so unbearable that suicide may result. If, therefore, one has the practice of Dzogchen in all such situations, it will be of vast benefit.

For that reason, if one has the habit of understanding suffering to be self-envisioned, one will thereby be able to make all occurrences of unwanted illnesses and suffering naturally dissolve. If we remain detached from taking external happiness and suffering to be real, even if some kind of calamity, such as an earthquake or war, suddenly occurs, our mind will be able to abide peacefully, naturally, and at ease. We will then be able to benefit others greatly. For these reasons, I consider this book to be something important.

Meeting with my gurus

My greatest fortune is having met solely with gurus who are enlightened beings appearing in human form. Although their conduct and lifestyle is something I cannot judge, nevertheless in my perception each guru has an amazing unique conduct and lifestyle. I have bowed at the feet of some fourteen guru lamas, and there are also a few more gurus with whom I have made dharma connections. My main gurus are Lord of Refuge, Dudjom Jigdral Yeshe Dorje Rinpoche, the master who was prophesied in the treasure scriptures to have the power to lead beings to Ngayab Ling merely by their seeing his body and hearing his name; Lord of Refuge, Dilgo Khyentse Rinpoche; Lord of Refuge, Dodrupchen Rinpoche; Lord of Refuge, Trulshik Rinpoche; Lord of Refuge, Dungse Thinley Norbu Rinpoche; Lord of Refuge, Drubwang Penor Rinpoche; Lord of Refuge, Domang Yangtang

Rinpoche; Khenchen Pema Tsewang Rinpoche; my sublime father, the second incarnation of Pema Dewai Gyelpo, Pema Jigme Namgyel Rinpoche; my paternal uncle Tsewang Rinpoche; Khenchen Dawai Wozer Rinpoche; and Khenchen Pema Choying Khyabdal Rinpoche. I will now describe the conduct and deeds of my lords of refuge.

Khenpo Choying Khyabdal Rinpoche

Before I met Khen Rinpoche, I had heard that he was totally carefree—free of all conventional responses—but when I met him, I saw that he was even more unpredictable than I had been told. At that time, he was old, thin, and not very strong. His room was an old wooden hut four meters square with nothing more than a small wooden box for his bed and a table in front of it, and he was just sitting there cross-legged on the bed. He was wearing old stained woolen robes, and when you looked at his possessions, there was not even five hundred rupees worth of things there in the room. When I had heard about his living conditions, I could not believe it: but now, when I saw it with my own eyes, I had no choice.

Having offered three prostrations, I presented my offering scarf and the letter of introduction from Khen Rinpoche (Khenchen Dawai Wozer) and requested teaching on *The Way of Entering the Mahayana* by Rongzompa. When I explained why and how I had come to meet him, he paid little attention, and combined with a scolding, he gave me oral instructions, pointing out my hidden faults. After looking for a few seconds at the envelope of Khen Rinpoche's introductory letter, he threw it away. "We used to call him 'Long Ears,'" he said. "I never called him 'Khenpo,' and he didn't like me calling him 'Khen Rinpoche.'"

When I think about it, Khenchen Pema Choying Khyabdal Rinpoche was totally different from worldly people. In general, it is the way of things that whoever one may be, one is happy when praised and angry when criticized. Khen Rinpoche was not like that. Even if one were to say to him, "Everyone praises your excellent qualities!" he would act deeply offended and say, "If they see excellent qualities in me, why can't they be like me? I have no need of praise. I know what I'm like. I have no need of criticism. I know who I am." When he would speak like that, I would feel like a debater sitting in front of the lord Nagarjuna—I had no idea what to say and could only sit and watch.

During that period, "perceiving the lama as buddha," as taught in the oral instructions and so on, came about naturally without any effort on my part, and tears would come to my eyes. I came to understand that his scolding of Khen Rinpoche Dawai Wozer was a skillful means to cut through my own pride.

In short, merely through his actions and way of living, I was also able to come to understand that samsara has no essence and that one needs only to cast aside self-grasping and the eight worldly obsessions. Sometimes when he gave oral instructions to students, he would look at a student's conduct and show anger and other emotions; it was clear that at all times he was never separate from Dzogchen's four modes of freely resting, abiding with the three doors naturally wide open, carefree and at ease.

While receiving *The Way of Entering the Mahayana*, it was, due to the text itself being a tremendous blessing and the teacher being highly skilled in explaining dharma, as if I had arrived in a totally new world. Previously, the assertions of the different systems of dogma and the various different explanations of the great scholars had seemed contradictory to me, and I had struggled a lot. But due to the teaching and great kindness and compassion of this teacher, it was as if I had been relieved of an illness, and I felt a great comfort.

From then on, I understood that all the teaching of sutra and mantra (the tantra class) is contained within Dzogchen above them and also that all the nine approaches are devolutions below Dzogchen. Having understood that, unbiased faith unlike anything I had felt before naturally arose in me toward the ocean of texts of sutra, mantra, and the tantra class.

I came to understand that everything is a means to lead us to the path of Dzogchen—the teaching was not just dry words to which I had to pay lip service, as I had thought before, but actually brings us to realization. I also came to understand that all approaches are contained within Dzogchen, and I realized why the crucial points of all practices just come down to Dzogchen.

As a result, a deep-rooted certainty arose within me, and I developed unshakable faith in the teaching and teacher. Sometimes, all of a sudden, the understanding of these present appearances as being unreal and illusory would arise in my mindstream.

While we were studying the fifth chapter of *The Way of Entering the*

Mahayana, at one point Khen Rinpoche's personal experience blazed forth, and, when asking questions, I arrived at a state of naked pure presence unlike anything I had experienced before. Afterward I gained a mountainlike certainty that, beyond this, there is nothing more to resolve and nothing new to understand.

Khen Rinpoche Dawai Wozer

Besides being learned in an infinity of textual traditions and having perfected the excellent qualities of a monk, Supreme Khen Rinpoche Dawai Wozer immersed himself in Dzogchen night and day. Unstained by the eight worldly obsessions, he stayed in solitude and there joyfully took hold of the victory banner of accomplishment. He lived as a hidden yogin-practitioner.

Whenever I met him, a special feeling would come over me. Whatever teaching and advice Khen Rinpoche gave, it was always extremely touching. For example, one day when he was speaking about the benefits of Longchenpa's *Seven Treasuries*, such strong faith was induced in me that my hair stood up on end, my eyes became wet with tears, and I said to Khen Rinpoche that I was going to try to have the *Seven Treasuries* written out in gold. He replied, "It is an excellent project to have the *Seven Treasuries* written out in gold, but the most important thing is to live what they teach, and it's best if you just get wooden printing blocks carved for them."

Similarly, one day he told the life story of Kunu Lama Tenzin Gyeltsen—how for thirteen years Kunu Lama wandered from place to place, meeting teachers, going on pilgrimage, listening, contemplating and meditating on an ocean of different texts, and staying in places where he was totally unknown. Khen Rinpoche praised this kind of lifestyle tremendously. I told him, "I'm also going to do that." He replied, "That is an admirable aspiration. But you should know that for those who are realized, it makes no difference whether they are on the move or stay in one place, and for people like us, it is best not to travel around to many different places; it's better if we stay in one place. Stay in one place and realize the dharma!" As everyone knows well, I am not subject to sudden impulsive thinking, but the way Khen Rinpoche used to teach, his proclamations of truth would shake me up and turn my mind around.

In short, the little knowledge I now have and my external appearance as a dharma practitioner, directly and indirectly, are solely due to the kindness of Khen Dawai Wozer Rinpoche. He has influenced me more than anyone else in my life, and I acknowledge him as one of my root gurus endowed with the threefold kindness I can never forget.

With regard to how I received Dzogchen pointing-out instructions, one time when I was receiving teaching on Longchenpa's *The Treasury of the Dharmadhatu*, I said to Khen Rinpoche, "We're already about halfway through the text, but so far, even though I understand the words, I don't have even the slightest understanding or experience about the real meaning of pure presence [*rigpa*]. What should I do?" Khen Rinpoche then said, "It's not a problem. Supplicate Longchenpa one-pointedly. Chant the root text continuously and then at some point, due to some adventitious condition, you will recognize rigpa.

"For example, the great scholar and undisputed reincarnation Dza Patrul Rinpoche, although he had relied for a very long time on genuine teachers without ever parting from them, he recognized rigpa, the nature of mind, in the following way: Once when Patrul Rinpoche was coming down from Shri Singha, he met Do Khyentse Yeshe Dorje, who was journeying along wearing a sheepskin with a sword hitched around his waist. Although Patrul Rinpoche didn't lack faith in Do Rinpoche, he thought, 'What's wrong with wearing clothes that are in accordance with the dharma?' Do Khyentse knew what he was thinking and all of a sudden grabbed him by the throat and shook him back and forth, shouting, 'Old dog! Old dog!' At that very moment, Patrul Rinpoche recognized rigpa, the nature of mind.

"Likewise, even when the famous Khenpo Tubten was made a Khenchen (teaching abbot) and was teaching sutra and mantra to a huge gathering of students, he had not recognized the nature of mind. One day when he was going to perform a ritual in a village, he slipped while walking over a small bridge and fell into the river below: at that very moment, he arrived at rigpa and came to know the nature of mind."

By telling me many such stories, he made my perception change so that I often thought, "That will happen to me one day." A few days later, in a dream I arrived in a transparent empty cave, like the small tunnels that they build on mountain roads these days. In the middle of the cave was a stone trough filled with fresh and old blood. I thought it must be a place where Hindus make sacrifices, like they do for the black goddess Kali in Nepal. I was terrified and revolted and thought, "I absolutely must drive these terrible spirits away!" With the divine dignity of Vajrakilaya, I uttered HUNG four times in order to expel the spirits, and I scattered oil-grain around. At the same time, sounds of horns, drums, trumpets, and so on, naturally resounded, and with my mind mixing with space, I remained in rigpa. After that my fear and revulsion completely vanished. The next morning, I told Khen Rinpoche, and he said, "What was the state of rigpa like?" I was left without anything whatsoever to say. Then Khen Rinpoche said, "Ah! That's it!" and he was extremely pleased. That recognition was attained through the blessing of the lama.

Dungse Thinley Norbu Rinpoche

Dungse Thinley Norbu Rinpoche is the lord of those skilled in the meaning of samsara and nirvana's being of equal taste as the dharmakaya and apparent existence appearing as instruction. He keeps the form of a great hidden yogin and bestows Dzogchen pith instructions on his fortunate disciples. He possesses some extraordinary qualities.

In 1997, one day Rinpoche came on pilgrimage to the Swayambhu and Boudhanath stupas with a large group of students. In the evening, after returning to his residence, he gave some advice and dharma talk. He acted slightly drunk from drinking wine and gave naked pointing-out instructions. The way he taught then was quite different from the way lamas normally teach. He taught how to sustain rigpa with great naturalness at the very moment attachment and aversion arise. Upon receiving Rinpoche's instructions, I thought, "Today all of these people recognized rigpa. How fortunate they are!" and I became inexpressibly happy and joyful.

Another time, when I met Rinpoche in California, in the evening, when we were making a feast offering and Rinpoche was teaching, he scolded me, saying, "It's true you're very learned, but you're too proud!" and he mocked me. One day he said not just once, but again and again, "It's no use being a great scholar. You need realization. Thinking you're very learned will only harm that, so it would probably be best if you stopped your textual teaching." It made me think that I should offer a pledge to practice, so I asked Rinpoche, "Would it be best to do a one-year Direct Crossing [*togel*] retreat, or a one-year long retreat reciting the entire Nyingma tantras? Please tell me, Rinpoche." "Both are excellent, so do both," he replied. "Which one should I do first?" I asked. He seemed displeased and the next day said again, "Teaching texts to students has spoiled you!"

I then thought to myself, "Before, when I knew nothing at all, and Khen Rinpoche Dawai Wozer told me to teach the dharma from texts, I said to him, 'I don't know anything myself, so how can I teach?' and he replied, 'When I first came to India, I wasn't as learned as you,' and he encouraged me and gave me confidence. As a result, for about seventeen years, I have been teaching fifty or so monks without a break. It seems that by now I have fulfilled Khen Rinpoche's instruction, and it is time to fulfill Dungse Rinpoche's command."

So I said to Rinpoche, "From now on, I vow not to teach even a single verse of dharma." For a little while, Rinpoche didn't say anything. Then he said, "If I tell you not to teach the dharma, won't I have negative karma? I'm not saying that. I'm saying you need to abandon the pride of thinking 'I'm so learned.'"

Later on that evening, after we had made the feast offering, and I had returned to my room, I sat in bed thinking. "Today, something really shocking occurred. I wonder what will happen if Rinpoche really makes me vow not to teach anymore? If I give up teaching the dharma, my life's work will be at an end. Why? Because the source of funding of the monastery is the West and Taiwan and other places where I teach the dharma. If I don't teach there, I'll stop going there. Likewise, if I stop teaching the monks at the monastery, even if I stay there, my whole purpose of being there will be over. I'll also have to give up explaining what to adopt and what to abandon, virtue and vice and moral conduct at the Vajra Guru Mantra Accumulation ceremonies and other dharma gatherings outside Humla. I'll have no work, and it'll be like I'm already old. From today on, I will have nothing to do other than stay in an uninhabited retreat place, and I would be committed to staying there for the rest of my life."

Pondering what would happen, I stayed awake for many hours. I felt very nervous, and when I thought about it carefully, I saw that, just as Rinpoche had said, I had a very strong attachment to teaching the meaning of texts. Even though I believed I was not proud about being learned, as Rinpoche had said, it became clear that I was actually so strongly attached to texts that

I could not bear to part from them. As a result, I understood that whether it was attachment to virtue or vice, it was still attachment and a direct obscuration of the dharmakaya. From then on, seeing my own faults, my attachment to texts decreased. The students of Dungse Rinpoche's lineage have an amazing understanding and quality.

Dodrup Rinpoche

Dodrup Rinpoche is one of the great gurus who showed me enormous kindness in bestowing upon me empowerment, oral transmission, and instruction. Not only that, but in particular, I received his blessings in dreams and visions. When I was staying in a three-year retreat and had almost finished the recitation of Vajrakilaya, one day, in my dream, Dodrup Rinpoche was sitting on top of a throne inside a small shrine room, chanting while playing the damaru and bell. I and a few other monks were there, and at one point in the chanting, Rinpoche said, "It's now time to pay homage, so make the mudras." Then all of a sudden I was naked. I fell on the floor, and my two legs went around my waist and reappeared at the front. My right leg extended over my left thigh, and my left leg extended over my right thigh. They wrapped behind my waist and reappeared at the front, forming a full knot around my waist, and I was transformed into Vajrakilaya. When I woke up, it was like I had no waist, and for a long time I had the experience of my body's being empty form.

Further, in another dream during that three-year retreat, Dodrup Rinpoche was sitting in a tent on top of several flower-covered mounds in a grassy meadow. I told him that I had completed the three-year retreat and its recitation, and he said, "Now you need to recite 1,100,000 *Arapatsana* [Manjushri] mantras. If you do that, it will be like a sharp sword that will cut through all obstacles to the accomplishment of your activities."

Later, when I told Dodrup Rinpoche about those dreams, he said they were very auspicious. I told him, "I want to practice the realization of Manjushri, but there are so many different texts. Which one would be best?" Rinpoche then replied, "My guru is Yugog Chadral. He considered the Manjushri meditation practice from the tantric tradition to be very precious, so do the entire recitation and accomplishment for that." So then I stayed in retreat for about three months, doing the recitation of the peaceful aspect of the tantric tradition of Manjushri. I accumulated exactly one million mantras in that recitation, and, together with the "amendment" recitation, the total was exactly 1,100,000. At the end I realized that the Dodrup Rinpoche who had appeared in my dreams was identical to the actual present Dodrup Rinpoche, and I believe that the guru actually came in person in my dreams.

Domang Yangtang Rinpoche

In general, in the context of the secret mantra Vajrayana and, in particular, in Dzogchen Ati, one sees one's root guru as the Buddha in person, the all-pervasive lord of the mandala, and places his or her commands at the crown of one's head. This is a crucial point, showing that the blessings of the wisdom lineage are transferred solely from the guru. You can see this clearly from whichever guru's life story you look at.

In 1959, during the terrible chaos in Tibet, the great beings who upheld the teaching, monasteries, and teaching centers were struck a vicious blow. During that time, placing his root guru, Lingtrul Rinpoche, on the crown of his head, Domang Yangtang Rinpoche remained in his monastery even though he knew his life was at risk, and he had the chance to escape to India. During the Cultural Revolution, though free of the slightest fault, he took upon himself all the hardships of the fighting and conflict. For twenty-three years, he was incarcerated in Dardo Ranga prison. During that time, the government imprisoned the great gurus, tulkus, khenpos, and most of the high-standing people under appalling conditions, deceiving them with lies, such as telling them that they would educate them in the Cultural Revolution, give them certain rights and different positions, and quickly release them. Some timid and jealous Tibetan people criticized the dharma and the gurus and pretended that they believed in the Cultural Revolution, and some humiliated the lamas, saying how shameful they were, while those with faith in the dharma, standing by, became extremely disheartened. During that time, Yangtang Rinpoche remained unmoving, like a great mountain in the face of snowstorms. He was victorious over all obstacles, and no matter how much they tortured and abused him, he remembered his guru's command and took Dzogchen as his heart practice.

At that time, secretly, he relied on Sera Yangtrul Rinpoche as a teacher and shared his experience and realization with him. Many signs of the qualities of experience and realization appeared increasingly, and those signs became legendary in that area.

Although Rinpoche has many mind treasures, from among the different texts he composed in this lifetime, the text entitled *Instructions on the Great Perfection: A Brief Summary of View, Meditation, and Conduct* has the power of inconceivable blessings. It is commensurate with Patrul Rinpoche's *The Three Incisive Precepts*, the sole practice of one hundred scholars and a thousand siddhas.

Although I was born in this period when the five degenerations are rampant, due to the blessings of having met with gurus such as Domang Yangtang Rinpoche, those who are fully endowed with the wisdom of Dzogchen, I can count myself as a being of great good fortune. I obtained the blessings of empowerment, oral transmission, and instruction from this Rinpoche, and in addition he gave me some profound advice and encouragement with regard to both dharma and mundane affairs. In particular, it was he who said to me, "If you can write a book, it will be highly beneficial to the young people of this age," and it was mainly because of that that I took on the work of composing this book.

The Great Secret of Mind

We bow to the Buddha
Bhagawan Samantabhadra!

1. The View

1.1 The Nature of the Physical World

All intelligent human beings are united in their desire for happiness in this lifetime and the next. But the cause of happiness, the way to obtain happiness, is a matter of broad disagreement. Some people try to obtain happiness in business, some in politics, some by farming the land, some in government jobs, and some with machines and technology. Others, driven by bad karma, even try to find it as thieves, gangsters, or terrorists.

All anyone ever wants is happiness, which first of all means freedom from present suffering. Most people want this for themselves, and they think that they know what is good for themselves and their community, and what is good for their children, partners, and family. Essentially they want just four things: to get rich and have money in the bank, to have a healthy body and a quick mind, to have a good reputation, and to be appreciated and respected by the people around them. What they get, however, is the contrary: poverty, pain, criticism, and anonymity, and they are bitterly disappointed. They find it extremely difficult to fulfill their desires according to their dreams, and, even if they do accomplish something, at the end of the day, they lapse into regret and remorse.

At the time of Shakyamuni Buddha, there was a rich landlord called "Pelkye." In those days, in the sacred land of India, princes, landowners, and those who could afford it had many consorts, and their status and renown was measured according to the number of women they possessed. Pelkye had eight consorts, and each of these bore him a son and a daughter, making sixteen children in all. His eight sons were given splendid wedding parties, and his eight daughters were married into rich families. For years he enjoyed community, wealth, and reputation together, but eventually he became old and senile. His eyes dimmed, his hearing faded, and, as his power diminished, he could not function as before. His lovely women, who previously had followed him like shadows, and his children, who had catered to his every whim, now ignored and despised him, and the old man became depressed. "I have cherished my children and given them everything," he thought, "both love and money. I have covered my women with expensive jewelry and designer clothes and now none of them, children or wives, pay me any attention." Unable to stand his situation, he was filled with deep frustration with the world. But then, spitting it out like a glob of phlegm, he made his way to the feet of the Buddha and there begged the master to accept him as his disciple. Shakyamuni ordained him, and at the end of his life, he attained constant happiness at the level of an arhat.

In *A Collection of Elegant Verses*, the wise Gendun Chophel expressed it like this:

> Constantly bemired in worldly affairs,
> Life is a cause of fatigue;
> The dharma is our only consolation,
> Arising adventitiously within the mind.

Kings, presidents, and politicians may rule for decades, but eventually some trivial adverse circumstance brings them down and costs them their status and perhaps their lives. People of wealth and fame have no concern for this life or the next while they accumulate their fortunes, even risking their lives and breaking the law. They quarrel with their parents and children, break up with their partners, and find themselves alienated from family and friends—all for the sake of money.

Even mountainous wealth and universal fame must be left behind at the time of our death. To give our money to others seems unthinkable, and we cannot spend it all upon ourselves. Our children may spend it lavishly and thoughtlessly, drinking and gambling and womanizing, and seeing how they behave, we lose our sleep and our appetite, and life becomes endless suffering. When we berate our children, they ignore us or tell us that it is none of our business. In the passage of time, partners who have been close to us and loving become estranged and seek new mates. Friends who have been intimate with us and in tune with each other become enemies for no good reason. Seeing that the world is changeable and undependable for these and many other reasons, people's minds are fraught with anxiety and world-weariness. In such circumstances, if we are aware of the Buddha Shakyamuni's teaching, we will surely apply it.

If, however, we are unaware of that teaching, we will be unable to overcome our suffering. We may try to drown it by consuming alcohol and drugs, or by gambling, or some other form of escapism, but although such remedies seem to give some happiness in the moment, actually the happiness they provide is superficial and temporary. To apply such false antidotes is like pouring oil on to fire, a fire that then burns with increased intensity. Besides, consuming alcohol and drugs destroys health and leads to sickness. It also takes away self-control, and we find ourselves roaming about like mad dogs, deprived of human society. Since that condition is self-afflicted, rather than imposed upon us by others, it is a cause for further grief. According to this logic, our faults derive from ignorance of Shakyamuni Buddha's teaching, ignorance of the message that has the potential to overcome suffering and to nourish the mind.

Recently I heard the news of the death of the famous dancer Michael Jackson. He was barely fifty years old. Hundreds of people from all over the world gathered to pay homage to him, and likewise I was moved when I heard of his death. But then the words of Shakyamuni Buddha flashed into my mind, that all beings in this world are bound by birth, old age, sickness, and death. If anyone could have escaped from the curse of sickness and subsequent death, it was Michael Jackson, who was one of the richest men in the United States and seemingly had all the wealth of the world at his disposal. People say that Michael had acquired immense wealth from the sale of his CDs and from his stage performances. How was it that someone like that who was admired the world over and was so fanatically worshipped by innumerable fans that some would die to see him perform—as almost happened in Taiwan in 1996—how was it that he could not escape the sickness that led to his early death? If money could extend life, surely in this case it would have done so. Because Michael had gained fame and started his fortune at the age of nine, we might assume that he had led a life of constant happiness. But as reported by the media, his life turned out to be a miserable catalog of litigation, personal tragedy, and grief. The medical records of his autopsy showed that he was a mere fifty kilograms at the time of his death, and his stomach was full of various medicines and completely empty of food. His disease seems to have been some kind of self-hatred, manifesting particularly as a dislike for his own skin color and facial features that was so deep that he had them modified in several surgical operations.

The truth is that fame and fortune could not provide him with any measure of satisfaction, and the lesson to be learned from Michael's life is that regardless of the effort we ourselves make to be like him in fame and fortune, we too are bound to fail in our quest for happiness. In the light of evidence of the absence of any substantial essence in the material world, therefore, Shakyamuni Buddha could say that, regardless of our status in this threefold world, none of us can escape the conditions of birth, old age, sickness, and death. Suffering is caused by emotional affliction—the six neurotic syndromes—and this in turn causes us to take rebirth in one of the six corresponding realms. Shakyamuni went on to say that from birth, old age, sickness, and death in those six states we suffer an endless diversity of suffering: separation from what we love, for example, or the misery of engagement with what we dislike, the pain of failing to find what we seek, and all the other sufferings of embodiment. Continuing, he then said that in order to escape from all that grief, we should depend upon the continuum of emptiness that is the true path. This is mentioned in *The Explanatory Sutra of Interdependent Origination*:

> Since the Buddha knows emotional affliction as the cause of suffering and shows us the antidote to karma and emotional affliction, so he tells us of the supreme liberation where the suffering of old age, sickness, and death is absent.

We should recognize clearly, therefore, that whether we abide in the human realm or are caught up in any of the six neurotic syndromes, we are still fenced in by immediate incontestable suffering. Entering the immaculate path defined by the master, Shakyamuni Buddha, we shall be released from the severe suffering of birth, sickness, old age, and death in both this life and the next, and with constant effort, we may attain the deathless peace of nirvana. All of us, regardless of status, are like Michael Jackson in that we are dominated by emotional traumas that cause suffering. Although on the face of it, the world may appear to offer pleasure and beauty, it is imperative that, by relying on buddha-dharma, we recognize that chasing after pleasure is the cause of suffering.

In his exposition of the four noble truths, Shakyamuni Buddha taught that suffering consists of birth, old age, sickness, and death. Further, there is the doctrine of threefold suffering: The first kind of suffering, the suffering of suffering, is, for example, the grief one feels upon the death of a loved one. The second kind of suffering, the suffering of change, is illustrated by change in one's financial status or by the change from enjoyment of good food to the sickness caused by that same food. The third kind of suffering, the suffering of conditioned existence or the suffering of embodiment, is the slow change of deterioration that accompanies all life, like the slow but sure change from youth to old age.

In general, Buddhism, Hinduism, Islam, Christianity—all religions—have the same potential to bring peace of mind and a happy state. All agree that, to achieve peace of mind, we need to practice some sort of shamata and vipasyana meditation, but having such high aspirations is as far from the actual realization as the earth is from the sky. Some religious practitioners are able to suppress the suffering of body and mind temporarily through the virtue of meditative absorption. Some practitioners of other religions are successful in securing rebirth in the higher realms of the gods or human beings, which is a little better. But what is the use of that? It is no better than treating the symptoms of the disease instead of its root cause. The same is true for suffering: we need to eliminate its root cause.

1.2 The difference between "insider" and "outsider" meditation

Most religions offer a simple-minded contemplation that is relevant to a worldly path defined by the "outsider" view. This type of meditation, which is found in various forms in different religions, can temporarily relieve superficial suffering. It may induce ordinary clairvoyance, the four levels of concentrated absorption, and even rebirth as a formless god. But what kind of liberation is that? What we need is the eradication of the ego-clinging that is the root cause of suffering. The way to do this has been provided in the teaching of the lord of beings, the Bhagawan, the Buddha Shakyamuni, who taught "insider" contemplation. On that path we understand that all experience is empty and unreal and that contemplation can accomplish the release wherein there is no longer any ego-clinging. Here the cause of suffering is eliminated at its very root.

The crucial difference between "outsider" and "insider" meditation is that the former seeks to cut off the branches of suffering, while the latter cuts through the root. Developing an understanding of ego-loss, we attain the various levels and stages, and training in the qualities of contemplation, we proceed to the attainment of buddha. To engage in such practice, we need to understand the nature of all phenomena, and since mind is the leader—the dominating factor—in that process, it is essential to know its secret. As the bodhisattva poet Shantideva says in *Entering the Way of the Bodhisattva*,

> Without knowing the secret of mind,
> Any pursuit of happiness,
> Any forsaking of suffering—
> All that is quite futile.

1.3 The Fallacy of Materialism: How the Actuality Contradicts Our Assumption That Our Happiness and Sadness Depend upon Material Things

No one in the sensual, aesthetic, or formless realms has revealed the secret essence of mind except the Buddha Shakyamuni. For anyone seeking happiness, the first crucial thing to know is that mind is the root of all happiness and suffering. This is contrary to our ordinary human assumption because through beginningless time to the present day, we all presume that our happiness and suffering depend upon external objects. Due to this false assumption, we all search for beautiful things to gaze upon, sweet sounds to listen to, fine aromas to enjoy, subtle tastes to savor, and soft clothes to wear, and so on. In short, everyone, from the highest to the lowest, from four-footed creatures to all the birds of the air and even down to the smallest insects, constantly, day and night, runs in search of objects that they believe will provide happiness. Likewise, we assume that suffering depends upon material objects or external phenomena, and we manufacture weapons to subdue those external forces that cause us such suffering. Thinking that this particular external cause can produce a particular disease and that particular external cause will hurt us, we are led to believe that if we could only destroy the external physical objects that appear to be the cause of our misery, we would be happy. Our assumption, therefore, that suffering and happiness inhere in external material objects is common to all six classes of beings. Many scientists, particularly, hold such a view.

Now let us consider the example of a beautiful woman. Such a woman is seen variously by different beings. To her father, she is a daughter. To her children, she is a mother. To her husband, she is a wife. To a tiger, she is not so much a beautiful woman but is instead something tasty to eat. To the exalted arhat, she is not a beautiful woman at all but rather something unclean and repulsive. If the body of a woman were a single substantial entity, there would not be such a multiplicity of concepts as to her identity. The key point here is that the multiplicity of concepts regarding each material object indicates that objects on their own have no substantial or definite reality.

If an object is defined by an immutable attribute, then no circumstance can change that attribute. If an object has the attribute of immutable happiness or immutable sorrow, then changing conditions will not be able to affect it. Its essential identity cannot change, just as fire cannot turn into water or water into fire. Even if innumerable people try to prove that fire is cool, it remains undeniably hot, and likewise no one in this world can prove that water has an inherent quality of heat. But happiness and sadness are not immutable attributes of a thing, for it is evident that, in the minds of different people, they arise variously from a single object. The crucial point here is that all phenomena are unreal and therefore can appear in different ways. They appear but in reality do not exist.

1.4 The unreality of material things

In the *Lankavatara Sutra* it is said,

> Outside, actually, no form is concrete—
> It is our mind appearing out there;

> Until they understand the mind,
> Babes conceive only the material world.

Our country, our homeland, and our own houses are like containers, and our children, our local and national community, all four-footed animals, birds of the air, and insects—in short, all sentient beings inhabiting this world—are like the contents of those containers. First, to analyze the container and the contents, we will look at the spatial existence of the container. To take a drinking cup as an example, if we ask where the cup exists, there is no doubt that it sits upon the table. And then when we ask where the table is, the answer would be that it rests inside the house. Then asking where the house is located, we hear that it stands in such and such place in such and such a country, and so on. Scientists believe that the world is round, that it was created by the "big bang," and that it revolves around the sun, like the other planets. If we ask them what the spatial location of this world is, their reply must be that it rests in space. And if they are asked where space rests, they answer that it rests upon its constituent invisible particles. And where do those particles rest? They sit upon other, smaller, invisible particles. And what is the ultimate basis of these particles? Even the most reputable scientists have no definitive answer to that.

A solid material object must contain some indestructible substance if it is to be described as truly existent. Without an essential substance, material objects cannot be said "to exist." If a thing is substantial, it needs to have substance. Without some other thing "to exist upon," it cannot be called an existent. It is an undeniable truth that the ultimate particles have no substance. Whatever thousands or millions of arguments there may be to prove otherwise, the conclusion, the valid truth, must be that physical reality is without substance and is therefore what, in this analysis, we call "unreal." But who believes this statement?

The inimitable Gendun Chophel says in *An Ornament of Nagarjuna's Mind*,

> The tiger's witness is the yak; the yak's witness is the goat; the goat's witness is the bird; the bird's witness is the worm: ultimately valid truth depends upon the worm.

In general, whether scholar or fool, we base our reasoning upon direct personal experience: this we consider ultimate. But how can it be trusted when, for example, many things that we thought good during childhood become intolerable when we grow up and when many principles in which we now adamantly believe will later become untenable? In the past, great scholars unanimously believed that this world was flat like a plate; in later centuries great scientists like Galileo believed that it was like a ball; still later scientists changed the concept, believing that the world is shaped like an orange, with the surface near the two poles flattened. Scientists are still investigating the matter. There is no certainty about its shape (maybe it is actually like the inside of a coconut), so we should not be dogmatic! Each year and each season a new concept becomes fashionable. At one time scientists were sure that the atom was the bedrock of materiality, but now they know it can be split. Until the mind's tendency to interfere and control is exhausted, its probing of the material world will be endless and without any possibility of settling definitively upon even a single concept.

Only when we realize the nature of mind as taught by Buddha Shakyamuni, then, and only then, can we acquire final certainty. That kind of certainty is immutable even in the face of the loud positive or negative arguments filling the sensual, aesthetic, and formless dimensions. If we do not possess the Buddha's absolute certainty, then we cannot be sure of anything and may even tend toward paranoia.

How, for instance, can we trust the mind that yesterday perceived a woman as a loving spouse but tomorrow will perceive her as the wife of an enemy who could kill our loved ones? How can we trust the mind that perceives a girl in her youth as an alluring goddess, perceives her later in life as suffering from leprosy or lost limbs, and perceives her in old age as repulsively ugly? The mind is not a single unchanging reality. When a close friend can turn into an enemy through some small slight, or when the man who killed my father can become a close friend by some positive chance gesture, the certainty of changeability is self-evident. We must look at our own experience and understand!

Some people try to have it both ways: though they can accept that objects "receive" our varying projections, they nonetheless believe that objects must have at least some inherent self-existence. Even though they acknowledge that different people can impute differing qualities to the "same" woman, they insist that her material body actually exists. The danger here is the positing of two female bodies, one inherently existent and the other labeled as this or that. Though some people distinguish between the thing in itself and how it appears (a woman, for example, may be perceived differently by different people), others hold that the elements themselves have both inherent existence and properties that cannot be changed by anyone: that is, the heat of fire, the liquidity of water, the solidity of earth, and the lightness and motility of air. So how can phenomena just be variable figments of mind? The question is valid. Certainly, if all phenomena are projections of mind, then the four elements cannot be exceptions to this rule.

If we consider this problem, examining and investigating phenomena using the logical reasoning of the Madhyamaka school, by demonstrating that phenomena have neither unity nor multiplicity, we can show that they have no substantial existence. For example, we all—high or low, clever or stupid—agree that what we call a "house" is a single entity. This unity is a nominal fact, universally accepted. The problem is that the door and the window are also single entities, and these entities are a part of the single house. A "house" therefore is an aggregation of many material parts. But if we admit that there exists a multiplicity, then the unitary whole, "the house," is nullified. Similarly, if a door, for example, is taken to be a single entity, no distinction is allowed between its upper and lower parts; if we posit separate upper and lower parts of the door as distinct entities, then we have lost the concept of the door as a single entity. If we accept the human body as a single composition of its upper and lower constituents, then the head and the feet become identical. This is clearly not rational. By the same token, if we investigate atoms or particles, by the logic of one and many (or singular and plural), we will find that insofar as they can exist neither as a unity nor a multiplicity, they are mere imputations of mind and are actually empty.

This emptiness is not a vacuum. It is always filled with the appearances of any kind of thing whatsoever—houses, possessions, mountains, creatures, feelings and judgments, and so forth. All these things, so full of expectation and apprehension, are nonexistent yet apparent, and they are called "samsaric phenomena" or "mental projections."

Consider another example: human beings believe that the earth is our supporting ground, but some animals, like rock-eating frogs, regard it as food. Similarly, water is considered by human beings to be a liquid for drinking and washing and a source of nourishment for plants; but for fish, this same water is regarded as a house or as clothes. Similarly, the differing karmic imprints in various beings determine different responses to the same substance. For example, meat creates pleasure in tigers and other carnivorous animals that regard it as food, whereas rabbits and other herbivorous animals regard it with fearful distaste. Likewise, people who smoke cigarettes gain pleasure from it, while the very smell of it creates headache and nausea in nonsmokers.

In this way different types of beings share a common collective karmic vision while at the same time experiencing differing personal karmic visions. Water, earth, and the other great elements appear similarly to all human beings as a common perception of the outer world, while the individual's personal vision is the product of his or her own dispositions, perspective, hearing, and experience. These latter dissimilar conditions lead us to see the very same thing as either a source of pleasure or a source of sorrow.

1.5 All things are figments of the mind

Appearances that in reality are not separate from our mental projections are mistaken for an objective and independent outer part, while our experience of what seems to be an independent inner reality is mistaken for an independent apprehending subject; yet neither of these apparent poles goes beyond the limits of the intellectual mind.

In *The Wish-Fulfilling Treasury*, Longchenpa says,

> Intoxicated by the psychedelic dhatura [thorn apple],
> In the vast gamut of appearances, no matter what arises for us,
> All is hallucination and thus nonexistent;
> The six classes of beings and all delusory appearances,
> Likewise, are pastiches of a mistaken intellect:
> Know every single one as an image of emptiness!

Things appear in many different ways when we are under the influence of alcohol or mind-changing substances. When drunk on alcohol, a single object may replicate and many things may appear as one. The ground may appear to shake, and it may seem that we are falling into a crevasse. Or it may feel like the house and its pillars are falling upon us. When people are completely drunk, they may sing and dance—even at their father's funeral, making rude noises and engaging in unseemly behavior. They cannot distinguish between good and bad, beneficial and harmful, clean and unclean. In short, when the drug controls them, they act like a beast within a human body. Such intoxication produces all kinds of senseless, unpleasant, dangerous, and shameful behavior. This is not the fault of the person; rather it is the drug that opens the door for it.

In the above verse, intoxication is a metaphor for delusion. So long as mind is deluded, the vision of the outer world and the vision of the beings that it contains are all—and only—delusion. The difference between intoxication and delusion is that the first is the insanity of a short-term drug experience, whereas the second is the insanity of our original ignorance.

According to the quality of suffering stemming from the variety of feelings dominant in the upper or lower places of rebirth, we are classified as an embodiment of one or another of the six classes of beings.

1.6 How this body emerges from the karmically conditioned mind, and how we may anticipate the next life

If we examine this body composed of the four great elements (earth, water, fire, and air), we will see that it is generated by mind. Its primary cause is the consciousness that has no origin, and its necessary condition is our father's semen and our mother's blood. According to each individual's karma, consciousness enters into an appropriate womb and that consciousness adheres to that womb. Slowly, through ignorance, a sense of self that creates the four aggregates of form, feeling, perception, and instincts is generated, and within nine or ten months, the sense-fields are formed. Birth is nothing other than the gross manifestation of an innate sense of "I" and "mine." We feel all alone, naked, and empty-handed. At that time we do not even have a name. When we feel cold, thirsty, or hungry, the only thing we can do is cry.

Then gradually we begin to recognize our mother, father, uncle, brother, sister, and other family members, which starts the conception of a grouping of "us" versus "them." Later we develop a gross sense of clean and unclean, good and bad, friend and foe, and we are no longer that nameless naked one. We assume permanence to be a reality and accumulate many material things, calling them "my" house, "my" wealth, "my" ancestor, "my" father and mother, "my" enemy, "my" country, "my" friend, and so forth, and desire, hatred, and ignorance emerge like boiling water. A deep strong clinging to the five aggregates compounded as an ego develops like an immovable nail. From then on, even if we have piles of food at hand, we still feel hunger; even if we have oceans of liquids to drink, we still feel thirst; even if we possess mountains of wealth, we still want to amass more; and even if we have the power of a king, we are not satisfied. Over time, life becomes exhausted, our youth is lost, our hair grows grey, our teeth fall out, and wrinkles line our face. Our eyesight becomes dim, and we can no longer see clearly; our ears become impaired, and we cannot hear well; our nose grows unable to distinguish different odors; our tongue no longer savors taste; our sense of touch diminishes; and our body becomes weak.

But in old age the mind itself does not grow old, and hatred of our enemies may increase, like a forest fire, while attachment to our children and partner billows like ocean waves. With neither mind-training nor thought of our next lives, we are trapped in a circle of delusion. Then one day, bearing a burden of sin, we die as we were born from our mother's womb—alone and empty-handed. The moment of our death is unpredictable; death strikes like lightning falling from the sky. As we die, we must leave our partner behind, though she is as beautiful as a goddess in paradise. Likewise, we have no power to take our sons with us, though they possess the power of kings, and no power to take in hand a penny of the wealth that we have accumulated, though it be as great as Mt. Meru. Our physical bodies left behind, our rebirth not yet determined, we find ourselves suddenly in the intermediate state possessing only a mental "bardo body." In that body we will undergo immense suffering out of fear of the bardo, and mentally we will get a rough and cold feeling. We move like a wave of the ocean with no time to sit for even a second, or we drift like a feather on the wind, moving here and there, obsessed by thoughts of how long this fear and suffering will last.

At the time of their death, those great leaders of the world and those scientists, who, during youth, firmly believed that there was no rebirth and shared that belief with many thousands of people, become unsure and faint voiced, and everyone can see them revert from depending upon the science of medicine to depending on their old religious beliefs. This shows the lack of conviction in their unbelief and, to the contrary, an acceptance of the greater likelihood of rebirth.

In *Entering the Way of the Bodhisattva*, the great bodhisattva Shantideva said,

> Although we may be surrounded by friends,
> The sensations of death
> Must be experienced alone.

If we examine the sensations of suffering as we experience them, nothing is found to be real. Certainly particles of subjective (*atman*) and objective aspect (atoms) with "pretensions" of being discrete entities are unreal. Insofar as we realize that what we see is actually unreal, it is reasonable for us to assume that therefore the inner experiences of elation and pain, too, are the illusory play of the mind.

With that understanding, in considering how to eradicate suffering with finality, we now know that mind is the sole root of both suffering and happiness. We also know that there is a distinction between mind and its essential nature. Even if we have not perfectly understood it, at least we can make the assumption that everything is merely a figment of the mind. We may free ourselves from gross and intolerable pain thereby. At the very least, if we understand that desire, anger, pride, jealousy, and stupidity (for all our emotions are subsumed within these five categories) are like last night's dream, then we achieve that freedom. Desire is the yearning never to lose our happiness; anger rears against fear of the pain of suffering that we try to avoid; through jealousy we compete with people of the same status to facilitate our own happiness; we envy the good fortune of others; through pride we presume to possess a clean, happy, eternal body, and this perception inspires us to challenge other people's systems of belief; and stupidity is a lack of percipience in the physical, energetic, and mental dimensions: these five are the principal causes of suffering for oneself and others. If we know, however, that these emotions are naturally without substantial existence, just like last night's dream, and that they are the illusory play of the mind, then the specific attribute of suffering—that intolerable sharp pain—will not arise.

In the dream state, if we dream that our beloved son has died, we grieve; but as soon as we wake up, we know that our son's death was just a dream image and our suffering is relieved. Similarly, if we understand that no matter what emotion we have—whether pride, anger, desire, or anything else—it has no substantial, inherent existence, that it is just a figment of mind, and if we let it dissolve in mind, then the basis for suffering vanishes. There is no need to depend upon intoxication to eradicate suffering. Nor is there any need of guidance from another; we ourselves are the guide. When we are happy, there is a tendency for pride to increase and that becomes a hook that drags us down. If at that time we know everything as magical illusion, the pride of wealth and power will become the means to bring greater peace, and the round of suffering will cease. In his *Exhortation to Read the Seven Treasuries*, Patrul Rinpoche says,

> With perseverance, tortured minds' chains are broken,
> Happiness is mellowed, frustration assuaged;
> This message is the one that cannot deceive,
> So chant *The Treasury of the Dharmadhatu* as a song!

In that way, all phenomena transcend their illusory dualistic nature.

1.7 Distinguishing between Impure Outer Appearances and the Pure Nature of Reality

Whatever people assert in ordinary conversation, positive or negative, is determined by the experience that has arisen in their own mind. If they make claims about what is neither visible nor obvious, they are questioned because their claims seem beyond proof and thus invalid. The mind works like speech in this respect. Because the mind accepts only what is seen clearly, what is evident, in Varanasi the Buddha Shakyamuni first taught the four noble truths, a message suitable to the minds of ordinary people. According to the perspective of cause and effect and what to accept and what to reject, the truth of suffering and the truth of the origin of suffering are the effect and the cause, respectively, of samsara, which is to be abandoned; and the truth of the cessation of suffering and the truth of the path to cessation are the effect and the cause, respectively, of nirvana, which is to be cultivated. Only gradually, later on, do we discover that the only effective way to proceed is by familiarizing ourselves with the unelaborated truth—the emptiness that is the true nature of all experience whatsoever. Buddha Shakyamuni said unequivocally that he taught the four noble truths for the common people. Of course, it is unthinkable that the Buddha Shakyamuni was incapable of teaching the inconceivable and inexpressible meaning of Dzogchen, but insofar as the moon's reflection needs a pool to shine in, so the recipients of the profound teaching of Dzogchen need primal awareness and a very broad mind to comprehend it. The eye cannot know a form unless it comes into the visual field. So it is with the other four senses: people cannot know what is beyond the field of their perception.

Modern youth might question that assertion. Airplanes and other wonderful things that were unknown to the senses in the past are now taken for granted. One can even fly to the moon. Many great things have already been invented, they may say, not to mention others—heretofore unperceived by the senses—that are in the process of being discovered.

Of course, they are right, but from the omniscient scientist to the ignorant fool, everyone's beliefs are based on their present knowledge, which is derived from the five senses and the mind. Whatever is newly invented is first projected in mind and then through close focus is developed; after this, based on various kinds of materials, it is manufactured. Whatever exists at present, whatever will exist in the future, whatever appears or will appear—it is all bound to the mind. For this reason, no one can go beyond the boundary of his or her mind, from famous scientist to ignoramus; in this we are just like a fly captured in a glass bottle—whether it flies up or down, it can never leave the bottle. And as long as we are bound by mental delusion, whether we are high or low, famous or anonymous, we will have no choice but to swim in the vast ocean of samsara's suffering. As it is said,

> Wealthy people complain of their suffering—
> Just like beggars:
> Every mind has a load of suffering—
> There is not a moment of happiness in samsara.

We give ourselves suffering all the time. And if we ask, "Is there a way out of it?" the answer comes, "Yes, there is!" The answer is the realization of the nature of mind, of reality itself. Our eyes, at present blind to primal awareness, need to borrow from the Buddha the eyes of supreme primal awareness. If we need to venture out into the complete darkness of a moonless night when we lack night vision, either we must obtain a torch or travel in darkness. Can we borrow the eyes of the Buddha's primal awareness? Shakyamuni Buddha himself said in *Ananda's Sutra*,

> I will show you the path of liberation,
> But you must walk down it by yourself.

As the sutras of definitive meaning say, we must rely upon the ultimate path taught by Shakyamuni Buddha as definitive meaning. Whatever form we see, whatever sound we hear, whatever aroma we smell, whatever taste we savor, whatever touch we encounter, whatever we are conscious of in the five sense fields—about these things we feel a certainty, a confidence in our knowledge. Consider the eyes, however; they cannot see more than their own capacity allows, and if the light is too bright, no matter how beautiful the object, we cannot look at it. If we try to look at such brightness directly, our eyes will be damaged. Likewise, the eardrum is very small and delicate and can hear only what is within its range of frequencies, and if we are too close to a sound that can be heard a thousand miles away, instantly we will go deaf, just as some people go deaf from the loud noise of thunder. So is it wise to trust in such feeble faculties? All ordinary persons insist that what exists should be proven through seeing, hearing, and mental perception. Whatever cannot be seen, heard, or perceived by mind is regarded as substantially nonexistent, as delusion. Incredulous critics call those fortunate persons who believe in the inexpressible and inconceivable exalted teaching superstitious fools with blind faith.

For those critics I would like to relate this anecdote. One day a man happened to stumble into the kingdom of monkeys. The monkeys caught and examined him. "This is a monkey," said an elder of the tribe, "but it is a monkey without a tail." And the tribe of monkeys sat around and laughed at the man because he had no tail.

Again, once during the time of Shakyamuni Buddha, the disciple

Sariputra, who was the most excellent in primal awareness, and Brahmajata, from the pure-land of the Buddha Ashoka, debated the qualities of the realm of the fourth universal guide, Shakyamuni. Sariputra argued that the realm of Shakyamuni, the fourth buddha, is an impure realm strewn with rocks and stones and covered in thorn bushes and that Shakyamuni Buddha and his retinue had shorter bodies than buddhas residing in other realms. Bodhisattva Brahmajata, who had reached the eighth level of the bodhisattva path, rejected Sariputra's claim about the inferiority of Shakyamuni's realm. He maintained that the realm of Shakyamuni, the fourth universal guide, has the same purity as the realm of the Buddha Vairochana (Gangchan Tso), the highest buddha-field and source of all buddha-fields. They could not agree upon this issue and decided to approach Shakyamuni Buddha himself for the answer. Buddha transformed the world and its beings into a pure realm with his miraculous power in order to dispel the notion of inferior and superior. "My realm is always like this," he said. Sariputra was amazed. Shakyamuni asked Sariputra, "Is it the fault of the sun or the inadequacy of the eye that a blind man cannot see things?" "It is the fault of the eye," Sariputra replied. "My realm will always be like the one perceived by Brahmajata," the Buddha told him. "The fault of not being able to see it is yours."

If the subjective "knower" is pure, then the objective field is experienced as pure. For example, people suffering from jaundice see a white conch as yellow. On recovery, however, they see it as white. Similarly, the clarity of one's faculties determines the beauty and the fineness of perception. Devils in hell see ordinary water as molten iron that tortures them. Hungry ghosts see the same water as pus and blood, filthy and loathsome. For animals water is merely for drinking, and for human beings it is for drinking and washing. For the gods this same water is experienced as nectar. And to the buddhas and bodhisattvas who reside in the pure-lands, water, as buddha consort Mamaki, appears as pure buddha-nature. It is similar with all the other elements.

Are all these various perceptions valid? Everything that appears to the six kinds of beings does so according to their various karma and is valid for themselves. But the higher the level of rebirth, the thinner the karmic obscuration and the greater the degree of validity of one's perceptions. In *Beacon of Certainty*, Jamgon Mipham says,

As more and more delusion is clarified,
According to the view from below,
The higher the level, the greater the validity:
And that proposition we may accept.

When Surchung Sherab Drakpa's fame was universal, a contentious scholar called "Bajetong" came to him to discuss the nature of reality. He found Sherab Drakpa doing circumambulation around a temple. Approaching, he asked permission to sit on the mat that he laid down, saying that he had some questions to ask. Surchung Sherab Drakpa gave him permission to question him about his doubt. The geshe picked up a stone and said, "You Nyingmapas believe this stone to be Buddhalochana. Isn't that so?" Surchung Sherab Drakpa replied, "In the ultimate vision, it is, of course, Buddhalochana." "Then it is not actually a stone?" the geshe asserted triumphantly. "If we look at its illusory appearance, it is solid stone," the master replied. He then asked the geshe, "Do you dare to deny or denigrate the power of karma?" At this, the geshe lost confidence in his hypothesis. Later he became one of Surchung Sherab Drakpa's eight lineage-holding disciples. It is very important, therefore, to know the distinction between the apparent condition and the true condition, between the conditioned state and the reality, between relative and ultimate, and between mental fabrication and the natural state of all material things.

1.8 All Phenomena Are Unreal: All Is Just a Delusive Display of Mind

Some people say that an event cannot be accepted if it has not been seen with the eyes. A couple of decades ago, the Nepalese teacher Kapil, a communist ideologue, maintained publicly that there was no rebirth because no one alive can personally vouch for it. If it truly existed, he maintained, then it could be positively affirmed through the powers of the senses: since no one has seen it, it doesn't exist. I say that this argument—that all unsensed things are thereby nonexistent—is not worthy of consideration. If we insist on believing only what we see or hear, then we must give up belief that our ancestors once existed in this world. Even if we were to live to the age of 150—and no one does—this world is so vast that it is highly unlikely that we would have actually met our ancestors and therefore be able to stand witness to their existence. If the absence of any living witness to our ancestors proves their never having existed, then how is it possible that our father came into existence? Is it possible for an effect to appear without a cause? If we believe there can't be an effect without a cause, then Kapil himself, were he sitting right in front of me, could not exist because he denies the existence of his causes, that is, his ancestors whom he has never seen. Is it proper to deny the evidence of the senses? There is no answer. Even though we cannot see the cause, if there is an indication, or logical evidence, that something exists, then even modern scientists and intellectuals must accept it.

Once, in 1998, I met a group of American tourists on their way to Mt. Kailash. They were skeptical about buddha-dharma, but most of them were interested in it. Among them was John, who sat quietly, saying nothing, just sitting with his legs stretched out. I asked him if he had any questions. He said straight away that he did not believe in buddha-dharma. I told him that he ought to believe in it because it dealt with the real nature of things. He said that religion maintains the truth of previous and future lives and of karmic cause and effect and that he did not believe in a future life because no one has been there and returned to tell the tale. I told him, "Tomorrow you are going to Mt. Kailash, but who has seen tomorrow? Just because no one in the world has seen tomorrow, not even your famous president Bill Clinton, does that mean that there is no tomorrow? Your only response can be that since there is a today, therefore the probability is that there will be a tomorrow. Likewise, if there is a present life, isn't it probable that there will be a future life?" "Your answer is interesting," John responded and clammed up. "If there is an indication or reason for it, even though it cannot be seen or heard, we should accept it as a possibility," I continued. "Material objects may be viewed in three ways—as form, as consciousness, or as neither form nor consciousness—each dependent upon its own causal stream, just as a sprout of barley comes from barley seed or a sprout of rice grows from the rice seed. There is no doubt that a perception arises from a previous similar moment of consciousness. So the previous life and the next life, karmic cause and effect, are common sense, and their connection may be directly inferred." Having listened to me, John seemed satisfied. "Very interesting!" he said as he departed.

If we examine the egoist consciousness of the personality in the present moment, by careful discrimination, dividing it into thousands of parts, we find nothing. Even if thousands of scientists subject this body of flesh and blood to dissection and microscopic analysis, they will not find any discrete consciousness, only various substances composed of the four elements. Simply because they cannot find consciousness, however, does not prove that it is nonexistent. To insist that it is nonexistent is a denial of common sense and just nonsense! Consistent with that, since there is a present life, so too there should be a next life. Because today exists, we can reasonably presume that there is a tomorrow.

In *The King of Samadhi Sutra*, it is said,

> Eyes, ear, and nose are undependable;
> Tongue, body, and mind are unreliable:
> If these senses were valid guides,
> Who would follow the noble path?

If seeing with our eyes and hearing with our ears were in themselves enough to establish valid cognition—if our five senses by themselves could see actual reality—then there would be no need of the Buddha's eye of awareness and the paths and levels. Moreover the microscopes that can see atoms would be pointless since we would have accepted that what we see with our eyes is the definitive truth. Shakyamuni Buddha said 2,500 years ago that upon an atom invisible to the eye reside thousands of beings. Scientists have validated this statement: there are, for example, innumerable germs in a single drop of blood of a tubercular patient. So the Buddha and the scientists are in agreement, except the Buddha did not depend upon a machine to see it but instead perceived it with his primal awareness.

In this twenty-first century, in Western countries, the outer world is highly developed and still developing, and it appears that people's lives are problem free, but at the same time, we see that many people are depressed and crying out in their pain. Anyone who visits the West from a less-developed country is amazed upon seeing how beautiful and well developed it is, for both Asians and Westerners think that happiness depends upon material things and money. To attain that happiness, people strive busily without food by day and without sleep at night. Besides that, if we see how animals, birds, and insects search for happiness in the material world day and night, we may assume that they, like humans, desire happiness and loathe suffering, want love and hate aggression and pain, and believe that happiness is derived from material things. Isn't that amazing!

Consider the example of a millionaire who has a very beautiful well-furnished house with a charming garden in front, a swimming pool behind, soft pillows and bedding, good Internet connection, a television for viewing the international news and entertainment, and a phone near his bed with which he can talk without disturbance to his father and mother living in a far-away country. If he feels cold, he can warm the room with a heater; if he feels hot, he can cool the room with an air-conditioner. He has a fine electricity service, owns many hectares of land around the house, has a vast variety of food and drink, owns a very fine automobile waiting in front of the house, and frequently engages in entertainment with beautiful women. Wherever he goes, he is escorted by servants.

If we listen to the news or reports from people who know these rich people, however, outer appearances and inner nature do not seem consistent. These rich people are very aggressive, it seems. Without relying on alcohol and drugs, how can they be at ease? The fires of jealousy burn against their superiors. They strive in competition with people of their own class and status. They try to undermine their inferiors. Sometimes, due to their bad habits, they engage in illegal actions and find themselves summoned to court and then imprisoned for years, and then their grief has no end. They may need to promise not to commit such acts again and beg forgiveness from the government.

Seeing all these things, the inherent fault of attaching oneself to material happiness as if it will last forever is clearly demonstrated. Such wealthy people should not need to do such things. But out of the root of ego grow the branches of pride from which hang virulent poisonous fruit that ruins oneself and others. If happiness depended upon objective material things, rich people would not undergo suffering as they do, but rather they would enjoy the pleasure of the gods. But happiness doesn't stay more than a moment; second by second it changes inexorably from happiness into suffering.

1.9 The Method of Eliminating Belief in Concrete Reality, the Cause of Suffering

The root of all suffering is the grasping at and clinging to a substantial essence in objects. First, we need to learn to apprehend the unreality of material things.

Happiness and suffering do not exist in the nature of things. What we consider to be a source of happiness—for example, our children, partner, wealth, and so on—sometimes becomes a source of suffering, such as the death of our beloved son, the infidelity of our beautiful wife, the theft of our cherished wealth, or even the loss of our own life. Sometimes, an event that we considered a source of suffering becomes a cause of pleasure. What about the enemy who by merely uttering a few chance words turns into a close friend ready to put his life at risk for us? Or take Mahatma Gandhi's experience of painful humiliation on a train, from which arose the heroic thought of struggling for Indian independence. Afterward the Mahatma pioneered the path of nonviolence, for which he would become world famous. In that case, the negative situation turned into a highly positive and favorable event.

Again, a long time ago in India there was a great poet called "Tulsi Das." One day his wife left his house to visit her parents. Tulsi Das could not sleep even a night without his wife beside him, so he went to her, a journey that involved crossing the great river between his village and his in-laws' house. When he reached the place where his wife was staying, she accosted him, saying, "You shameless sex-starved beggar! You even risk your life to come to me." He was so saddened by his wife's attitude that he left her and went to Mt. Bikche, where he meditated for many years. One day he had a vision of a deity and obtained from him the power of literary composition. He composed the versified *Ramayana,* beloved by all India, and his fame spread far and wide. Thus humiliation by his wife created the condition for the composition of a literary masterpiece.

During the Maoist insurgency in Nepal, the cadres burnt down the people's huts in some small villages. After peace was made, the Nepali government gave large sums of money as compensation to the owners of those huts, and with that money, they built big houses in the city. The tragedy of their homes' being destroyed became a source of happiness for them.

In this way, one particular event can give rise to either happiness or suffering. Further, when we feel happy, wherever we look, we take delight in what we see and derive feelings of happiness and beauty from everything. When we suffer, everything we see or hear is unpleasant. When our blood is boiling, we will reject, break, or destroy anything we see in front of us. We know that sometimes a person will burn down his or her own house in anger and even incinerate his or her own body. When we are angry, everything we perceive is a source of anger and displeasure; wherever our gaze falls, we see the root cause of our suffering.

All appearances may well be our own projections, but their particularity is not predictable or invariable. How things look in childhood is quite different from how they look in old age. Moreover, what appears undoubtedly pleasant and true in the morning may become quite unpleasant by evening. Each of us can recall examples from personal experience of such change, of diverse, unpredictable, equivocal experiences arising from an undefined source. This fact helps demonstrate that all phenomena are projections of our minds. On the other hand, if we are unable to comprehend phenomena as illusion, as mere appearance manifesting without any substantiality, we tend to believe that our enemy's enmity is immutable and that our friend's loving regard will last forever.

When famous and rich people believe their fame and wealth to be something truly existent, they are deluded, and the opportunity for release from samsara never arises. So what is the meaning of "truly existent"? What is truly existent must be intrinsically substantial, with a permanent, unchangeable, firm, stable, and indestructible essence. If apparent objects are not truly existent, how can they be a constant and certain source of suffering? How can suffering arise invariably from an object that is not inherently substantially existent? Similarly, if thoughts about an event that is inherently illusory are understood to be untrue, then there can be no foundation for belief that causes suffering. Only if the essentially unstable event is taken to have substantial existence can thoughts arise as beliefs that cause suffering. Consider the case of a dark-colored rope mistaken for a terror-inducing snake. Here it is the belief that a delusory creation of mind is real that provokes our fear. Suffering arises from delusory perception of things, from a failure to see their true nature.

Moreover, consider the experience of a man who spends a moonless night in a place where there is no electricity or any other source of light. Covering his head with a blanket, he dreams that he enters a large garden filled with flowers, where a party is in full swing. He joins the crowd and converses happily with them amid all those beautiful flowers, eating tasty food and touching and smelling those beautiful flowers. At the time, he experiences the beautiful garden, the talking, and the seeing as real. When he wakens, he knows that the dream was unreal and that the garden had no substantial existence.

Suppose we assume that what we see in the light of day is true and what we see in dream is unreal. Then consider first, where our daytime perceptions come from; second, where they abide; and third, where they go. This examination should result in the realization of the unreality of our ordinary experience and an increase in the sense of illusion. What we ordinary people perceive as real, enlightened beings see as in a dream world. Since they know that every atom is substantially nonexistent, their perception of the illusory nature of reality is constant. For this reason they can never be distracted by the apprehension that happiness resides externally.

Ordinary people hold the view that the perceiver and the objective field are truly existent—and thus they suffer. Noble beings, on the other hand, realizing that the perceiver and the objective field are untrue and unreal, go on in every life from happiness to happiness. The difference between these two is the vast difference between the mundane materialistic path and the transcendental dharma path. In *Entering the Way of the Bodhisattva*, Shantideva says,

> An ordinary person looking at external objects
> Believes them to be genuine and true,
> While the yogin sees them as magical illusion:
> That is why yogins and laymen disagree.

The many religious schools of this world, whether Buddhist, Hindu, Christian, or Muslim, the great scientists who analyze the nature of things, and the atheists too do not argue about whether things are perceived or not. If things cannot be perceived, then there is nothing to argue about; if what is seen is the same to all, then no argument arises. But they do argue. Each school has its own opinion about the origin and nature of appearances. They argue whether appearances are determined by the objective or the subjective aspect and whether the appearances we perceive in the moment coincide with the actuality. The argument is about the cause of external appearances, about who or what produces those appearances. "Scientists"—rational, Western intellectuals—need to examine the different philosophical opinions determined by divergent views about how appearances are perceived. Everyone can accept that the nature of appearances is what is disputed and is the necessary focus of examination. The belief that appearances are nonexistent contradicts common sense, since if they did not exist, all putatively perceptible, material things would be like space. The crucial question that scientists must address is whether the object that appearances depend upon is truly existent or not. The answer necessarily must always be "No object upon which any appearance may depend has a true existence!" as explained above.

1.10 The Ways of Establishing the Unreal World as Magical Illusion in the Different Levels of Approach

Even the early Buddhist Relativist (Vaibhashika) and Traditionalist (Sautrantika) schools accepted that gross phenomena like mountains, houses, and so forth, exist only as imputation. According to them, what we perceive, speak, or do—both mind and mental functions—are fictional truths: whatever is established by the application of gross labels is considered to be fictional and illusory. But they also believe that there are basic particles that are not just nominal imputation but have actual substantial existence—that are ultimately real. An instant of consciousness, for example, is deemed to be a discrete indivisible entity, and therefore an ultimate truth.

The Mahayana Mind-Only school (Chittamatra) holds that, primordially, the appearance of all things has been determined by the various habitual imprints upon the basic ground of being of the mind's positive and negative thoughts. Gradually, the power of habitual tendencies increases and the entire world with its various beings appears. They do not assert that collections of atoms are the basis of reality as in the Relativist and Traditionalist schools. Such atoms cannot withstand analysis, as Asanga points out in *The Thirty Stanzas*,

> If its six sides are considered as separate,
> The basic atom would be sixfold;
> If the six sides are considered a unity,
> The universe would be one single atom.

For this reason the Mind-Only school posits the existence of appearances only as mental. Perception of the subject/object dichotomy as empty is considered to be the absolute truth of intrinsic presence and light itself. If all external phenomena, established as emptiness, are insubstantial and not inherently existent, then the consciousness of the subjective knower, and even intrinsic presence and its radiance, remain groundless and unestablished, although real. If there is no color blue in the objective field, there can be no eye-consciousness of blueness. If we know that the empty consciousness of dualistic perception is actually intrinsic presence and its radiance, then the imputations of the analytic mind are seen to be without foundation.

The Middle Way school (Madhyamaka) holds that the objective aspect of perceptual events—the object itself—is unreal. But unlike the Mind-Only school, it does not accept that the intrinsic presence and radiance of an objectless perception is real. It maintains that "the perception of the emptiness of subject and object as intrinsic presence and light" is merely another label pasted by the discursive mind upon a fictive experience. It maintains that, if one examines closely this supposed reality of intrinsic presence and light with analytic logic, one discovers that there is not the slightest truth in it. Chandrakirti in his *Entry into the Middle Way* says,

> Do not think that form can exist without mind;
> Do not think that mind can exist without form:
> Accept neither both nor neither, said the Buddha,
> And that is elaborated in the Abhidharma.

All the phenomena of samsara and nirvana that arise as undeceiving appearances of interdependent causes and conditions are thus relatively real. In absolute reality, both subjective and objective aspects are inherently emptiness, which cannot be established, and which cannot be confirmed or elaborated as existence, nonexistence, both, or neither.

From the perspective of the resultant tantra, the Middle Way school makes an invidious distinction between the two truths, relative and absolute, by emphasizing what is seen. In this perspective, the Middle Way school accepts that appearing material objects are, in absolute terms, absolutely empty and unreal already, but it maintains that the relative truth—our ordinary delusory perception of appearances as solid material objects—is to be investigated, purified, and eventually abandoned. In the absolute view, all phenomena are emptiness free of conceptual elaboration and free of any agent of purification, but from the relative view, one needs to cultivate what is desirable and reject what is undesirable in terms of karmic propensity. In the resultant tantra, on the contrary, there is no basis for holding an uncompromising classification of what is valid and what is not since both relative and absolute views are just the same nominal imputation. All views are only notional-conceptual because in the natural or essential state of reality neither the relative nor the absolute can ever exist.

In his *Great Memorandum of View*, the peerless pandita Je Rongzompa says,

> If buddha is our essential identity,
> Our attributes can be no other than buddha;
> Since an attribute is a part of identity,
> The attribute and the identity are both buddha.

With the realization that we and buddha are inseparable, reality abides nowhere in particular, wanting nothing. Just so, as taught in the sutras of definitive meaning, perfect insight and meditative absorption are the path of Shakyamuni Buddha.

In neither relative nor absolute reality is anything good or bad, and there is nothing in either to cultivate or reject. Consider dream experience: therein we can infer that events arise from causes and conditions, that sowing crops brings forth a harvest, that consuming poison results in death, and that taking medicine assists recovery. But even though such events appear in sequence, neither the death after taking poison nor the healing after taking medicine, for example, can be said to be connected because the taking of poison and the death and the taking of medicine and the healing are all dream events. Each moment of perception of dream events is equal and the same, free of any imputation of causal linkage. Since in the waking state every event is of the same dreamlike nature, any preferential judgment we make regarding relative or absolute reality is a function of delusion within delusion. As Je Rongzompa said in *Applying the Mahayana Method*, "As inside a dream, so outside: there is no essential distinction between a functional and a nonfunctional illusion. All phenomena in our waking state are also without reality and without foundation, like mirage, like dream, like reflection, like apparition." Although, in a dream, a pot appears to function as a water container, it has no more functional capacity than does the reflection of a pot in a mirror. There is no need to prove that dream appearances and their attributes are indeterminate, or have or do not have any functional capacity. Likewise, there is no need to prove that the appearances of relative delusion—our ordinary perceptions of inner and outer objects—arise as the products of causes and conditions, or that they are functional or nonfunctional: they all appear the same to both the wise man and the fool. Appearances may be imputed as pure or defiled, but there is no need to label them either way because, in reality, cause and effect and truth and falsehood are mere intellectual imputation. In this way relative and absolute are the same.

Unlike Middle Way scholars, tantric yogins do not hold that in relative reality the two truths are different while in absolute reality they are inseparable. Rather, for the tantric yogin, the relative is absolutely pure, and the absolute is absolute sameness—purity and sameness being identical. The unique sustaining view of the dharmakaya as unitary awareness and emptiness sees the absolute inseparability of the relative and the absolute. In *The Wish-Fulfilling Treasury*, Longchenpa says,

> The relative is beyond distinctions,
> Beyond the two nominal truths,
> And therefore any elaboration is redundant.
> The truth of inseparability cannot be proven or denied.
> In spaciousness, appearances and emptiness are nondual
> And therefore truth is one.

No matter what arises in samsara and nirvana, at the very moment of its appearing, it arises in ultimate timeless emptiness. There is not an iota of good to be cultivated or bad to be rejected. This is called "great timeless inseparable truth." Empty when appearing, appearing when empty, this magnificent timeless sameness of emptiness and appearance is called "the view of Dzogchen" and also "the view of the ultimate sacrifice" or "the view free of all propositions." In reality, therefore, all phenomena are merely mental labels, and in reality not even the smallest thing exists to be cultivated or rejected. Yogins and yoginis who have this view pay no attention to their own level of accomplishment regarding either attachment to the objective, material aspect of nominal experience or to the degree of any emotional attachment. Such yogins and yoginis make no distinction between high and low views, nor do they pay heed to the speed of accomplishment on the path.

Consider these examples from *Applying the Mahayana Method* by Rongzompa: Seeing the reflection of a snake in water, people have varying reactions: some are afraid and run away; some see its poison and take it as medicine; some perceive it as a reflection in the water and relate this to others but do not touch it; some perceive it as a reflection in the water and not only tell others about it but demonstrate its unreality by touching it. Still others, when encountering any manifestation of a snake, consider that seeing it as real and running away or perceiving it as a reflection and touching it and so on are no more than the play of children. Making no gesture either toward acceptance or rejection, they remain at ease, demonstrating by this their view that all judgments and reactions of any kind are delusory.

Consider another example: monks of the two early Buddhist schools, the Relativists and the Traditionalists, strive to release themselves from samsara by avoiding the causes of emotional affliction. Mahayana aspirants of both Mind-Only and Middle Way schools search for the compassionate aspect of emptiness as the antidote to all emotional affliction. Exoteric tantric yogins and yoginis perceive that the causes of affliction are indemonstrable, and to face fear, they visualize buddha-deities and recite mantras. Esoteric tantric yogins and yoginis, knowing the inherent insubstantiality of affliction and endeavoring to get rid of any small fear they have of it, make those emotional afflictions into the path and trample upon them. The anonymous Dzogchen yogins and yoginis, however, know that any emotional affliction is merely nominal delusion, without substance. Realizing the futility of showing menace and threat toward it, and playing with it like a triumphant crow flying in circles above a dead snake, such yogins and yoginis abide in a state of natural relaxation quite beyond any reaction of acceptance or rejection to the qualities of the objective field because they have taken hold of the unchanging citadel of intrinsic presence.

1.11 People ignorant of the illusory nature of their own unreal mind spin around in confusion

If all phenomena are primordially and reflexively released without the necessity of cultivating what is positive or rejecting what is negative, why do sentient beings wander in samsara? *The King of Samadhi Sutra* says, "The seed of enlightenment pervades all beings." And in the tantra *The Secret Core: Illusory Display*, it is said,

> We may search the four directions,
> But we will not find perfect buddha;
> The very mind itself is perfect buddha,
> So do not search for him anywhere!

If the nature of mind is perfect buddha, how then can delusion arise? Discursive thought in an individual sentient being arises unbidden and, exacerbated by ego-clinging, projects the universe of samsara. Samsara is therefore a dreamlike self-envisionment.

Here's an old story from Japan: Many thousands of years ago, long before the mirror was known, there lived a farmer and his wife. Every day the farmer went to his fields to work. As time went by, his wife noticed that he had begun to spend a long time each day looking down at one place in the field. At the same time, she heard him repeating a single phrase over and over. Wondering what was so special about the place that constantly drew his gaze, she quietly followed him one day to spy on him and saw with amazement that he was looking into a piece of broken glass. She snatched it from his hand and, looking into it, she found, staring back at her, the face of a beautiful woman. She became angry and upbraided him. "Now I know what you have been doing all the time in the field," she shouted, "You have found another woman to admire!" "That would be quite wrong," he responded. "I am not interested in another woman. It is my deceased father in this glass that I have been concerned with." She took the glass and looked into it again, and again saw the beautiful woman. "Here! Who do you see in this glass?" she demanded, returning it to him. "It's my father," he assured her. She chided him for his duplicity, for his refusal to admit what was clear to her eye. While they were quarreling in this way, a yogin happened along and stopped, asking them what was the matter. The wife answered him, saying, "There is plainly a woman in this glass, and he is telling me that it's his father. That's the issue." "Let me see," said the yogin, taking the glass and looking into it. Seeing a good-looking young yogin in it, he told them, "There is neither a woman nor an old man in it, but rather a handsome young yogin. Don't quarrel! Anyhow, this is something I need," he said, and respectfully touching the mirror to the crown of his head, he took it away with him.

As this anecdote demonstrates, due to our failure to recognize the nature of our mental processes, we exteriorize whatever is grasped at and apprehend an object "out there." The one who grasps that object, interiorized, is apprehended as a subject, while form, sound, smell, taste, and tactile sensations are conceived as external objects. Then a welter of concepts of desire, aversion, or disinterest arises toward attractive, aversive, or neutral objects. Nonduality is thus apprehended as duality, and due to our particular karmas of accumulated virtue and vice, we are reborn in one of the six classes of beings, each with its unique environment. The cause of our projection into samsara has nothing concrete about it, nothing constant or substantial; the surface of the mirror showed three versions of reality as perceived respectively by the farmer, his wife, and the yogin. The yogin reacted with attachment, the wife with aversion, and the farmer with disinterest.

In short, out of confused thought, we believe that insubstantial, unfounded illusion is existent: this is only delusion. So long as we do not understand that what appears in the mirror is our own image, endless disputation arises. Until the contrivances of magical illusion brought about by a sense of ego dissolve and so long as there is dispute about the image in the mirror, we are stuck in samsara.

The gods, demons, humans, animals, hungry ghosts, and the devils of hell, each in their own different bodies, with their own pleasures, and in their own various environments, experience their own peculiar happiness and suffering. As vast varieties of images ceaselessly appear before us, just as in a movie, we all cling to "I" and "mine," to "my" possessions, "my" parents, "my" lover, "my" child, "my" country, and so forth. Because of this, we become bound by what certainly seems to be a separate subject and object and, stuck in this belief, we are like criminals bound in chains, never to taste release and never to attain freedom from samsara.

If we think that those chains of the dualistic perception of delusive appearances are concrete and substantial, then, of course, again we are mistaken. There is no bondage or liberation in the moment of delusion: just like a magician's binding an illusory elephant to an illusory pillar, no one binds and no one is bound. The emotional afflictions and the suffering that appear like chains, when examined by reason, do not have any substantial existence. What is the source of this appearance of bondage? The answer is that it is the adventitious thought of the egoist personality that makes the illusion. For example, let us imagine a rope in the sky in front of us into which we tie and untie knots. The rope is the nature of our own mind, buddha-nature, pure from the beginning, like the sky. The knots are the tangles of dualistic perception, made by the negations "no" and "is not" and the affirmations "yes" and "is," which create the delusive appearances of samsara, like a vision of a vast magical country. Until the magician interrupts the magical illusion that he creates by mantra and props, we believe it to be real, when actually all along it has been without foundation or base. Until we abandon the attachments of dualistic perception, we will fall for the terrific illusions of samsara, thinking them to be real when in fact there is nothing substantial out there at all.

1.12 Pure presence itself is buddha

The root cause of suffering in beginningless samsara is the emotional affliction of desire and aversion. Insofar as we need to rid ourselves of the delusive mental projections that emerge from those emotions, perhaps the first thing we ought to do is make a distinction between what is to be extinguished and the healing antidote. For example, there is the wood that is to be cut, and the axe; there is the sickness to be cured, and the medicine; and there are the delusive visions of emotivity, and the antidote that removes them. The antidote is the realization of egolessness, or primal awareness, wherein dualistic appearances do not arise. But if we believe that we need to depend upon an antidote in the sense of isolating, following, and practicing it, we are mistaken. No matter which thoughts of desire or other emotions arise or which delusory projections appear, they are all the nature of samsara, complete and perfect in the total sameness of reality, primordially released, beyond error or fault. Why? Because samsara's nature is emptiness. In *The King of Samadhi Sutra*, it is said,

> The bodhisattva undermines materialism,
> Because all existence is primordially empty.
> The wise do not contend with children,
> Or with extremists whose emptiness is a void.

Further, in the very moment that samsara appears, it has in actuality no substantial existence—it is immaculate natural perfection. Dream phenomena and the mind of the dreamer are one in the mind, just as dualistic appearances, if examined, are seen to be the magical illusion of relativity. In the same way, both the ego that turns the wheel and the reified objective field of samsara and nirvana are the nature of mind because the nature of mind is appearance itself. Nagarjuna, in *The Root Stanzas of the Middle Way*, says,

> There is not even a fine distinction
> Between samsara and nirvana;
> There is not the slightest difference between them.

With respect to samsara and nirvana, when we understand that all of the notions of antidote and abandonment, acceptance and rejection, and affirmation and negation of nirvana and samsara, respectively, are merely elaborated mental concepts, we realize that all discursive concepts are empty in themselves and are the sameness of reality itself. There is no view and meditation more profound or superior to this. In *In Union with Buddha*, Padmasambhava is recorded as having said,

> If conceptual thought is reality,
> The only meditation is upon the dharmadhatu.

In a dream, the subjective aspect of dualistic perception mistakes itself for an objective field; in like manner, mistakenly conceiving the dualistic appearances of samsara as an external objective field is delusion. Actually, the nature of mind is never other than the natural perfection that is the suchness of things. Just as the reflections of stars in the ocean can never be separated from the ocean itself, so all positive and negative thoughts can never leave the nature of mind. When one is settled in the relaxed, unfabricated space of mind's nature, realization of the thought-free dharmakaya will arise by itself. In the tantra *The Supreme Source*, it is said,

> Whatsoever appears is one in suchness,
> So do not try to modify it!
> With the king of unmodified sameness,
> Spontaneity arises in the thought-free dharmakaya.

After first settling into the unmodified space of pure presence, we will experience the sudden arising of adventitious thought. This is what we call the creativity of pure presence. If our attachment to this creativity seems to arise in the form of causes producing effects, and we investigate, we find that there is actually no connection between what we consider a preceding causal instant and a subsequent effected one. This is because the face of awareness abides in primordially pure natural perfection, in rootless and baseless spaciousness (dharmadhatu). In the arising of the multifarious expressions of creativity, there is actually no continuity because an instant is by nature fragmented. A radio wave can circle the globe three times in one second, serially, through successive instants of time; an instant of creativity, on the other hand, is an instantaneous unfolding, not a process where time exists in or as an unbroken stream. Each fragment of time, each instant, is incapable of activity because it has no extension. Activity, and therefore karma, cannot occur in a single instant; it is possible only in a temporal continuum, which is extended across time in a series of many moments. Conceptions of substantial existence arise through the mistaken notion that such a continuum is the case. But the past moment has ceased, a future moment can never be found, and if we examine the present moment, we see that it has neither substantial existence nor duration in any of its aspects, outer, inner, or intermediate. We see that an instant vanishes as it arises, and it is thus the nature of pure presence's primordial timeless awareness, which is skylike spaciousness (dharmadhatu).

Looking out from the subjective pole in the unitary field of seeming subject and object, we see an apparent objective field: we mistake our own true face—primordial buddha, primordially pure reality—as projected mental appearances. The subjective aspect of the conditioned mind overwhelms the objective aspect and seems to arise as the display of multiform appearances, but in reality this is primal awareness enjoying its own self-manifestation. Just as the waves of the ocean, however rough, always remain a part of the ocean, in actuality the continuity of thought, laced by the five poisons, is the display of primal awareness, primordially pure. This is the contemplation of the supreme incomparable approach. In *The Supreme Source*, it is said,

> Without thinking, without practicing, in reality
> From thought itself, primal awareness is born.

Dudjom Rinpoche has said in his *Calling the Lama from Afar*,

> Whatever arises as the dharmakaya's creativity
> Is neither good nor bad:
> Present knowledge is direct buddha.

In short, in direct, ordinary perception of the here and now, free of the adulteration of dualistic perception, straight, just as it is, without the slightest modification, kept in its normal state, we settle into the natural state of being, and intrinsic awareness, timelessly present, reveals the true face of Samantabhadra.

The victorious, perfect Buddha Bhagawan's principal message, foremost in all approaches to buddha, is that all phenomena are inherently insubstantial emptiness, mere nominal imputation.

1.13 Illustrating the Similarity of the World and Magical Illusion

All knowledge may be no more than a bunch of conceptual labels, and there is nothing concrete or predictable anywhere. But what about our knowledge of the good we can do to benefit sentient beings and the harm that we can avoid? What about knowledge of the universal benefits of medicine and the effects of poison? Such knowledge is garnered by indisputable common sense or inductive thinking. To take the example of plant or vegetable growth: depending upon seven interrelated causes (seeds, shoots, stem, leaf, sprout, flower, and fruit) and the six interconnected conditions (earth, water, fire, air, space, and time), the plant grows in congruence with its seed. That we know by direct observation. Or take the example of the stages of life of sentient beings: they develop according to the twelve links of interdependent origination starting with ignorance and ending in old age and death, as taught in the texts.

What should we do with such conventional information? The answer is that so long as we are saddled with the delusions of dualistic perception, like a shaman under the influence of the psychedelic dhatura [thorn apple, jimson weed, used in Shaiva yoga and American Indian shamanism], whenever appearances arise—and they arise unceasingly—we take the world of labeled phenomena as a given. Then, depending upon those conceptual imputations and making analyses based on the notional-conceptual world, we have no other recourse than to accept and endure.

Once there was a great king, and one day he asked a great magician for a demonstration of magic. The magician inquired whether the king minded some embarrassment, and the king assured him that he could tolerate it. So the magician began. Just then, an attendant approached with tea, and while it was being poured, the king heard a neighing, and looking out of the window, he saw a beautiful pasture with many flowers and gently flowing streams. In the pasture the king also saw a beautiful light blue horse running here and there. The king, seeing this beautiful horse, knew that he must ride it at any cost, and thinking thus, he ran to mount it. With the king on its back, the horse ran up and down and then, gaining speed, it took off from the pasture and flew into the sky. On and on it flew for thousands of miles until it reached a barren place without grass, a seeming land of demons; there the king dismounted. The blue horse that had brought him there then vanished, and the king became worried. What should he do? He had no supplies with him, nothing to eat, and he had no idea at all of the way back to his kingdom. While he was musing in this way, he noticed some smoke far down the valley and decided to go down there in the hope of finding something to eat and something to wear. As he came nearer, he saw that the smoke was coming out of a ravine. Descending further, he called out and a middle-aged woman appeared, and he requested a bed for the night. She agreed to give him lodging, and he thought that perhaps he would return to his kingdom at daybreak, but of course he did not know the way back to his far-away kingdom. So he stayed there for days, which soon became months, which, as time rolled by, became years. He stayed on with the woman, who in good time gave birth to nine children. The family depended on the milk from six goats, who became his responsibility. But these produced so little milk for so large a family that the children were always crying from hunger. On top of this, their clothes were threadbare. Eventually the woman grew old and lost her teeth, and her hair turned grey. Eighteen years passed in this way, and there was only suffering and misery. But suddenly, without any forewarning, like awakening from sleep, he found himself back on his throne. He immediately cursed the magician, berating him for burdening him with so much suffering for so long, and he wept. Then the magician comforted him. "I have shown you a magical illusion," he said. "You have not actually left your throne, nor have eighteen years passed. It was all illusion, and the tea that your attendant set in front of you is not yet cold. Hearing this, and seeing the steam still rising from his tea, the king was astonished.

Just as in that story, wherein the king was convinced of the reality of the illusion of raising a family in a ravine with an old woman, regarding the children as his own children, and experiencing all kinds of happiness and sufferings, when in fact he had not moved from his throne, so too we see our world as a concrete material reality, when in fact it is nothing other than magical illusion. Even the experiences of seeing and hearing in a dream, which do not depend upon our actual sense organs, our eyes and ears and so forth, are just imprints conditioning the mind. Other than by the imposition of labels, not a scintilla exists, and that is the truth.

1.14 The Conviction That All Is Unreal Accords with the Sutras

We are told that the projected appearances of delusory mind are nonexistent: let us look, then, at harm from enemies and help from friends, at the offense rising from insults, at rampant sexual desire, and so on. As with the dream state, look at them and search first for the place where they come from, second, the place where they now abide, and finally, the place where they go to. You will find no specific locations of such places.

Then where do our present feelings of happiness or sadness, as well as our feelings in the dream state, come from? The answer is that those appearances arise from karmically induced tendencies of the mind. If they are examined, they are seen to have no substantial existence; if they remain unexplored, they seem to be real, concrete, and true.

This story is taken from the sutra *The Pile of Jewels*: Once in the kingdom of Magadha, there was a clever magician called "Bhadra," and his fame spread far and wide. "If I could fool the Lord Buddha with my magic, I would be the most famous magician of this world." Thinking this, he went to see the lord with the intention to deceive him. Arriving in the district where the Buddha resided at that time, Bhadra sent him and his retinue a luncheon invitation for the next day, and the Lord Buddha accepted. The morrow arrived, and Bhadra conjured a beautiful house decorated with flower garlands, with a throne and tables displaying many delicious foods. The people living nearby were amazed to see such things. Bhadra reasoned that this enterprise was a good test of the Buddha's omniscience because, if omniscient, the Buddha would naturally avoid coming to lunch for fear of looking foolish and subjecting himself to ridicule. But at noon that day the lord with his retinue of five hundred monks arrived for lunch. Bhadra ushered them in and begged them to sit down. Then he served them his illusory food and drink, and the Lord Buddha blessed the offerings as if they were real and began to eat. Bhadra decided at that moment to dismantle the illusion of his magic and expose the Buddha as a fool, but however hard he tried, he could not dissolve the illusion. The Lord Buddha enjoyed the lunch with his retinue and, having finished the feast, he recited a dedication prayer:

Both the giver and the recipient,
As also the gift, are unknowable;
Through the sameness of those three,
May Bhadra attain perfection.

This fine dedication prayer means that the three—giver, receiver, and gift (Bhadra, the Lord Buddha, and the lunch)—should not be reified as separate entities or imaged as individual objects. These three are the same in being unknowable, and by this recognition—that in deepest reality no one thing is necessarily more real than another—the accumulation of virtue and primal awareness can be completed for the magician Bhadra, despite the fact that his intention was deluded and the luncheon was magically produced. In deepest reality, there is not the slightest difference between a "magical" luncheon and a "real" one. Due to the inadequacy of the blessing power of his mantra, Bhadra was unable to dissolve the appearance of his magical illusion, while the superior power of the Buddha's real blessing gave what would otherwise be a magical illusion the same perceptual continuity as the conventionally real. But the specifics of the magical illusion created as "illusion" by Bhadra and made "real" by the Buddha are identical. The appearances of the waking state do not actually differ even a whit from the appearances of the dream state, and if we recognize dream as dream, then release from suffering is instantaneous.

If right now we recognize our fixated attachment to friends, reputation, and possessions, our hatred for enemies, and all other emotivity as dream appearances and understand them as nonexistent, as mere notional-conceptual products of mind, then external, material things will not be able to disturb us. Realizing that everything is apparent yet nonexistent—just images of emptiness—we attain the great citadel of everlasting pure pleasure.

At present we may have neither heard nor understood Dzogchen, or perhaps we have heard only its echo. Because of our lack of familiarity with Dzogchen, and because of our credulous minds, we run after various good objects or run away from bad objects of perception. Consciousness is like a dog following in his master's footsteps, and the objective field is like the play of the objects of the five senses projected by a magician. When these two—consciousness and object—coincide, that coincidence is called "attachment of pure presence to an object." That apparently objective aspect, flowing uninterruptedly like a deep river, although a mentally projected delusion, may nevertheless be experienced as real for days and months, for years and lifetimes. Thus an old man, a hundred years old, might see his life from birth to dying as the daydream of a single day. We experience the objective and subjective poles that never exist separately from each other as duality, and everything we perceive becomes in this way a meaningless distraction, a chasing after what is not there in the first place. In that way we are inveigled by stupidity into immersing ourselves in the ongoing continuum of samsara. In *The Treasury of the Dharmadhatu*, Longchenpa says,

> With the mind preoccupied by different petty concerns,
> A moment of inconsequential fixation becomes a habit,
> And a day, a month, a year—a lifetime—goes by unheeded.
> We deceive ourselves by construing the nondual as duality.

So, first, absorb the excellent view and gradually become familiar with it. Until that is done, no matter how much we listen to the teaching and accumulate knowledge, and no matter how deep the teaching, there will be no benefit whatsoever. The mind training is explained later in the section on meditation, but, in short, we must first recognize the view itself, then gain conviction in it, and finally thereby realize our potential. Until we are stabilized in our attainment, we must meditate.

Pleasure and pain are there for all, from high officials and the rich to beggars and small children. No matter what the degree of suffering, everyone—intellectual, fool, even the animals that know nothing—tries to solve problems by various methods requiring continuous struggle. Some are able to ameliorate their suffering a little by skillful means, while others, ignorant of technique, cannot even begin to solve their own problems. Whether it's the frustration of getting situations and things they don't want, or the frustration of not getting the ones they do want—not to mention violence, sickness, starvation, and so on—all beings are perpetually under the heel of suffering. The antidote to all this suffering—the single panacea or "white" medicine that cures all ills—is the understanding that no matter what feelings of happiness and sorrow we experience, none have substantial existence and none are anything more than mental projections and labels.

Whatever experiences of suffering or happiness we encounter, we should allow the natural ease and calm of pure presence to just suffuse and permeate them without allowing our own pure presence, in a process of reification, to arise as objects and attachments to objects. If we gaze at these experiences directly, seeing them clearly, the entire field of suffering and happiness will then vanish like haze melting into the sky. When, in this way, apparent substantiality has been ultimately penetrated, not once or twice but again and again, suffering and happiness and all the experiences of samsara and nirvana will be experienced as the magical illusion of a skillful magician, or like a dream, an echo, and the rest of the eight analogies of phantasmagorical illusion. Whosoever is without hope of happiness or fear of suffering, understanding that all experience is the great illusionary display of mind itself, he or she will become a Dzogchen yogin or yogini. If we understand that all appearances of our present life are naturally insubstantial, then even the happiness and sufferings of dreamtime will be recognized as dream. If dream is understood as dream again and again, then the bardo will be recognized as bardo. More details on this topic will found in the following chapter.

1.15 An Introduction to the Secret of Mind

The mind can be considered under two aspects: relative mind and mind-in-itself—what we call "the nature of mind." According to the glorious Rongzompa's view in *Applying the Mahayana Method*, the two terms are "mind" and "luminous mind," or "enlightened mind." "Mind," the relative mind, is the intellect, characterized as fictive and notional-conceptual; it is that mind which divides experience into an apparent subject and apparent object. Luminous mind, on the other hand, is nondual primal awareness, primordial spontaneity, the mind as it actually is. To address the question of whether the intellect and luminous mind are one or two, take the example of a firebrand and its circle of fire. When the firebrand is held in the hand and whirled around at night, a wheel of fire appears. This wheel of fire seems to be independent of the firebrand itself because nothing can be observed in the dark other than the wheel of fire, but it actually has no independent existence at all—it is totally dependent upon the firebrand and the properties of the eye. The subjective intellect—our sense or experience of a self separate from an observed "objective" field—is like the wheel of fire: we can say upon reflection that though it appears and is experienced, it has no substantial existence whatsoever beyond this appearance. When luminous mind self-manifests as a condition of dualistic perception, it is called "fictive mind" and is just like the wheel of fire, arising in dependence on something else and having no true existence of its own. Primal awareness, free of dualistic perception, is called "luminous mind" and is just like the light of the firebrand, on the basis of which the illusion of a wheel can arise.

The basis of the illusion of the wheel of fire is nothing other than the firebrand, but the firebrand itself does not partake of the illusion of the wheel of fire—the firebrand does not "see" the wheel and is not "deluded." So be sure that while the intellectual mind's delusions are not other than the nature of mind and the creativity of pure presence, luminous mind itself should not be mistaken for the intellect—it could not be the intellect because luminous mind is free of adulterating dualistic perception. In *The Medium Matrix Perfection of Wisdom Sutra in Eight Thousand Verses*, it is said,

> The mind has no substantial existence—
> The nature of mind is clear light.

Mind can be understood as manifesting under two aspects: the delusive mind that is the intellect and the real mind that is its nature. These two aspects are like the wheel of fire and the firebrand, respectively. The fictive mind is primordially insubstantial and without inherent existence. It is limited by conceptual delusions of dualistic perception that appear everywhere and move constantly, never standing still. Leading us all, self-righteously, this fictive mind believes itself lord of everything, and, as a result, through the concepts of "I" and "mine," it finds samsara everywhere.

Real mind, the nature of mind, mind in its natural aspect, is primordially free of the discursive elaboration of subject and object, of grasper and the grasped. It does not consist of substance or material things. On the contrary, the essence of the nature of mind is uncompounded and immutable. The primal awareness that is the true nature of mind is profound clarity abiding in the Vase Body of Eternal Youth, the dimension of eternal life in pure being and primal awareness.

Just as a wheel of fire is nothing other than the firebrand, the fictive intellectual mind is nothing other than the real luminous mind. As Longchenpa says in *The Treasury of the Supreme Approach*, "The appearance of external objects arises naturally from mind's magical display; internal appearances of mind arise naturally from the creativity of pure presence."

All external seemingly concrete phenomena arise from mind's magical display, while the internal appearance of mind, our seeming subjectivity, arises from pure presence's creativity. In mistaking what is nondual as two, in mistaking the field of experience as object and subject, attachment arises, along with the rest of our emotional afflictions.

To cure human illness, first we must diagnose the disease; only then can we take appropriate medicine. In the *Supreme Tantra*, Lord Maitreya says, "To know the disease is to eradicate its cause." So, first, investigate this fictive intellectual mind. Our mind in this present moment is seemingly seeing and knowing appearances very clearly, but the mind is not at all what it seems to be. It cannot be found on top or under our flesh or fat, or in the blood or lymph, or in the hair or nails, and so forth. Likewise, it cannot be found in the forms of material objects, in white, yellow, red, or green colors, or in square, triangular, half-moon, or circular shapes. It is not merely that our eyes cannot see it, but its discovery is beyond even the most advanced technology. It cannot be found inside or outside or in between. Although we cannot say for certain that it existed in the past, that it exists in the present, or that it will exist in the future, what we are perceiving now as felt knowledge, bright and aware, is called "perception."

This perception is a projection of our mind—self-envisionment. If we know that objects of dualistic perception are rootless and baseless, then they can be recognized without attachment or reification as simply raw presence, pellucid emptiness. The foregoing is called "the introduction to real luminous mind" or "dharmakaya awareness." If you think that this secret of mind is difficult to understand by ordinary people, of course, you are right!

The principal objective of the three turnings of the wheel by our teacher Shakyamuni Buddha is stated in *The Sutra of Individual Liberation*,

Abandon all vice,
Cultivate every virtue,
And tame the mind:
That is buddha-dharma.

Shakyamuni Buddha taught many methods of taming the delusory mind. But left to ourselves, we do not feel any compulsion to look back at and examine what we call "mind" or any desire to discover its nature; for that reason a doubt about it never arises. What feels happiness or sadness, guides us in life, is the source of all modern scientific knowledge, and discriminates between good and bad—in short, what sees, knows, expresses, and experiences all knowledge—is the ordinary mind. If we turn back and look at it for a moment, examining it, we will find it to be like a motor car without brakes, running at more than a hundred miles an hour, an accident always imminent. The mind, in its deluded attachment to the five sensory objects, is like a runaway vehicle, completely out of control. The consequence of a serious motor accident is at worst that we die or at best that we are injured; the consequence of an accident of an uncontrolled mind fuelled by attachment, hatred, and ignorance is untold suffering in this life and the next. On the other hand, if our motor car is serviced by good mechanics, and if we are competent drivers, we will arrive at our destination without injury. Similarly, if our mind is serviced at the service station of buddha-dharma by a lama skillful in introducing the nature of mind, a lama who can effectively repair the mind, we will live in complete happiness in both this life and the next.

To know the nature of one's own mind—mind's reality—is to see the face of buddha oneself. If such realization is nothing else than the actuality of knowing the natural perfection of seemingly concrete phenomena, then the purpose of Shakyamuni Buddha's many hundred volumes of sutra and tantra, in their inconceivably varied and vast scope, is nothing other than the elucidation of this very essence—what else could it be? The principal teaching of all the buddhas of past, present, and future concerns taming the mind. It is difficult to know the nature of mind but not impossible. Just as the butter in milk will not precipitate out unless the milk is churned, just as the gold in its ore cannot be amassed unless the ore is refined, just as we cannot access underground water unless we dig a hole in the ground, and just as we cannot see the sun unless the clouds disperse, so too until thoughts dissolve, luminous mind is trapped in the dualistically grasping intellect. When all discursive thought and concepts and all constructs of the dualistic mind dissolve into their spaciousness, the real luminous mind in all its clarity shines in its own space, and there is no need to look for it anywhere else. If we churn milk, butter forms; if we refine the ore, we amass the gold; if we dig a well, we find the water; if the cloud disperses, the light of the sun shines through. Similarly, if we keep our mind in genuine ease in its natural state at any moment of happiness or sadness, or while thinking, whether in joy, or fear, and so on, then from within the intellectual mind shines a bright intensity, and right there is mind's peaceful reality, the dharmakaya, a dimension that is free of the attributes of face, limbs, and so on. In this way, nondual intrinsic awareness is revealed as the true unitary nature of the perceived objective field and the perceiving subject, free of all reference points.

All sentient beings have buddha-nature, intrinsic awareness, in their mindstream. As it is said in *The King of Samadhi Sutra*, "Buddha-nature pervades all." Just as its oil permeates a sesame seed, so the identity or essence of all sentient beings is no other than buddha. If we do not recognize this, we consider one as many and many as one; we regard suffering as happiness and vice versa; we cling to a self though there is no self to cling to, and so forth, and by the power of mistaken identity, we are stuck perennially in samsara.

1.16 The Dualistic Nature of the Intellect Illustrated in the Question-Answer Method of the Sutras

This story is taken from the sutra *The Teaching of the Noble Youth "Incredible Light."* Once in Sravasti when the Bhagawan Buddha was collecting alms, he passed an empty house by a cemetery where a number of people had gathered. An extraordinarily beautiful child had been abandoned there, and the people had gathered to stare. Bhagawan sent his close disciple Ananda to see what was happening, and, upon hearing Ananda's report, he said that he thought the child was a highly fortunate being who had the potential to understand his teaching and who had previously accumulated immense merit. He went into the house in order to lead the people on to the path of virtue and to show love for the child. When he arrived, he asked the child if he was not afraid of snakes, *yaksha* spirits, wolves, and other animals living in the cemetery.

"Who needs to fear when all things are selfless and empty?" the child replied.

"Due to your past sins you are here to suffer in this empty house," said Bhagawan.

"Do you, Bhagawan Buddha, still have a solid concept of an empty house?" asked the child. "Haven't we abandoned all such ideas?"

"I have no such idea," replied Bhagawan. "I came here because I love you."

"There is no substantive atom existing in any entity called 'sentient being,'" said the child. "So what is the object of your love and where will you put it?"

"Nonself and emptiness are not understood by many people," replied Bhagawan. "With a singular intention toward them, in order to create the great love, I accumulate merit through wise discriminating activity."

"You know your own emptiness, and you have peace of mind," said the child, "but have you actually abandoned misconceptions such as 'sentient beings' and 'suffering' in the light of the primal awareness of emptiness?"

"Realizing emptiness and the peace of nirvana, in order to mature beings and allow them to attain the nirvana that is beyond both samsara and nirvana, the buddhas teach them out of their great love for them."

"You, the Tathagata, have not yet rid yourself of erroneous concepts," insisted the child. "If the concept of 'sentient beings' is investigated, it is found to be inconsistent with what is concrete. So where is the object of your love?"

"When sentient beings fully apprehend the luminous mind and attain buddha, through their analysis they find that sentient beings no longer exist. Even so, the Buddha, with indomitable patience and great compassion, seeks to help all those beings who without analyzing or examining the nature of dualistic delusionary appearances are tortured by suffering."

"Dualistic thought and attendant emotions have no substantial root. If both outer and inner body are investigated, no substantial cause of either can be found. Since afflictions cannot be discovered as anything substantial, what is the need of an antidote?" asked the child.

"All the misconceptions about emotional affliction arise from the labeling mind," said Bhagawan. "So that they may discard all the gross and subtle afflictions, the profound and vast teaching is given to beings."

"Why do we need so many investigations? The nature of mind is clear light and thus emotional adulteration cannot arise in it," said the child. "Although erroneous thoughts may give rise to reification, they can never affect the natural clear light that is the nature of unconditioned mind."

"What you say is true," admitted Bhagawan. "The mind always stays in the clear light of great bliss, but adventitiously, due to delusory dualistic perception, ordinary beings are afflicted."

"Emotions are immaterial things," said the child. "And they lack spatial extension. How do those emotions arise so adventitiously?" asked the child. "Please tell me!"

"Let's take the example of clouds appearing in the sky," replied Bhagawan. "They are not different from the nature of the sky, but suddenly they obscure the sky. Emotions arise in the same way. The luminous nature of mind is seemingly suddenly obscured by emotion, but in reality it is never obscured."

Finally, the child said "By your grace, I have gained full self-confidence. I have spoken my mind without hesitation, and now I seek your forgiveness."

> Then the Bhagawan Buddha took out his right hand from his robe, and the child took hold of a finger of his hand and stood up. Bhagawan took him out of that empty house and put him on the path. The people were surprised that the Bhagawan answered the questions of a mere child who was so afflicted, and the people were amazed and paid homage to the Buddha.
>
> "You have purified your karma," he said to the child. "Now remember the root of your past virtue and let it be known to the people gathered here by a display of some miracle." Then the child sprang from the ground to a spot seven feet high in the sky and light radiated from him and that light spread over Sravasti and throughout the whole world.

That story is told in verse in the sutra. Here it is simplified in prose. Read the sutra if you would like to know more.

As in the sutra *The Teaching of the Noble Youth "Incredible Light," The Supreme Tantra* of Lord Maitreya notes that the mind has the quality of clear light but is obscured by adventitious emotional afflictions. Nine similes illustrating our ignorance of the hidden luminous mind are given there: (i) ignorance of buddha wrapped within a closed lotus; (ii) ignorance of honey within a flower; (iii) ignorance of a seed within its chaff; (iv) ignorance of gold in a cesspit; (v) ignorance of treasure beneath the earth; (vi) ignorance of a tree inside the bark; (vii) ignorance of a jewel inside tattered clothes; (viii) ignorance of a king inside the womb of a poor woman; (ix) ignorance of solid gold in the mud. Like that, the buddhas guide us by metaphor. Buddha-nature is wrapped within desire, hatred, and ignorance as illustrated by the nine examples above. Those who do not realize it are like an elephant keeper who keeps his elephant in a stable and then goes searching for it in the jungle—a totally futile exercise. Knowing that buddha is within but looking for him outside is like sitting beside a lake and begging for water, or like having a feast spread in front of one and yet dying of hunger, and so on.

Believing that happiness and sadness depend on external objects, those who do not understand that buddha is within are, as we say, deluded. So all human beings, great, small, and middling, always strive to attain happiness and abandon sadness only through external objects. We search for objects, argue about objects, wander around objects, but we do not investigate where happiness and sorrow come from, their cause, or who experiences them. Failing to investigate the source of happiness and sadness and searching for them instead in the objective field is just like ignoring the root and focusing on the branch, putting a jewel aside and buying glass trinkets, refusing fine food in preference to muck, or refusing medicine and taking poison. When we realize everything as our own envisionment, baseless and rootless, it is like the poor finding wealth, the hungry finding a feast, and the sick finding healing medicine. When we realize that both happiness and sadness arise from the mind as self-envisionment, no attachment to happiness or aversion to suffering can occur. When we understand everything as mental illusion, both happiness and sadness are like a child's play.

We elders regard a sand castle built by children as an imaginary castle and have no attachment to it, while the children consider it to be real and may become quite attached; when by chance it is destroyed, the children are saddened and cry. When we see the children becoming upset, we console them and urge them to stop crying, because their sand castle was imaginary; we give them proof of that in order to relieve them of attachment to it. When the children come to understand that the castle was a fiction, they are relieved of their sadness. Knowing that the sand castle has no real value, we elders were neither moved to sadness by its destruction nor moved to happiness by its beauty. What we ordinary sentient beings consider to be real—the objects upon which our happiness and sadness depend—are to the noble ones like the sand castles of children. They have realized that unpredictable and unreliable happiness and suffering are without essence, and thus avoid attachment to them.

In general, happiness and suffering arise due to attachment to objects in the sensory fields. When we understand that objects in the sensory fields are unreal, without substantial existence, just like the reflection of the moon in water, then external things no longer have power to hurt the mind. In the same way, other people's suffering has no power to affect us deeply. We are not so affected by the suffering of someone else's child, whereas the suffering of our own creates deep sorrow, although in neither case is there a direct connection with our own mind. There is no cause for sadness in either case except when the mind generates the illusion of a sense of self. Different feelings thus arise from the same incident.

When we understand such ideas, we can be free from both temporal suffering in this life and ultimate suffering in the lower realms.

1.17 Reasonable proof that buddha-nature exists in our mindstream

The sutras and tantras of definitive meaning (as opposed to the scriptures of provisional meaning) teach that the ordinary mind of all sentient beings is buddha-potential. Direct perception verifies that buddha-nature saturates mind just as oil suffuses the sesame seed. Experience on the path leads to the accomplishment of the fruit of the ultimate level of buddha. Here, where buddha-potential is revealed, knowledge, love, and power become fully mature. Sentient beings in the three lower realms of samsara are ignorant of the natural perfection of things and wander as the devils of hell, hungry ghosts, and animals. The same is true for beings of the three higher realms—gods, demigods, and human beings. Yet all possess the potential for attaining buddha right here and now.

We can see that knowledge, love, and power exist in the animal realm (I use the animal realm as an example because the devils of hell and the hungry ghosts are invisible to us). For example, even though no one taught ants how to care for their babies, they still do it very well. When fire or water destroys their nest, without concern for their own precious lives, they try to save their eggs by carrying them to a safe place. Have you seen that? This is proof right in front of our eyes that all sentient beings have compassionate mind.

In the human realm, we have knowledge to the extent that when we feel cold, we move into the sun; when we become hot, we look for a cool place; and when there is danger of fire, water, or wild animals, we escape to a safe place. Moreover, animal researchers have found that each animal or bird species has its own unique knowledge. Elephants can tell where there is underground water in the desert through the sensation in their feet. Birds can tell when it is going to rain. Creatures living underground can tell when an earthquake will occur, and they come out from their holes and make strange noises. This proves that beings have knowledge.

Animals also have power. Each animal is capable of helping or harming its group. Creatures that are more powerful snatch food from inferiors and take it to their own place. Ants, though smaller than tiny pebbles, associate in thousands to build their huge and beautiful nests up to two or three feet in height. This is evidence of their power.

In 1979, at Nakchuka in Tibet, a nomad encampment was threatened by wolves. In a meeting to discuss the problem, the community decided to kill the wolves; accordingly, they began a hunt. But the pair of wolves that threatened them escaped. The hunters, enlarging the area of their search, finally found three wolf cubs. But before they could kill the cubs, one sinful elder objected that that was not the best thing to do. "We should tie the cubs to a pole," he suggested, "and in the night light a fire around them. This will bring the mother wolf, which we will then also kill." They did as he suggested, and at about ten o'clock, they lit a big fire and hid nearby with swords, guns, and stones. When the wolf cubs cried, the mother wolf came to help her poor babies, jumping within the circle of fire to save them, and the hunters emerged from their hiding places shouting, shooting, and throwing stones. At first the wolf retreated, but when she heard her cubs crying, she returned to save them, challenging guns and stones: she became trapped inside the circle of fire, and the mother and cubs were then killed.

This example shows that a wolf, like any animal, naturally, without need of instruction, treats its young with love, understanding what is beneficial and what is harmful. We can infer thereby that we all possess buddhanature of primal awareness, compassion, and power. Certainly if we do not possess the seed of buddha, then it is impossible to attain buddha. It is universally known that without the seed of barley, for example, there cannot be a barley shoot. If we do not possess the seed of buddha, no matter how we strive, all effort is useless. No matter how much we squeeze sand, there is no chance of obtaining juice. In his *In Praise of the Dharmadhatu*, the second buddha, Nagarjuna, says,

> If a stratum of gold exists,
> Gold may be discovered;
> If there is no buddha basis, whatever you do,
> Only emotivity is engendered.

~

Furthermore, in the second turning of the wheel, in the sutrayana, as also in the final turning, the victorious, perfected Buddha Shakyamuni, in accord with the supreme view of definitive meaning that was taught to show the potential of buddha-nature, says in *The Medium Matrix Perfection of Wisdom Sutra in Eight Thousand Verses*,

> The luminous mind is not dualistic mind;
> Its nature is clear light.

And also,

> Absolute buddha-nature is empty in essence, and its nature is without any substance, without any intention, and without any attribute. Luminous mind is not relative mind.

And in the final turning of the wheel it is said,

> It is not like the emptiness of nothingness—like a vacuum—but rather it is natural radiance; appearing by itself as knowledge, compassion, and power, it is clear light in its nature.

Its clear light nature is first evoked in the final turning of the wheel. The emptiness of the second turning and the clear light of the final turning are completely consistent. Emptiness and clear light are inseparable, and therein arises the spontaneity of primal awareness that is all-embracing compassion. In the presentation of the causal basis, buddha-nature is threefold—empty in essence, clear in its nature, and compassionate in its all-pervading emanation. If we examine buddha-nature from the absolute perspective, since it cannot be established as anything that is not emptiness, and it is neither impermanent nor permanent, its essence is identified as emptiness.

If we apply ordinary sensory cognition and inferential cognition to discover buddha-nature, it is like congenitally blind people exploring an elephant with their hands—they can never know the beast in its entirety.

We might assume then that buddha-nature cannot be established by logic, but this is not so. After we establish that the unity of emptiness and appearances has neither existence nor nonexistence, nor both existence and nonexistence, nor neither existence nor nonexistence, so that it is without ontological status and that as such it has no sensorially perceptible attributes, we have proven buddha-nature to be emptiness itself, an absolute. The natural radiance of the emptiness of buddha-nature is uncrystallizing clear light. Appearances and the absolute spaciousness and primal awareness of the natural perfection self-arise like the sun and its rays. This pure conventional logic of the primal awareness of appearances establishes the reality of the clear light. As the omniscient Botrul Dongak Tenpai Nyima says in his *Analysis of View and Doctrine*,

> Buddha-nature cannot be established by absolute proof;
> And ordinary sensory perception cannot prove it:
> It is proven by inferential logic
> And by the direct insight of the noble ones.

~

In the tantras of the mantrayana, such as the *Guhyagarbha Tantra*, the path of liberation and omniscience is taught by means of the four kinds of appearances: appearances in the ground of natural perfection, impure delusory appearances, appearances while traveling the path, and ultimate appearance as the fruit.

Appearances in the ground of natural perfection as immaculate, undefiled illusion show that primal awareness abides in the mindstream of all sentient beings like oil suffusing a sesame seed.

Impure delusory appearances arise out of the ground of being, unrecognized as primal awareness. This absence of recognition is called "inborn or innate ignorance." When conceptual thought becomes increasingly gross and rough and we misconceive our own envisionment, that ignorance is called "the ignorance of imputation." Through innate ignorance, the primal awareness of our self-envisioned appearances is not understood, and thus we become attached to the name and form of our personality, which is composed of the five aggregates. Through attachment to a self, desire for beauty and hostility to ugliness arise, and thoughts of desire and hatred are generated, like the gathering of black clouds. Since we do not understand the nature of the objective field just as it is, we discriminate between enemies and friends, good and bad, right and wrong, and between what is to be cultivated and rejected, and through such biased preferential labeling, we wander continuously in samsara. Grasping at objects where there is nothing, clinging to illusions, holding unity as a multiplicity, and taking variety as a singularity evince the beginning of impure delusory appearances, like the credits at the beginning of a movie.

When appearances are taken as the path or the process, from objective form to the buddha's omniscience, they have no foundation or inherent existence, and our envisionment of them as empty form is nothing but magical illusion. Envisionment is explained as either pure or impure according to its authentic or inauthentic nature, as either nondelusive or delusive, as primal awareness or mind, as buddha or as sentient being. In the vision of the noble ones' primal awareness, the nature of being and appearance coincide in the great purity of relativity and absolute sameness, which is the inseparable reality of purity and sameness and other similar formulae expressing the unity of being and appearance. Many means of attaining liberation and buddha are taught, but we must have certainty in the view of the inseparable reality of purity and sameness. Here, without depending upon the relative path of illusory training in mudra, mantra, samadhi, and so on, there is no way to attain the level of ultimate nirvana. This is the path of the yogin.

Lord Maitreya, in *The Supreme Tantra*, says,

> Impure, impurely pure, and perfectly pure
> Are the three degrees of purity
> Relating to sentient beings, bodhisattvas, and sugatas.

Impure delusory appearance refers to sentient beings' appearances. Impurely pure appearances are of being and pure-lands, increasing in light and intensity from the first bodhisattva level to the tenth, which is the bodhisattva's envisionment. The perfectly pure is the buddha's envisionment with the twenty-five resultant dharmas, the twenty-five aspects of buddha-potential in fruition (see section 4.1). This last is the fourth, the ultimate appearance as the fruit.

~

Chandrakirti in his *Entry into the Middle Way* says,

> Without dependence upon the relatively real
> The ultimate meaning cannot be realized;
> If the ultimate meaning is not understood,
> Nirvana cannot be achieved.

Appearances manifest according to karmically conditioned propensities, like clouds of impure delusion; through the power of the meditation process, they dissolve into the sky. After the purification that leaves no residue, the potential of the five modes of being and the five modes of primal awareness arise like the sun shining through a gap in the clouds. But in actuality, the intrinsic awareness of Dzogchen is not produced or initiated by causes and conditions, for the potential of pure being and primal awareness is intrinsically present and manifests spontaneously.

All knowledge of things is unreal; appearances are like miracles of the mind, no more than the cloud display of the rootless all-pervading sky. This is illustrated and explained by many different metaphors. There is a Tibetan saying: "Don't parrot arrant nonsense; repeat only what is important." Do not irritate intelligent people by foolishly addressing a trivial point over and over again. On the other hand, what is crucial and vital should be reiterated. If an attendant is to be sent away on an important mission, he must first be instructed about the work a few days before he leaves, and instructed then again a few days later; finally, we need to give him instruction one last time while seeing him off at the airport. Until we have a genuine realization that our envisionment of samsara and nirvana is rootless and baseless, we need to be reminded a hundred times in various ways. And we shouldn't feel any irritation about that! As Shabkhar Lama says in his *Flight of the Garuda*,

> Emaho! My lucky heart-sons!
> If the horse is not spurred, it will not gallop;
> If the milk is not churned, butter will not congeal.
> The meaning of this epic song,

> If unelaborated, could not be told,
> So listen contentedly without irritation!

So just as Lama Shabkhar advises, read with equanimity!

1.18 When the Natural Perfection of Mind Is Realized, There Is No Need to Apply an Appropriate Antidote to Each Karmic Impulse

The purpose of any elucidation of the four philosophical views and the nine approaches in buddha-dharma is to reveal and illuminate the natural perfection of mind. If we understand the natural perfection of mind, then the keys to the philosophical views are revealed, and the nine approaches are completed. Realize the natural perfection of mind, and all our sinful obscurations, accumulated over many eons, are purified in an instant. The karmas that we have accumulated in previous eons are countless: a pile of karmas higher than Mt. Meru and wider than the ocean is purified in a moment if only we realize the nature of mind.

Consider how obscurations can be purified. If each particularity needs a separate antidote in order to be purified, since the karma of beginningless and endless births has no limit, there can no possibility of exhausting it. As emotional afflictions have no substantial existence but nonetheless appear through dualistic delusion, just like mirage and dream, with the arising of the conditions that cause them to vanish, they too disappear automatically. So a separate antidote need not be applied to each emotion. Whatever needs correction is released just as it is if only we can arrive at the natural place of intrinsic presence, where past, present, and future are identical.

In *Applying the Mahayana Method*, Rongzompa introduces this discussion: A man's father was killed by a tree, and thereafter the man hated all trees. Does this hatred depend upon or arise from the tree, or does it arise as an independent phenomenon or separate entity? If it is the former, then burning down trees will assuage the hatred. But we know that such activity does not facilitate the desired result. If it is the latter, then the incidences of hatred would be beyond number; even if they were counted to the limit of the eon, hatred would not come to an end. Likewise, the process of abandoning each arising of hatred would proceed endlessly, and we would never come to the end of abandonment.

In the tantra *Recitation of the Names of Manjushri*, it is said,

> Instantaneous differentiation,
> And also instantaneous buddha!

Consider a lamp that illuminates a north-facing cave that has been in darkness for a thousand years. We cannot say that the darkness of eons is beyond illumination, for the instant a lamp is brought into it, the cave is surely illuminated. Once we realize the natural perfection of mind, then there is no doubt that all the obscurations of beginningless lives along with accumulated karmic imprints will be removed instantaneously.

The peerless Rongzompa, quoting from a Mahayana sutra in *Applying the Mahayana Method*, says, "Through an understanding of the nonexistence of karma and its nonmaturation, the obscurations of the bodhisattva's primal awareness are removed." Consider the case of king Indrabodhi, whose realization of pure presence and release were simultaneous. Of course, if it is suggested that this renders meaningless whatever Shakyamuni Buddha taught in the four noble truths about karma and its effect, what is to be cultivated and what is to abandoned, and so on, that is not so. Renunciation, antidotes, and the doctrine of the four noble truths regarding what to adopt and what to abandon are taught to less intelligent individuals and to academics and intellectuals so that they may be led into the Mahayana. Once they enter into the Mahayana and study well, they will gradually attain realization.

1.19 Reconciliation of the view that the world is an empty, unreal subjective delusion with the scientific view that it is composed of atoms

Those who want to enter fully into the buddha-dharma should have faith in the ineffable, unvocalized side of the Buddha's message. Of the two types of student, the dull and the bright, the dull have faith in the inexpressible due to trust in their lama and the Buddhist scriptures. The bright explore the nature of phenomena and realize that appearances are merely nominal concepts of the mind, like the reflection of the moon in water that appears to be real but cannot be located in the upper, lower, or middle part of a container. Although they see the same object in different ways, many people mistakenly believe that the object has some substantial existence. This is like a person sleeping in a very small house who, while dreaming, believes that hundreds of dream elephants are able to fit inside it.

Scientists believe that all things are made of collections of atoms. Water, for example, is an aggregation of three atoms—one atom of oxygen and two atoms of hydrogen. The world and the beings residing in it are all similar aggregations. Buddha, too, accepted the appearance of things even though all phenomena are of the nature of emptiness. In *The Heart Sutra*, it is said, "Form is emptiness; emptiness is form. Emptiness is not other than form; form is not other than emptiness." All experience arises from emptiness. Emptiness is nothing other than the nature of appearances. What appears is thus the ultimate nature of experience.

Buddhists assert that no matter what particle nuclear physicists might discover in the future, it will not possess a solid core, no matter how small, but will be empty of any substantial essence. It is simply impossible to find an apparent material entity that is not in actuality unreal and empty. This is established as the nature of reality. In his *Beacon of Certainty*, the very wise Ju Mipham says,

> Inclining toward neither emptiness nor appearance,
> No basis whatsoever can be established;
> Due to the equality of that pair, in whatever appears,
> The objective field may be seen in many ways.

Emptiness appears in many forms, but if we try to analyze those illusory forms, nothing is there.

The whole world is surely an envisionment. When we are intoxicated, we feel the house collapsing or shaking. When we are in a happy mood, we think that the moon and the trees are singing. When we are sad, we think that the moon and the lotus flowers are crying. These situations are all subjectively envisioned and actually have no continuity or substantiality. The moon and the lotus lack all concepts of happiness or sorrow or beauty or ugliness. Even though we investigate each and every part of them a hundred times, we will not find beauty and happiness anywhere. They are nothing but envisionment. They do not exist in truth. Buddha shows that the three dimensions of spatial extension exist in a single mustard seed in such a way that the mustard seed does not expand and those dimensions do not contract. This is not an illusion that is out of accord with nature as is, say, the performance of a magician; it is the actual state of seemingly concrete objects. In *The Treasury of the Dharmadhatu*, Longchenpa says,

> The creativity of luminous mind, pulsating outward and inward,
> Being nothing at all, yet appearing as everything whatsoever,
> Paints magnificent, amazing, magical emanation.

We need a little confidence. If we demand visible and audible proof, then perforce we remain in samsara. In *The Wish-Fulfilling Treasury*, Longchenpa says,

> Dzogchen—
> Shown but not visible;
> Explained but not comprehended.

Buddha's ineffable meaning cannot be expressed in words, and when it is spoken, it is as if it were being heard by cattle. Even the tongue of primal awareness cannot express it. It cannot become anyone's object of perception. People may think, therefore, that primal awareness of intrinsic presence as such is an aberration of the mind, but of course that is not so. The ineffable is the objective field of perception of the primal awareness of intrinsic presence in each and every individual being; it cannot be understood as an object "out there" or a subject "within" or as something that has color and shape—it can be perceived only by the Buddha. Based on Shakyamuni Buddha's teaching, if by logic we establish all things, from form to omniscience, as mere illusory mental projection or mental labels, then there is no way whatsoever to avoid gaining confidence in the inexpressible teaching. Even though there is no substantial existence in objects of knowledge, according to the manner in which the ground of being is defined by the particular inclinations of the various schools, there are many different varieties of appearance—samsara and nirvana, good and bad, rejection and adoption, god and demon, happiness and suffering, beautiful and ugly, inner and outer philosophical views, and so on—labeled and held by the mind. The mind's functions assert the actual existence of mind and all those various imputations, and the mind provides thousands of reasons, with scriptural authority, to support this contention and prove itself right, as well as thousands of reasons, with scriptural authority, to prove others wrong. Mind is thus convinced of its own existence and proclaims it with a loud voice in every corner of the country. Now check whether the distinctions we make and the imputations and beliefs we insist upon are mental projections or not.

1.20 Sickness and Physical Pain Are Relieved by Making a Habit of Recognizing Pure Empty Presence

Knowing that the world is a magical display of mind, convinced that the world is a magical display of mind, realizing experientially that the world is a magical display of mind, with no trace of disbelief remaining, trust in the ineffable arises automatically. If we have such trust, we are not surprised when we hear that sentient beings are the Buddha and that there is no pain in hell and no happiness in the buddha fields.

Shantideva, in *Entering the Way of the Bodhisattva*, says,

> Who made the blazing grounds of hell?
> Whence do these fires come?
> All such things are created
> By the sin-ridden mind.

As mentioned above, "Our ordinary perception is similar to perception when we are under the influence of dhatura," and, as quoted from *The King of Samadhi Sutra*, "Eyes, nose, and ears cannot be trusted." We grow strong in confidence through such statements. By force of understanding that the six kinds of beings are figments of mind, we gain confidence in the undeniable evidence that an individual's different actions produce variable experience of happiness or suffering. Without needing to examine cause and effect, we will know indisputably that this is so.

In *The Treasury of the Dharmadhatu*, Longchenpa says,

> Creativity is projected as display into another dimension,
> Where it appears as the multifarious variety of the universe.
> Never say categorically that there is no cause and effect!

When we gain full confidence in the interdependence of outer and inner causes and conditions, the knot of hope and fear regarding acceptance of nirvana and rejection of samsara will be untied instantaneously. At that moment we become great yogins and yoginis, perfected in the matrix of pure presence that is the sameness of samsara and nirvana. Anyone, man or woman, who hears, experiences, and realizes such a view will remain in the state of permanent supreme blissfulness or enjoy the happiness of uncontaminated primal awareness as the most fortunate of noble beings. Though such beings appear outwardly human, their mind is the same as Buddha. These yogins and yoginis experience everything—both suffering and happiness—as happiness.

How do ordinary beings experience suffering and happiness? When our daily work goes well, whether business, manufacturing, education, farming, office management, politics, or anything else, we feel pleasure. When it goes badly, we feel unhappiness. Sometimes unwanted things occur, and we suffer. Like a revolving wheel, happiness and suffering alternate continuously in ordinary people's experience no matter whether they are leaders or common people, rich or poor. Obviously, every individual experiences both suffering and happiness.

In this world, at this very present moment, some are singing out of happiness, and some are crying out of frustration. Since both happiness and suffering are free from causality, we always tend to feel joy in pleasure and sorrow in suffering, and if we are happy, we see all as pleasure, and if we suffer, we see all as sorrow. Ignorant of our own self-envisionment, we see pleasure as continuous, and likewise we regard suffering as true and unremitting whenever we are stuck in it. Due to this, if we get a little happiness, arrogance increases, and if we get a little suffering, aversion increases, and so forth. Arrogance and aversion are like the roots of a tree out of which the branches of suffering grow.

This happens because we do not know that both happiness and suffering are figments of mind. As mentioned above, yogins' and yoginis' own envisionment of illusion cannot torment them because they have understood that all happiness and suffering are merely mental appearances, and that, free of all marks of referential focus, the nature of mind is nonexistent and sealed by the impress of the dharmakaya. Right from the start, free of attachment, whatever appears is released in the matrix of pure presence. Yogins and yoginis do not try to alter the complexion of present suffering, nor do they try to change its color. The suffering dissolves by itself in its own place and vanishes.

Suppose travelers arrive on an island of gold. Even if they search for common earth and stone, they will not be able to find it. Likewise, even if the Dzogchen yogins and yoginis look for suffering, they will not find it. This does not mean that they never experience the external sufferings of birth, old age, sickness, and death, because suffering still arises, but such yogins and yoginis are free of the dense specific unalleviated suffering that habitually invades the mind.

For example, in a book by Dr. Sadhed Kumar Pahadi on painkilling medicines, in the chapter on benefits and detriments, before listing the various painkilling medicines, he explains how pain arises. The part of the body associated with pain sends a message to the brain, and it is in the brain that the pain is suffered, not in the body part that sent the message. No matter where the pain arises, the brain is where it is experienced: this is asserted by modern science. This is highly relevant to our topic. Analogously, no matter what the cause of joy or sorrow, it is all felt in the mind. If we can abide only in the nature—the essence—of mind, therefore, not only will internal suffering be eliminated, but external suffering also.

These days the disease of lost memory (which may, perhaps, be identified with Alzheimer's disease) is increasing. In the past such disease affected mostly people who were more than sixty years of age. As the saying goes, "A person of sixty forgets even his own name," and it was normal for people over sixty to start losing their memory. Sometimes they would talk without meaning or react with either excessive joy or sadness to minor issues. These days not only people over sixty but forty-year-olds also suffer from such memory loss. The main causes of the disease are severe pain, too much useless thinking, and so much input that the brain cannot rest. Too much time spent on the computer is one reason that the mind fails to rest. Further, people who party a lot, attend large gatherings, or work day and night in business or politics without eating or sleeping do not rest enough. They spend too much time thinking about concerns, large and small, and their minds cannot relax. Due to this, the blood cannot flow properly through the brain, and the "all-pervading wind" inhibits the subtle movements of mind, allowing fever and headache to develop. Sometimes we may feel that "wind" gets into the heart and makes us uneasy. These are all symptoms of the disease of memory loss. When we leave these symptoms without treatment for too long, we may lose our memory completely. Sometimes these symptoms will become more recognizable between the ages of sixty and seventy, when even the way to perform routine actions like eating and sleeping are forgotten and help is needed just to survive. Experts may advise physical exercise and strict dietary discipline, but there is no special medicine for memory loss. When we type on a computer faster than its capacity to process, it slows down and sometimes freezes, although it returns to normal if we delete some already programmed functions. If we could throw out some of the unwanted thoughts from our minds and give it a good rest, then, just like the computer, it might slowly return to normal. The best method of resting the mind, forsaking unwanted thoughts and clearing them from the mind, is meditation. The antidote to an absent mind is mindfulness.

For Dzogchen meditation, we need constant mindfulness, and there are two kinds. The first is conditioned mindfulness, the second ultimate mindfulness. For beginners, conditioned mindfulness is remembering what the lama taught and then applying it; that is meditation with a cause, which entails effort. Once that outer or preliminary meditation has been accomplished, the main practice is to abide in pure presence, where effort is unnecessary and meditation is natural and automatic. This is called "mindfulness of reality" and since it is effortless, we do not need to strive in any way to arrive there.

The main cause of absent-mindedness is failure to rest the mind, a theory that is supported by doctors. Meditation is the method of resting the mind. In meditation, through conditioned mindfulness, we first train to keep the mind in its own nature without grasping. If we return to that point again and again, thought—good or bad—will naturally disappear. Through this process, the mind becomes rested. If we can keep that up for a few hours, we will be in constant mindfulness, and no matter what happiness or sadness arises, attention will not be distracted. Through this practice, we will become mindful of reality, and thus more gentle, peaceful, and naturally happy.

Through mindfulness of reality, we can rest the mind. The brain and the heart relax thereby and stress-induced damage is eliminated. The mind becomes sharper, and in old age we will not encounter the problem of absent-mindedness. We can see this in Dzogchen yogins and yoginis who are ninety years or more in age and who still have sharp memories. When they teach, they can quote many texts that they had learned by heart. Moreover, they can challenge others on the topic of the nature of mind. This is not merely a contemporary phenomenon; it has been happening for thousands of years.

In 2001, I heard on the radio that in Malaysia many religious leaders and important scientists had gathered to discuss whether religion could help sick people. They had examined the condition of both religious and nonreligious persons suffering from HIV/AIDS and TB, and they had found that viral diseases spread slower among religious people than nonreligious. The nonreligious were found to be more anxious, and among them, viral contagion was greater. It was established by the religious leaders and great scientists at that conference that the degree of suffering varies inversely with the individual's degree of religious commitment.

Consider the relationship between mind and body. When we have peace of mind, we feel healthy. When we are anxious, we feel unhappy. We can actually observe this. But when we have tamed our minds and see all phenomena as self-envisioned baseless delusion, we will feel neither happiness nor sorrow. Just like the king seated majestically upon his own throne, beyond any need of chasing after desirable material things, we sit upon our own imperial seat of intrinsic awareness, enjoying the nature of intrinsic presence.

In the autobiography of the rigzin Jigme Lingpa, it is related that once when Pemo Dharma was practicing Vajrakilaya, accumulating a hundred million recitations in silent retreat, he became sick and suffered acutely from his illness. Jigme Lingpa visited him and gave him the oral instruction called "Making Sickness Itself the Path with Automatic Release into the Trikaya":

> Don't reify the sickness; look into the one who suffers.
> Don't fix your neurotic mind on the symptoms;
> Focus instead on the naked pure presence of the illness:
> That is oral instruction on illness as dharmakaya.

When we are diseased or wounded, we should not conceive of the illness as a real substantial entity. Rather, look at the one who thinks "I am sick," or take on the pain itself directly and gaze into that. The illness is just an envisionment that actually has no substantial existence. So do not fixate upon the misconception of the grasping mind that thinks "I am tortured by this disease." Loosely fix the naked, unmodified, here-and-now pure presence on the baseless envisionment of the sickness. Thereby that very illness will appear as the intrinsic creativity of the dharmakaya. This is the supreme oral instruction of Dzogchen. Pemo Dharma relied upon this Dzogchen instruction and, recovering from the illness, heightened his accomplishment.

1.21 Mind is the root of all experience

We may comprehend the absence of any substantial nature in both outer and inner forms, in sound, taste, or touch, and so forth, through intellectual investigation. We may then abandon objects of desire, such as a man's or woman's body, by seeing that body as unclean and ugly. But if the inner mental attachment is not released, the grasping that is at the root of attachment will not be eliminated.

Consider, for example, a dog hit by a stone. Instead of locating and chasing the stone-thrower, the dog will bite the stone. In the same way, no benefit will accrue by attacking the immediate form to which we are attached. When a stone is thrown at a lion, the lion will attack the person who threw it, not the stone. The root of all desire, aversion, and stupidity is the mind alone. If we keep the mind itself in a state of nongrasping, the emotions such as desire, aversion, and so on, will automatically be pacified. In *The Words of My Perfect Teacher,* Patrul Rinpoche quotes Tilopa saying to Naropa,

> Not the appearance—it is attachment that binds.
> Cut through the attachment, Naropa!

1.22 Knowing the whole world as figments of mind, undisturbed at the time of death, we are released in the bardo

We may not have full realization of the magical, illusory nature of the world as figments of mind, but with just a modicum of understanding of it, we will be free of fear at the moment of death.

In August 1985, I went on a pilgrimage to Mt. Kailash. There I met a woman from Khyungpo Tongchen who was so weak that we felt that she was on the verge of death. I will tell you her story. She was from a mid-status family in her village. She had three daughters, but because she had no sons, she had gone to Mt. Kailash for pilgrimage. It is a Tibetan tradition that women without male children should go to Mt. Kailash so that their womb-blood could give birth to sons. She had gone there together with some people from her village, vowing to perform a hundred circumambulations around Mt. Kailash to obtain the boon of a son. She stayed behind at Kailash to fulfill her commitment after her party left for home. Later she gave birth to a healthy son, but after three or four months she contracted serious dysentery. Day by day she became thinner and thinner, so that within six weeks she was like a skeleton. She could not even get out of bed to go to the lavatory. When she was doing her prostrations around Kailash, however, she had met a nun who took on the task of caring for her and her baby. The gossipy people who knew her said that, because of the strong attachment she had to her baby, if she died, she would surely be reborn as an evil spirit.

Then one day the nun came to me crying and told me the story. She told me that the woman was sure to die, that she had given up hope, that she was constantly asking the nun to bring the baby to her just to touch his face, and that she was weeping and moaning that she did not want to die. "This woman is on a wrong path because of her strong attachment to her son," the nun complained. "I tell her that I will take care of her son, but she seems to have no trust in me. She becomes unconscious several times a day, and then all of a sudden she regains consciousness with wide open eyes." She asked me to visit the dying woman.

Touched by this story, I went to see her and found her in a pitiful state, her complexion pale, her eyes sunken, her nose just skin and bone, and her mouth wizened. Her thin skin hung loosely on her body, she had lost her hair, and an unpleasant smell of sickness moved in the air. She could speak only a few words. I taught her some buddha-dharma, but she was just looking at her baby and moaning, "I cannot die!" I told her that attachment to her son brought no benefit to anybody and that moreover her attachment was a hindrance on the buddha-dharma path. I reminded her that the nun had promised that she would take good care of her son and that she should trust her, and I gave her this sermon.

> Death is for all, from celebrities to beggars. Sooner or later we all have to die, like sheep slaughtered by the butcher. At the time of death, even great leaders with a retinue of a thousand people have no power to take even a single person with them. If we have a pile of wealth as large as a mountain, we cannot take even so little a thing as a needle with us. We leave behind our children and our beloved spouse at the time of death. Death occurs to everyone, including you. So you need not worry too much about it.
>
> Buddha taught that all things are without substantial existence, like a dream. This is true regardless of the realm into which we are born, and we must sustain that feeling of illusion and trust in it. In this illusion, we differentiate friend and foe and distinguish between what is to be rejected and what is to be adopted. But all existence is actually empty, just like last night's dream. Whatever presumptions we make in the dream, all vanish in the morning. The same is true in the six bardos—nothing is real, everything is just a figment of mind. In the bardo there is no need to be afraid of any peaceful or wrathful appearances. Understand that they are all momentary subjective envisionment, and then you can certainly pass through the bardo without fear. Trust me! Just now you dream of being human, and within a few seconds, you will dream of the bardo. At that time pray deeply to the lama in whom you have faith! Be sure that everything is like magical illusion or dream. Merge your mind with the lama and rest easily in that space and you will be released.

Then I put some blessing-pills in her mouth and asked her if she had heard my words. She nodded and tried to place her palms together and then stretched her left hand toward me. Then I left her. But within fifteen minutes or so the nun caught up with me and, after telling me that the woman had just died, requested that I perform the ritual of consciousness sublimation. So together with Tashi, a monk from Tamkye, I returned to do the *phowa* ritual.

The woman was lying there in the same position as before, as if asleep but with her face aglow. She had died peacefully and many saw it. The nun thanked me and prostrated before me. I performed the consciousness sublimation ritual according to the tradition of Dudjom Rinpoche's Wrathful Dakini of the New Revelation. The nun had no one to carry the corpse for sky-burial, so I asked a man to loan her his yak for the task, and I sent Tashi and Lama Sonam Tashi, a disciple of my late serene father, to help the nun in the sky-burial. According to Tashi's statement, blood was oozing from the fontanel spot on the top of her head. I asked Lama Sonam Tashi to confirm it, and he told me that it was possible that blood from her nose had been smeared over her head. According to phowa texts, blood oozing from the head or the nose is the sign of success of consciousness sublimation. I have little experience of applications of the consciousness sublimation ritual; nonetheless, the clear signs displayed in this illusory scenario of the dead woman are undeniable. I never heard any rumors of the woman's having become an evil spirit or that there was any fear hanging over that place, but to the contrary there was peace, and many people grew strong in their faith in buddha-dharma.

If we are sure that the appearances of this life—relatives and friends, parents and children—are not other than figments of mind, then in the bardo and hell realms, if we could understand all appearances as mental projections, we could be sure of release from samsara. If, on the other hand, we yield to even our slightest tendencies to grasp at the appearances arising in this present lifetime, then we will not be able to attain liberation in the bardo or from the lower realms. If happiness and sadness arise and are mistaken for real and true things in this present envisionment of insubstantial appearances, then bardo appearances and bardo circumstances will seem to be real and substantial too. Through that belief, karma and karmic maturation will evolve, and suffering will ensue.

1.23 The creative and fulfillment phases are complete and perfect in the space of basic empty presence

On the various paths of the Mahayana and Theravada schools, different methods have been developed to train us in the understanding that phenomena are unreal and to make available to us experiential realization of this fact. In tantrayana, our impure bodies in themselves are visualized as pure divine bodies; stabilizing this through familiarization over a long period with a buddha-deity's color, attributes, face, arms, and so forth, is the main practice. Over time, our attachment to the present body gradually diminishes, pure divine appearance increases naturally, and eventually attachment to our physical body vanishes. Further, due to our recitation of the divine secret mantra, when slander, flattery, or abuse come our way, we hear such sounds merely as echo, and we suffer neither increase of conceit nor loss of self-esteem. Whatever happiness or sadness we experience appears as the display of the real nature of thought, and mind cannot waver from that. Whatever concepts arise we see as children's play, and, free of intellectual imperatives, we are released from the round of temporal happiness and suffering and become buddha. Because our minds are buddha in nature, we can see our own bodies as divine bodies. In *The Secret Core*, it is said,

> Emaho! The elements of the body-mind,
> To be known as the five perfect buddhas . . .

If we cultivate the recognition of our own body as divine, and stabilize this, then it is quite possible that we will truly realize the five buddhas.

In *Aspiration on the Gradual Path of the Wrathful Dakini*, Dudjom Rinpoche says,

> The creative phase, primordially perfected in the ground of being,
> And the fulfillment phase of the spontaneous clear light seed:
> These two in supreme secret union—
> May this crux of the vajra point take us to the matrix of the sky.

Once, in the kingdom of Varanasi, an old woman engaging only in shamata meditation visualized a tiger, and it actually manifested in the flesh and terrorized the city, which then became deserted. Further, once when Do Khyentse Yeshe Dorje was giving the empowerment of the Great Compassionate One at Menyag Lhagang, all the people present saw him on his seat as the real Thousand-Armed Avalokiteshvara rather than as the lama himself. That occurred because the lama visualized himself in the empty pure presence form of the deity and momentarily created an envisionment of total sameness, thus blessing his fortunate, devoted disciples. The key point here is that such transformations can be achieved only if the world is insubstantial and equivocal, just an illusory display of the mind. By such reasoning, we arrive at the insight that the root of all phenomena is insubstantial and nonexistent and that ordinary people suffer constantly from perceiving things as substantial and real.

The more wealth and fame we have, the more we are attached to them. They may temporarily give us happiness, but attachment to those things that give us pleasure will surely induce the suffering that arises from the fear of losing them. Further, if we use and enjoy our pleasure-providing possessions over a long period, eventually we will become bored and irritated with them, and they will become a source of anxiety. This suffering comes from our proclivity to cling to something that we believe to be substantial and true. But no matter what satisfaction occurs, great or small, everything changes in a moment. Consider poison concealed in delicious food: even though the food smells and tastes delicious, once it enters the throat, it brings only severe pain.

Nothing has essence, not even an essence as small as a sesame seed. Hearing good news, enjoying wealth and possessions, associating with friends—when we can experience such pleasures without attachment, with benign disinterest, only then can we fully enjoy them. When we are detached from pleasure—knowing the true nature of happiness and wise in the experience of happiness through true enjoyment—we will suffer less. To experience happiness yet remain detached from it, like a duck floating on a pond, in this way avoiding its otherwise inevitable transformation into suffering, is called "wise in the experience of pleasure."

Simplistically speaking, what we call happiness and suffering are attributes of nirvana and samsara, respectively. What we call "samsara" is suffering. Whoever, high or low, falls into samsara is bound by suffering just as if he or she had fallen into a pit of fire. What we call "nirvana" is happiness.

If we search there for suffering, we will not find it. Just as a chunk of molasses is sweet on every side, no matter from which side we approach nirvana, there is the sweet taste of happiness.

In *The Supreme Tantra*, Lord Maitreya, the buddha-regent, says,

> Know the disease, then eradicate its cause;
> To obtain the cure, depend upon the medicine.
> Know suffering, abandon its cause;
> Attain cessation by relying upon the path.

If samsara is suffering and nirvana is happiness, unless we know the actuality of both samsara and nirvana, we will neither be able to free ourselves from suffering nor attain any real happiness.

1.24 Why all beings are continuously bound in samsara

First, we should know the characteristics of this samsara that has suffering as its nature. This so-called samsara is a delusion. How is it delusory? Due to dualistic perception, we see one as two, we see unity as multiplicity, we see unclean as clean, we see suffering as happiness, we see nonself as a self, and we see impermanence as permanence, and so on. Through such misconceptions that deny the natural perfection of the sensory fields, attachment is generated, and we are fully deluded. The dualistic egoist mind, claiming superiority, arrogates to itself the lordship of reason and righteousness while pretending to know how things should be done. Taking the lead, in fact it knows nothing.

Like the eyes that see external things but cannot see themselves, we cannot see ourselves. At first, this body was created from the juice of our parent's sperm and blood and the elixir of the four elements, so right from the start, it is a multiplicity. But we see this aggregation as a singular entity and call it "I"; perceiving it as real and true, we label those who produced us "parents," and our mother's and father's brothers and sisters we label "uncle" and "auntie." As an extension of this process, those who help us are considered "friends" and those who seek to harm us are regarded as "enemies." To the former, we attach "love" and to the latter "hatred," and these imputations are considered to be indisputably valid. Not only that, but even the different delusory beings of the six realms are considered real and true, and our concepts of beings as truly existent become as solid and inflexible as iron pillars. In this way, trying to subdue enemies and assist friends, our short life ends like a lamp's being switched off. Then the delusory dualistic mind provides a primary cause, our specific karmic propensities gathered in previous lives provide the conditions, and we are born into suffering in one of the six realms.

If we analyze what we call "I," we see that it does not exist as a discrete entity. It depends upon our parents' sperm and blood, the four elements, and atoms. This aggregation of many components is called "I." It does not exist concretely, yet knowing it to be delusion, we still hold to it and say "I" and "mine." A multistory structure built on a frozen lake in the winter will collapse when the ice melts under the spring sunshine; in the same way, if we depend upon the "I" as a foundation, when we explore it and find that it has no true existence, it will collapse. Then, since the "I" does not exist, so parents, relatives, and spouse also do not exist, and the entire structure comes tumbling down. Our enemies and friends likewise do not exist. A patient suffering from jaundice sees a white conch as yellow in color; so too we perceive illusory mental projections as real and nonexistent objects as existing. If we cover a wall with realistic drawings, which look three-dimensional, of animals sporting in a landscape, the depth is mere illusion; there is no actual foreground and background, no inside and outside on the wall. When we look at the picture and say the deer are standing on the mountain slope, it is mere verbal convention; even so, we perceive the picture as three-dimensional. In the same way, the mind takes specific characteristics of the objective field as real even though no substantial existent can be found anywhere. Suffering arises from our fixation upon "I" and "mine" as definitely real.

If the tree's root is not cut, no matter how much we cut its leaves and branches, it will continue to grow. Likewise, unless the root of the ego is severed, we will be unable to free ourselves from suffering. Egoist concepts arise from the mind; if we investigate the phenomena that arise in the mind, we find that the mind is like a supreme judge who decides everything but does not have a true frame of reference. It has not so much as a moment of peace because it is constantly running after the good and avoiding the bad. When suddenly it hears a sound, it runs after it to find out what might be there. Is it the sound of a person or a natural sound? Is it good or bad? Is it useful or not? If it is considered useful, we seek its source, listen to it, figure out how long it will last, where it exists, and try to analyze it in terms of past, present, and future. If the sound we hear turns out to be from a person of the opposite sex, we might consider it good and that person attractive; then we might evaluate that person's height, sexuality, complexion, moral standards, financial condition, and so on. While listening to that voice we may deduce the identity of his or her parents, close relatives, class status, friends, enemies, and so on. Then, bored with this train of thought, we may move on and think of our current concerns: our business, our land, and so on. This linear conceptual thought is called a "chain of mental delusion." From the perception of an initial concrete sound, after a long series of connected discursive concepts, the mind finally moves on to another unrelated place. Isn't that so?

We are constantly deluded, and, in each of us, mental concepts are arising continuously. Sometimes we look inside and just assume that our conceptualizations are right. If we wonder about some thoughts and are able to thoroughly examine them, then it is possible we may understand that they are mental delusion. Just as in a conversation, we might begin by talking about a business issue and at the end find ourselves talking about some other issue, like war. Isn't that right? Associations arise from one to another in a stream of thought dominated by desire or some other emotional affliction. Insofar as such thought streams are repeated, this linear pattern becomes a circular one and is known as "cyclic existence" or "samsara." The first emotive thought in the series is the cause and each successive momentary thought creates a condition; the cause connected with its conditions develops into a delusion, and that is the beginning of endless wandering in samsara.

In *The Treasury of the Dharmadhatu*, Longchenpa says,

> With the mind preoccupied by different petty concerns,
> A moment of inconsequential fixation becomes a habit,
> And a day, a month, a year—a lifetime—goes by unheeded.
> We deceive ourselves by construing the nondual as duality.

It is a characteristic habit of our mind to criticize and correct others and to blame them for our own sins. But when we need to attain some objective, we first devise a plan and then implement it. Take a thief, for example, who knows that stealing others' possessions is both illegal and immoral, and who becomes active at nighttime when everyone is asleep. He knows the difficulties for thieves these days, with dogs in the compound and security guards and alarms inside the house, and he knows full well the heavy penalties that will fall upon him if he is caught. But he is undeterred by such considerations and forges ahead—whatever the mind instructs, the body performs without argument. When the thief is successful, his mind takes the glory, inflating with self-congratulatory pride. If he is caught red-handed, then his mind scolds his body, complaining that it did this and that wrongly, and it was because of a physical fault that the body was tortured by the police.

Once a man called "Thangpa," while drunk, decided to thrash his old dad. The next day, during his hangover, he was so ashamed that he cut off the fingers of his own hand. The mind made the mistake, but the hand received the punishment.

Theft and violence are initiated by mind. The body and speech are physical things and possess no will of their own. Possession of wealth, for example, does not make the body happy. It may be argued that the body and speech also love money, as evinced by rich people dancing and singing. But it is the mind that commands the body to dance and the voice to sing. The body itself is not affected by wealth. Body and speech are pathetic slaves of mind.

When someone performs a service for us, we are obliged to thank the giver and offer him or her a gift. But the mind does not thank the body for any service performed, and if the mind makes an error, it punishes body and speech. These days there is much talk about human rights—actually it is the mind that abuses our rights!!

1.25 Delusion dissolves when we look at the essence of mind

Now what if we simply depend upon Dzogchen alone? Do not pay any attention to thoughts or to whatever arises in the mind, but instead examine where the thought or the image comes from, where it abides, and where it goes. If we do this for long enough, we will discover that all thought forms are empty and that there is nothing substantial in the mind. Keep the mind in its own place, unmodified and without distraction, at ease in its state of clear naked emptiness. Do not attempt to stop the mind and do not follow it. In this way, we are freed of all the suffering of emotional affliction, and we go in peace. The happiness engendered is a deep calm, and we call it "serenity." This is not the same as a pleasurable feeling that accompanies a materialist's mental event, which, through a slight change of conditions, may become sadness. This happiness is derived from a connection to the space of great bliss that is thought-free primal awareness. "Great bliss" is the primal awareness of the nonduality of bliss and emptiness, and just as a weapon cannot damage the sky, so too that bliss cannot be affected negatively by circumstance, whereas pleasurable feelings of happiness that are based on mental events will, through changing circumstances, always turn into suffering.

Here is a real-life story that I want to relate to you. In a village in Bihar, India, there was boy called "Prakash" and a girl called "Babita." These two went to school together and then to college, and they were in love. After graduation they were happily married. They lived in felicity, never even using bad words to one another. Their love drew them closer, and they vowed to remain together even in death. In due course, they had a daughter. One day Prakash's friend Rabin, handsome and smart, came to visit them, and Babita welcomed him and gave him good hospitality; thereafter he came to visit frequently. One day when Prakash returned from work, he found cigarette ends in the house, and, asking her where they came from, he was told of Rabin's visits.

When their daughter was about three years old, Prakash's suspicions about his wife deepened, and he decided to test her. He told her that he was leaving for Delhi on some business and would not be back for ten days. Babita thought that this was a good opportunity to go to Rabin's house and ask him to paint their marriage photo—Rabin was a painter by profession. So she went to Rabin's and asked him to make the painting; she returned each day to see how the work was progressing, hoping to surprise Prakash upon his return. On the third day, upon returning home, she was surprised to see her husband there. "You told me you would be away for ten days," she said, "and only three days have passed. Plus, you didn't call me, and I was worried." Prakash was furious, his worst fears confirmed. "If you have Rabin, there is no need of me," he told her. "You are a shameless whore!" Babita protested her innocence and told him that she had done nothing to offend him. He told her that he knew that she had been visiting Rabin every day and that he did not need her any more. She swore that she had done nothing wrong with Rabin. She begged him to back off. They had a fight, and he beat her and kicked her out of the house. She lost hope and made a final request for her daughter. He told her that a whore does not have any rights and refused her. Babita left home weeping.

Believing that Babita had deceived him, Prakash was very depressed. His daughter cried constantly for her mother and would not sleep. He started drinking and became a little mad. After a few days, someone knocked on his door, and when Prakash opened it, there stood Rabin. Rabin asked Prakash in a friendly manner when he had returned from Delhi, but Prakash was angry and immediately was sharp tongued with Rabin, asking abruptly what he had come for and what he wanted. Rabin replied in amazement, "What is the matter, Prakash?" "You have ruined my life, and I am not going to let you live," Prakash shouted, trying to take him by the throat. While they were fighting, the painting that Rabin had come to deliver to Babita dropped from under his arm and, seeing that Rabin had brought his wedding picture, Prakash stopped short. Then Rabin told him about Babita's intention, but Prakash was not convinced. "You are my best friend, Prakash, and I don't want to ruin your life. If you don't believe me, then kill me—here's a knife." Prakash took the proffered knife but could not plunge it into his friend's breast. Instead, now convinced of his wife's innocence and realizing his own foolish jealous delusion, he turned the knife on himself, thrust it into his heart, and died.

Through his jealous attachment and deep delusion, Prakash ruined three lives: his own, his wife's, and his daughter's. Jealousy, desire, and delusion are all mental factors, and ignorance of this leads to our punishing the body. In this way, second by second, the mind is making errors that result in physical pain for oneself and others. It is vital to examine where error lies and decide what to do about it: to eradicate it or ignore it. When storm waves of thought overwhelm us and we do whatever comes into our mind without any consideration, we end up with so much regret. As the saying goes, "Be slow in the busy moment!" The more we find ourselves possessed of urgency or apprehension, the greater is our need for a moment of recollection and consideration. Only after this should we get to work.

Regarding the story of Prakash and Babita, in the first place, it would have been best to avoid unworthy suspicion of the loving wife. But when suspicion arose, it should have been examined carefully. Later on, when that suspicion was discovered to have been ill founded, forgiveness should have been sought from the wife: it is quite possible that she would have offered it. Without such consideration, just following a mind stuck on a single track may lead to destruction of a happy family and end in suicide. There is nothing more pernicious in the world than that sort of bad thinking.

Further, these days some imagine that suicide is the best way to end suffering, and they actually propagate such notions on websites, in books, and so on. These are works of fools and not at all correct. As it has been said,

> Those who find no meaning in life,
> Thwarted, seek happiness in death.

Suicide, however, will not end suffering. At the time of death, first there is heavy suffering in the gradual dissolution of the four elements. Happiness and suffering and even temporal duration are just subjective illusions. Happiness can seem eternal; but even the five-hundred-year life span of a god expires in a moment. Likewise a moment of suffering may seem like an eon. When our lives are full of anxiety and we cannot sleep at night, a day may seem like a month. Look at the pain that we endure when we simply try to stop our breath for one minute; each second seems an eternity. At the time of death, considering only the suffering caused by the cessation of the outer breath, our suffering is immense. Then, immediately after the moment of death, when outer appearances have ceased and the sound of the bardo hits us like thunder, we are terror struck. When rays of heat and light vastly more powerful than the rays of our sun strike our body, we are terrified. With knowledge of the body's insubstantiality and transparency, we are paralyzed with fear. Although all this fear is mental delusion, the suffering is seven times greater than mundane suffering. Consciousness is now moving like a feather on the wind, without any control at all. Beset by the illusions of the after-death bardo, we must go alone and friendless through the narrow defile of rebirth. To find more about the bardos, read *Liberation by Hearing in the Bardo* (*The Tibetan Book of the Dead*).

If, mentally, we look into the bardo, we find that some dead people become evil spirits. There are many stories about them, of course, but such spirits can actually be seen with the eyes. Rationalists may not believe in the existence of beings like this, but they cannot prove they do not exist. On December 20th, 2003, on the BBC Hindi program, it was reported that, in an old castle that had been turned into an exhibition hall, a video had been shot of a strange old man wearing clothes dating from a thousand years ago. Moreover strange voices had been heard several times in that castle. Such stories may provide information from which we may deduce that there are beings in the bardo. Moreover, a being of that type may actually enter the mind of a person still living and cause the person possessed to recognize relatives, a house, locations, and so forth, that the living person had no previous knowledge of. Certain occurrences can be cataloged. Just recently at Limi Til in Humla, Nepal, a woman's spirit possessed a man, and this was witnessed by many people.

Anyway, the point is that suicide does not end suffering. After death we must enter the bardo of becoming, the bardo of rebirth, and its suffering, so those who believe that suicide ends their pain are fools. Not only that but Shakyamuni Buddha tells us that the karmic maturation of the act of suicide is suffering first for eons in hell and then, for most suicides, rebirth as a ghost. Beyond this, they will commit suicide in each of five hundred lifetimes. It is very important, therefore, that we should know the results of our actions and engage in training that gives meaning to this embodiment.

If we are convinced that mind training is not an appropriate activity to pursue during our leisure time, when it comes to shouldering responsibility, we will have no mental base from which to proceed. When our leaders challenge other nations, for example, but have not confronted the deceptive nature of their own mind or even turned within to inspect or discuss it, they will surely find themselves at a loss. If their anger and aggression are strong, and they have the means, they may kill their enemies; and if not, perhaps they will end their life in suicide. In brief, the ignorant activity that follows upon our leaders' chasing after their emotional impulses is a disaster for everyone, including themselves. For examples of these things, look into the history of imperial dynasties and of the Second World War.

The root cause of such delusion is belief in fame, name, wealth, and power as a valid and substantial reality and belief that if we lose them, those virtues will be beyond recovery. The fault lies in perceiving temporary situations as permanent, predictable, unchangeable, and nondeceptive. When we were cast out of our mother's womb, we were not strong, famous, or wealthy. There was no way to recognize our parents or relatives, as neither their bodily forms nor their names appeared for a moment in our previous life's dreams. "Father," "mother," "close relatives," "friends," husband," and "wife" are all labels. Our egos, believing them to be real, create "my country," "my wealth," "my ancestral place." In reality all these things are without substance and without any certain extension in time. Whom we now label as "son" may be our "wife" in the next lifetime, our present "wife" may become our "daughter," and our best friend our murderer. The house or land we own at present and even our social position and reputation will have been owned in the past by others. For these reasons, it is nonsense to believe that nominal abstractions are valid and true. Whatever unfavorable conditions arise, such as sickness, conflict with an enemy, loss of property, or a lawsuit, and so forth, should be understood as illusion. With this perspective, just let go and rest in pure presence, and all experience will become one taste in dharmakaya mind.

1.26 The Advantage of Perceiving All Things as Mere Conceptual Labels

Tibetans consider comets to be bad omens, whereas other peoples think that they are auspicious signs and pray to them. "Auspicious" and "inauspicious" are labels applied to external signs or events, but actually there is no need for any positive or negative reaction to comets. Happiness has no essential existence; rather it is a contingent current label. We should not miss it, therefore, when it vanishes, and there is no need for us to suffer at its loss. Nothing can be gained through our endeavors because nothing substantial can be achieved; by the same token, nothing can be lost. If there is something to be gained, it will arise naturally and dissolve naturally. Whatever happens, there is no need for concern.

Once when the Dharma King of Derge, Tenpa Tsering, initiated the work of carving the woodblocks for printing the Kanjur, he asked Palpung Situ Rinpoche to lend him his edition of the canon for reprinting. This request did not please several scholars, and they conspired to frustrate it. Assuming that, as a high lama, he would firmly believe in omens, they arranged for him to observe some women carrying empty vessels to fetch water in the opposite direction of his grand arrival the next morning. When Rinpoche saw them, he did indeed feel it presaged a bad omen, but suddenly he asked the monks who accompanied him to count the empty vessels. There were eighteen, and when this was reported to Rinpoche, he was delighted since the number eighteen is the auspicious number of the different types of emptiness counted in the Middle Way metapsychology. He took this as an excellent omen for the unimpeded work of printing the Kanjur. Because for Dzogchen yogins bad situations become favorable, misfortune for them becoming good fortune, it is said that not a single obstruction can impede them. All phenomena are just labels.

In *The Heart Sutra*, Bhagawan Buddha said, "There is no path, no primal awareness, no obtainment, no nonobtainment." If there can be no obtainment of happiness in perfect reality, how can there be any nonobtainment? Since obtainment is the flip side of nonobtainment, if one of these is established, the other naturally comes with it as potential. If we can see the gain or loss of happiness and sadness as deceptive magical illusion, we are yogins and yoginis who have gained the space of nonaction. If we can see the components of each experience as conceptual labels and if whenever happiness or suffering arises, we can examine the actual present state of mind and stay with it without grasping, we will experience an awareness of great bliss that we have never experienced before. When we feel exalted, this primal awareness of great bliss can subdue our pride, and when we are miserable, it can undermine our suffering. Surely this nonconceptual bliss will replace both our happiness and our sadness.

1.27 When Pure Presence Is Spontaneously Recognized, Its Veils Naturally Dissolve

When we realize the reality of the mind free of dualistic perception, that is what is called "buddha." In *The Treasury of the Dharmadhatu*, Longchenpa says,

> Simple recognition of the nature of being is labeled "buddha"
> And with that realization, there is nothing to adopt or to abandon
> Because everything is smoothed out into the sole reality—
> On the Isle of Gold, everything is only gold.

The moment that we realize the nature of mind, buddha-nature, the natural perfection of being, there is no need to look anywhere else for it because we have found buddha in our own bed. We know that from beginningless time in samsara we have taken innumerable births and accumulated various good and bad karmas from the twin veils of emotivity and unawareness; in this way, our karmic propensities have become mountainous. Is it possible that our obscurations might evaporate without difficulty and we could become buddha in a moment? Even our Shakyamuni attained buddha only after collecting merit over three countless eons, and if you think that the sutras and tantras assert that buddha cannot be attained without effort, you are indeed right! Those scriptures maintain that without purifying defilements we will not attain buddha, and that logic is irrefutable.

However, as discussed above, what we call "obscuration," "defilement," or "veil" is not a concrete thing with a substantial nature; if it were so, it could not be eliminated by any antidote, because no antidote will be effective against something permanent and truly existent. The antidote as skillful means is recognized not only in tantra but also in sutra as the method of purifying all defilements accumulated over eons; defilements accumulated over eighty thousand years can be purified in a moment. The degree of the method's efficacy determines the speed at which the defilements can be removed. A thousand men's labor can be performed by a machine in a few hours, and similarly when we enter upon the tantric path of skillful means, the introduction to naked empty pure presence instantaneously purifies the defilements. Eons of accumulated defilements are removed in an instant, just as a cave that has been in darkness for centuries is illuminated in a moment if we simply light a lamp. Is it more difficult for a lamp to light the darkness of centuries than the darkness of a single day? Of course not. The point here is that the illumination depends upon the power of the antidote not upon how deep the darkness or how long it has reigned: a mere instant of pure presence in its spaciousness purifies, and buddha is attained.

The primal awareness of that instant of pure presence is "intrinsic." In the *Voice of Vajra Awareness*, Ju Mipham says,

> It's so simple that we miss the point,
> So difficult that it is above our heads.

Primal awareness does not require any effort or exertion on our part; it is inherently spontaneous. This crucial point is taught by the lama in secret because it is self-evident and easily understood. We consider that the teaching of the Buddha is so profound that it must be, we think, impossible to understand so easily; what is so easy to come by does not inspire confidence, and therefore the secrecy is necessary. On the other hand, through a lack of education, we may not be able to understand the explanations according to the scriptures or the logic of sutra and tantra.

If we could originate intrinsic presence by effort and exertion, then necessarily it would be something material, and, if material, then impermanent. If it is impermanent, it partakes of suffering. If pure presence could actually be established anew by effort, the implication is that reality could be realized by dependence upon a path. But it is not the case that pure presence can be established anew. Although conventionally it may appear that we need to learn something on a temporal path, in actuality the path, purification, and the traversing have no substantial existence. When clouds vanish from the sky, it is not the case that new sky is produced. The sky is primordially clear and unchangeable by nature, the clouds are adventitious.

When we train on a path over time, what to abandon and what to cultivate, what to realize and realization itself—all these are conventionally distinguished. In reality, intrinsic awareness has never been produced from a cause or conditions but abides naturally, absolutely unconditioned. It is seen as nondual subject and object, and this seeing that is nonseeing is called "the realization of the essence of buddha-nature."

In the tantra *The Lamp of Immaculate View*, it is said.

> Inasmuch as the inconceivable
> Appears as an object of mind,
> The experience is true
> But the object is not real.

Just as we say we see form with the eyes, implying that the object and subject are separate when in reality they are not, we may say that we see the essence of unelaborated pure presence, reality itself. But that is not yet the realization of the real pure presence, it's only recognition of subtle mental attachment. Until there is complete exhaustion of mental concepts, there is no realization of the dharmakaya. But it is a good sign that self-arising primal awareness has been understood. When we have sufficient faith to see our lama as a real buddha, when we see him as a siddha who has the power of blessing of the three transmissions—mind to mind, symbolic, and oral—in the instant of meeting him face to face, we may taste that profound reality that otherwise would remain unknown to us for eons. In that instant, we can experience the spaciousness of intrinsic presence in which subject and object are nondual.

Belief may be difficult because the broad exposition—innumerable transmissions and very subtle logic—in this and previous lifetimes has been unequal to the task of spurring sufficient and effective exertion in hearing, reflecting, and meditating. But even if we strive in training through these, still we cannot absorb the meaning of reality just as it is. Logic is sufficient to establish what is here and what is not here; if we examine that logic, its root is the rational mind of the ordinary being. But when we compare that rational mind with the primal awareness of the noble ones, it is seen to be merely the delusive dialyzing mind. In *Entry into the Middle Way*, Chandrakirti says,

> If worldly cognitive truth is valid
> What need of the noble one's vision?
> What use is the noble path?
> Worldly truth has no ultimate validity.

Furthermore, *The King of Samadhi Sutra* states, "The eyes, ears, and nose are not ultimately valid." As Chandrakirti said, the inferences of mundane logic are not ultimately valid. In short, ordinary people cannot cross the fence of dualistic perception, just like a fly in a sealed jam jar cannot fly out of it. Until all thoughts dissolve in the matrix of the great dharmakaya, pure from the beginning, even the noble ones have no choice but to remain in samsara, much less the rest of us.

Without the profound secret instruction of the lama, an individual trying to establish the sutric view by study is left only with the intellect to ponder the meaning of reality. Despite his or her study, his or her thought, even if straight and clear, will not go beyond the parameters of discursive reasoning. Is it possible that such an individual can gain introduction to the authentic mind—which is reality free of propositions, pure presence itself—by means of direct indication by the lama? Without accumulation of merit and without overcoming difficulties, due to doubts regarding direct perception of pure presence, it is not possible to gain such confidence in one's own mind. It is possible that through an innate understanding of the oceanlike teaching of Shakyamuni Buddha and the power of practice one person in a hundred might enter the ultimate arena of the five places of pure presence and attain buddha through direct perception. For that reason it is said that the meaning is not understood because of its difficulty.

In this short life of ours, because we have not finished our study of the broad exposition and innumerable transmissions, we think that we are unable to understand the dharmakaya's voice of logic, and we cannot encounter the rigzin-lama's blessings or his direct introduction to pure presence. We are like the dung sweeper who cannot believe that he could ever find a piece of gold in the dung. In that way the easiness of attainment cannot be believed and its difficulty cannot be plumbed. In *The Essential Heruka Tantra*, it is said,

> The fool depends on faith
> And comes close to siddhi;
> The brilliant scholar with wisdom
> Attains supreme accomplishment.

The root lama with realized wisdom, able to transmit the various kinds of blessing, is the single form of all the buddhas. With faith and trust in him, seeing him as a real buddha, we should contemplate single-pointedly what he introduces to our mind. By the power of that lama's blessing, together with our faith, we will gradually realize pure presence itself; we will thus gain confidence, optimize our creativity, and attain continuity in nonmeditation. In the tantra *The Discourse of the General Assembly*, it is said,

Without serving a teacher
Buddha will never be accomplished;
I have never seen it happen otherwise;
If it happens, it contradicts prophecy.

By serving a rigzin-lama and keeping the realization in our mindstream, obscurations are purified by themselves, and in one lifetime, we will attain the domain of Samantabhadra. Even if we fail in that attainment, without doubt within three or seven lifetimes we will reach the palace of Samantabhadra.

In *The Three Incisive Precepts*, Patrul Rinpoche says,

I may attain the Great Perfection in this lifetime,
But if not, at least I'll have been happy! Wah!

1.28 Creativity is necessarily released in pure presence

In the pellucid mirrorlike pure presence that is free of all conceptual intrusion, when suddenly a vivid thought arises, it is called "creativity." This creativity arises out of basic pure presence. It is the shifting nature of pure presence. Abiding naturally in that supreme cognition, creativity and display are rootless and baseless. When we awaken from a dream, both the objective field and the subjective knower vanish into their own space. So too from our own bed of unchangeable intrinsically aware dharmakaya, from where they cannot move even a hair's breadth, the concepts of materiality and specific characteristics dissolve in release.

If we fail to realize that the vivid thoughts, which arise in mirrorlike basic pure presence, are the natural creativity of pure presence itself, from that point onward delusive samsara, as an apparently true objective stream, beguiles us, as illustrated by the story of father Dawa Drakpa.

Once Dawa Drakpa went to work in another man's house, and by the time he returned home, he had earned a ten-kilo bag of barley. Concerned that it might be eaten by mice, he hung the heavy bag up on a beam just above his bed. Then he stretched out on the bed and began to think, "I will sell the barley and buy a hen. The hen will give many eggs, and from them many chicks will hatch. When the chicks grow up, they will also give many eggs. When I sell all those eggs, I will become rich and take a woman and get married. She will bear me a son, and when he is delivered, I will give him an honest name." Lying on his bed, thinking of a name for his son, he saw the moon rise and decided to name his son "Famous Moon." At that very moment a mouse finished nibbling through the thread that held the barley bag to the beam, and the bag fell upon Dawa Drakpa's head, killing him.

Each and every being's thoughts, chasing each other along, are delusory at the beginning, in the middle, and through to this very moment, and no one can measure the delusion, not even the noble ones. Even a magician, who can perform innumerable illusions and sleights of hand, when he investigates where the illusory objects come from, where they abide, and where they vanish, must remain unconvinced of the objects' reality when the nature of the illusion itself is emptiness.

A man dreamt so vividly that a very handsome son was born to him that, in the dream, when the son fell sick, he grieved, and when the son died, he was so sad that he cried aloud. When he awoke, he realized that he did not have a wife, so he could not possibly have fathered a son, and thus there was no way he could be happy at the son's birth, sad at his sickness, or grief-stricken at his death. In the dream, at the beginning, the son's birth seemed real, in the middle, the son's sickness seemed real, and at the end, his death seemed real. The circumstances of dream make us suffer exceedingly. When we awake and understand that the beginning, middle, and end of the dream are all figments of the mind and that there is not an iota of substance or a specific attribute that exists, then our suffering dissolves like mist in the morning sun. To overcome that suffering, it is imperative to strive on the path of awakening, to understand that the dream is unfounded and that there is no other way than this path to defeat it. To that end we rest all the creative appearances of dualistic samsara in pure presence and thus release them.

Until we recognize creativity itself as the magical illusion of pure presence, until we have gained confidence, optimized our creativity, and attained release, we must train on a gradual path.

1.29 Samsara never existed except as mere creative visions

Some people ask urgently, "Where did the very first sentient being come from?" and "What was the cause?" I would like to address that question here. Metaphorically speaking, samsara consists of the universe as the container and living beings as the nectar that it contains. According to both the Theravada and Mahayana traditions, the cause of both the universe as container and the beings living within it are emotional afflictions. The emotions are the source of both karma and the source of further affliction. The external universe as container has innumerable associated causes, and these seven—seed, shoot, leaf, trunk, stem, pith, flower, and fruit—serve as examples of the causal process, while the six associated conditions — earth, water, fire, air, space, and time—serve as examples of the conditions in which that process operates. The living beings that are the elixir in the container emerge from the sources of karma and emotion: ignorance, volition, consciousness, name and form, sense fields, contact, sensation, craving, grasping, becoming, birth, old age, and death. From these interrelated causes and conditions, the six elemental physical qualities of beings arise, namely, earth, water, fire, air, space, and consciousness. And where does the current karmic seed come from? It originates from the previous seed. And where does the previous seed come from? It originates from the one preceding the previous and so on without end. Neither religion nor science has any credible answer to the question of the origination of an original seed, and thus we may infer that there is continuity or that it is beginningless like a circle. For that reason our Buddha Shakyamuni has called the outer container "cyclic existence" or "samsara."

Therefore, in response to the question, "Where do the living beings within the container come from?" the answer is that rebirth follows from old age and death. "Where does old age and death come from?" They follow from birth. "Where does birth come from?" It arises from becoming and then successively in reverse through all the twelve interdependent links of origination until we arrive once again at the question "Where does ignorance come from?" It arises from old age and death. In this way we circle continuously in samsara, which is like a wheel. So it is called "cyclic." Since everything always depends upon a previous concatenating cause, we call it a "cycle." If we think, however, that this circular progression is true and real, it is definitely not so!

In *The Great Matrix Perfection of Wisdom Sutra in One Hundred Thousand Verses*, at the time of his teaching on the twentyfold emptiness, Shakyamuni Buddha said, "There is neither beginning nor end in emptiness." There is nothing in samsara that can be called either a beginning or an end. If we investigate this samsara that is without beginning or end and in which live the beings whose appearances arise out of their own karma, we find it to be like a dream and an illusion. In its identity, it has no going or coming, and it abides in its own empty essence in the emptiness that has neither beginning nor end. The attachment that arises out of desire for samsara, and the terror of it that arises out of apprehension is eliminated. The Buddha does not speak of a beginning or an end to samsara because he knows no beginning or end. Just as samsara has neither beginning nor end, there is no beginning nor end to emptiness.

In the tantra *The Discourse of the General Assembly*, it is said,

> Air is established in the sky,
> And the water aggregate is established in air;
> In water earth is established,
> And beings are established on earth.
> Beings depend on karma,
> So their causes are as stated thus.
> What supports the sky?
> This is the point to examine!

Asked "What do human beings depend upon?" we can answer: the earth. "Upon what does earth depend?" Water. "Upon what does water depend? Air. "Upon what does air depend?" The sky. But if we are asked upon what does space depend, ordinary people cannot answer, and even great scientists are left dumb. Shakyamuni Buddha, knowing the reality of all things, said that nothing has any true existence. Thus he is known as omniscient, praised by all gods and people.

In the tantras it is understood that all external, mundane things like mountains, houses, wealth, and so on, cannot be known and experienced and proven to exist as more than mental projections or mental appearances. Internally, the mind itself cannot be established as anything other than the creativity of pure presence, the essential nature of mind. That spontaneously arisen pure presence, timelessly free of any blemish, abides in its own space as the buddha-potential of the dharmakaya. We must understand that it always stays in the space of the unconditioned essence.

1.30 In Unconditioned Pure Presence, All Buddha-Potential Is Spontaneously Manifest

The primal awareness of intrinsic presence, beyond expression and understanding, is said in all the tantras to be essentially unconditioned. In the tantra *Magnificent Unelaborated Clear Meaning*, it is said,

> In all definitive teaching, in the agamas and tantras,
> The great intrinsic awareness
> Is expressed in vajralike words,
> Unchangeable and unconditioned.

Furthermore, in the sutra *The Inexhaustible Mind*, it is said,

> Consciousness passes;
> Primal awareness lasts.

While the *Gandavyuha Sutra* states,

> Although in the mundane world
> Everything conceivable may burn,
> The sky will not perish,
> Nor will intrinsic awareness.

Intrinsic primal awareness, timelessly undeluded, is buddha. If we believe that delusion must always arise in sentient beings, consider that it can never enter the ground of being. It is not possible for the ground of being to be deluded. Then how does delusion arise? Delusion arises through the dualistic perception of subject and object in the creative visions that appear in the ground of being. With realization of the gestalt imagery of the ground of being as just that—naturally envisioned appearances—we are released into the all-good ground. In the spaciousness of the ground of being, both release and delusion are pure from the beginning. Whatever in samsara or nirvana appears in the ground can never move from that ground, and the ground can never be anything other than the essence of purity. Thus the distinctions of "ground," "path and fruit," "the world," "beings," "nirvana," "pure realms," and any infinite spaces that appear can never escape the spaciousness of the ground of being. In that space both ornamentation and display appear.

In *The Treasury of the Dharmadhatu*, Longchenpa says,

> In brief, in the spontaneity of this vast womblike spaciousness,
> What seems to be samsara or nirvana is a display of creativity,
> Which at its inception can be known as neither samsara nor
> nirvana.
> No matter what dream arises in the creativity of sleep,
> In truth, it is only a pleasant moment of intrinsic presence,
> The all-pervasive smoothness of the vastness of ubiquitous
> sameness!

In this Great Completion, there is not a single experience in samsara, nirvana, or the path from one to the other that has not been included. Therefore it is called "complete." If we could only hold to the dharmakaya crux of empty pure presence, we would abide naturally and spontaneously in the vision of Direct Crossing. With the dharmakaya mind of pure presence and the sambhogakaya radiance of pure presence, we abide in ultimacy. Here the radiance of pure presence is spontaneously arisen vision because the inner light of the central pathway that hits the eye is not adulterated by delusion. On the path of the four lamps (the lamp of pure spaciousness, the lamp of empty seed-essence, the lamp of intrinsic wisdom, and the lamp of continual pure presence), if we take the fructified trikaya, the three dimensions of being, as the path, there is no doubt that we will attain the mature body of light that is the rainbow body. Pure presence and the radiance of pure presence are just like fire and its heat or the sun and its light, which cannot be separated at all.

These distinctions of Cutting Through [*trekcho*] and Direct Crossing [*togel*] are resolved in intrinsic awareness, which is their sole root, so it is crucially important at the beginning, in the middle, and at the end to realize that we abide therein. When unconditioned intrinsic awareness exists in the mindstream of all sentient beings, how can defilements and obscurations arise? We may think that we need the power of the sun or a lamp or electricity to remove darkness, but actually that is not true. A wolf does not need light to see in the dark. And, actually, nothing need be abandoned as nothing has substantial existence. The sky is completely clear and primordially free of dark and light. If we know that darkness is not an object of rejection, since it is the nature of the clear light of the sky, there is no need to eliminate anything. When primal awareness is revealed, there is not the slightest thing called "defilement" or "obscuration" that is to be rejected!

We will be released by the realization that everything is the intrinsic creativity of pure presence. When we fail in this understanding, holding object and subject as two, we wander in samsara where we need to depend upon antidotes and gradual progress on a path of cultivating the good and rejecting the bad. Applying ourselves to a process with the impure delusions of the vision of ordinary beings, or with the pure or impure vision of yogins or yoginis, as the case may be, or even with the Buddha's pure vision, there is no way to avoid the distinctions inherent in the rejection of some sensory appearances, the acceptance of antidotes, the graduation of stages and paths, and the difference between karmic cause and effect.

In the ultimate analysis, the stages and paths and the categories of what to cultivate and what to reject have never existed as an ordered structure in the sky's nature.

1.31 When we abide in unchangeable mind, there is enormous instant advantage

Whether we are concerned about this life or the next, we need to become familiar with the unchangeable aspect of mind. If we do not remain constantly in that unchangeable mind, even mundane work, let alone worship, will never be finished in this lifetime, whether it is trade, farming, politics, and so forth. No matter what our endeavor, given that the plan is deemed doable by the experts, if we work resolutely and with constancy, then one day it will be completed. Fickle-minded people, even if knowledgeable, may fail to first investigate the project properly, and if they do investigate it, the investigation may be incomplete. When difficulties arise and the work is postponed, it will not be finished. Later such people regret that the investigation was not done properly. In car accidents, even a slight distraction of mind allows a fatal accident to happen. Or, in construction of a building, if a slight error occurs in the measurement of the horizontal level, a huge difference in the proportion of the structure can result. Likewise, when we are afraid and anxious and become overexcited and lose our cool, grave disaster can strike just at that moment. In the same way that we cannot see what is at the bottom of the pail if we stir the water, and just as the more we rub our eyes, the less we can see, when mind is overstimulated and overexcited when solving a problem, the work stops, and we are left unable to proceed, without a sliver of attention remaining. Just as when we wind a thread too tightly, it will break, so if we put too much pressure on the mind, its continuity will break, and we will be left in utter puzzlement. The root error here in all these situations is an absence of knowledge about mind. If our mind is at ease and at the same time alert, then any work we perform happens with mindfulness and acuity, and our mind will remain unchanged. If we perform our work with unchanging and unfailing concentration, the result must always be excellence.

Once there was man called "Riklhun" who one day was returning to his house through the forest when two men suddenly attacked him. One caught him from behind and the other, standing in front of him, took out an axe and struck out at his head. Riklhun reacted like greased lightning, bending his head just enough so that the axe struck the man holding him from behind, killing him. The axe man fled. Riklhun laughed and continued on to his house. Later, the would-be murderer, though Riklhun's enemy, praised his courage.

Riklhun's slight but fast movement of the head saved his life. Whatever the emergency may be, it is mindfulness that makes the big difference. Another example: at the moment of being carried away by floodwater, we need mindfulness to keep ourselves from panic and save ourselves from drowning.

Once, in Nepal, the prime minister, Man Mohan, was flying in a helicopter with his four escorts to an outlying destination. While the helicopter was is in the air, its tail fan stopped working, and within two or three minutes, there was a danger of fire. The prime minister ordered the pilot to throw out all the gasoline from the helicopter and to land immediately. The pilot did as he was told, and the helicopter landed safely on the ground; thereby the pilot saved his own life as well as the others'. Later the prime minister gave a press conference, saying that a quick decision was needed in the couple of minutes during which their lives could be saved, and that decision, together with the resolve of the pilot, saved their lives. If a firm mind is required in a practical situation, then how much more so is it needed in taming our minds, and how great a benefit could accrue from that in this lifetime!

The best method of stabilizing the mind—realizing its unchangeable aspect—is the Dzogchen meditation of nonaction. Not only does it facilitate the accomplishment of mundane activities, it also releases us from the sufferings of samsara. Anyway, we need to attain constancy in pure presence.

1.32 Uncontrolled emotion effects severe ecological damage

If we believe that the material world should be controlled and manipulated for our pleasure and ease, and we act accordingly, we should consider the collateral damage we cause. In the past few centuries, scientists have invented machines that can travel through the air, under water, and under the earth. This has allowed us to travel easily, eat better food, and wear better clothes, and it has facilitated communication through e-mail, television, and video. We have better furniture, better heating in winter and cooling in summer, and, with electricity, we can turn night into day. Scientists are still improving their inventions and contriving new ones.

All this activity is admirable. But if we look at the other side of the coin, excessive production brings many negative side effects and an imbalance in the four elements. These negative effects are becoming increasingly evident. The earth is becoming warmer and warmer, and the ice of many centuries is melting, and some countries may eventually be flooded. Moreover, some kinds of birds, animals, trees, and grasses will become extinct. The majority of scientists are now predicting such results. An imbalance of the four elements will produce catastrophe. Predictions are that the suffering will be a hundred times greater than that of the Second World War.

The root cause here is people's greed. Even though this world belongs to all the sentient beings who live in it, human beings monopolize and utilize its resources for their own exclusive benefit, at the same time producing chemicals that pollute air, water, and earth. Through an imbalance of the elements, many animals, insects, trees, and plants that reside and grow in water and earth will become extinct. Ignorant of the fact that we are accelerating our own demise in this world, we proceed with "development" without the least concern for others. And this development is related to the fame and strength of the countries called "superpowers." Consider the person who puts himself or herself on the wrong side of the saw and cuts off the branch of the tree that he or she is sitting on. This is an example of crass foolishness, and it is not appropriate to compare the development work of the wise people of our world with such idiocy. On the other hand, to consciously ignore protecting the endangered environment and the four elements is very stupid.

What Shakyamuni Buddha teaches is that moderation and self-contentment is much more acceptable to the noble ones than the path of greed. Such teaching is like the white medicine that acts as a panacea, balancing the four elements and bringing peace to the world and harmony to its people. This path brings happiness in this life and the next, and for that reason we should all follow it.

1.33 The Dzogchen process necessarily and naturally preserves the environment

It is important to keep both outer and inner things unmodified. Until the mind is kept in its authentic state without modification and without fabrication, neither the external nor the internal worlds can be kept in the same natural manner. Mental contrivance is the main cause of ecological imbalance. For this reason, first, we need to keep pure presence unmodified and free of greedy thoughts and other emotions so that we remain empty of any need for control of the exterior. Then gradually the imbalance of the external ecology will be rectified, and the mind will be free of attachment, aversion, ignorance, and delusion so that contentment arises naturally. With this contentment, striving for development will decrease, and this will help to reduce global warming.

About contentment, Sri Saraha sang,

> Contentment is the ultimate wealth;
> Detachment is the final happiness.

This is surely true. So we need to strive to tame the mind and give it stability. There are many experts in this world who presume to train the mind, but there is none better than the Buddha.

Once king Bimbisara of Magadha gave an elephant to an elephant trainer and asked him to train it well, promising that he would be handsomely rewarded. After many months of training, the elephant was completely obedient. The trainer then presented the elephant to the king, and the king was delighted, and gave the trainer a large gift. But one day when the king and his two queens were riding the elephant in the forest, enjoying the beauty of nature, the elephant, suddenly paying no attention to the king's commands, went mad and stampeded. The king and his queens thought that they would be thrown off and killed, but they were lucky enough to become caught up in the branches of a tree, which surely saved their lives. The elephant was lost in the forest. Back at the palace, the king ordered the elephant trainer brought before him and accused him of lying and incompetently training the elephant. The king threatened a dire punishment. The trainer protested that he had trained the elephant's body but that he could not control its mind. "When the smell of a female elephant entered his nostrils, he went mad and had to run to her," he said "Wait a few days, and after the elephant has mated with the female, he will return." The king gave the trainer the benefit of the doubt and waited for a few days, and the elephant did indeed return. When presented before the king, the trainer ordered the elephant to pick up a bar of burning iron. The elephant did this without hesitation. The king thus regained faith in the trainer. "Who is the best mind-trainer?" the king asked the trainer. "Shakyamuni Buddha!" came the reply.

Practicing buddha-dharma, we should tame the mind; thereby we will gain the wealth of contentment as well as release from both attachment to external objects and striving after them. The ecological balance will be redressed thereby, and the environment will benefit.

Consider these events: my enemy has harmed me, so I am going to confront him, fight him, defeat him, and teach him a lesson; my girlfriend is having an affair with another man, so I am going to beat her so that she will not do it again. We think that through aggression we can control the external world and be happy, but such thinking is just the common error of ordinary people. In *The Thirty-Seven Practices of the Bodhisattva*, Ngulchu Tokme says,

> If the inner enemy "Hatred" remains untamed,
> Though the external enemy is defeated,
> The hatred toward him will increase.

Unless we tame our own minds, there is no possibility of controlling the external world. The male drunk who staggers down the road thinks that the ground is shaking and sees one thing as two things and two things as one. All kinds of thoughts pass through his head: sometimes he feels happy and sings, sometimes he feels sad and cries, sometimes he gets angry, and so on. But like the sensation of the ground moving, it is all subjective delusion. The concepts that arise in the drunk's mind are all due to inebriation. Regarding the shaking of the ground, it is said in *The King of Samadhi Sutra*,

> When one is intoxicated by tainted *chang*,
> Though the ground is still,
> It appears to be shaking:
> Regard all phenomena as delusory!

Though external objects have no substantial existence, attachment to them grows by presuming their permanence and concrete reality. It is adulterating dualistic perception that imputes concreteness and permanence to things and then labels them as intrinsically happy or sad, depending upon the subjective bias. The intellectualizing mind generates the imputation, the delusion appears in mind, and this mistake about the nature of mind initiates perpetual wandering in samsara. For this reason, we need to identify with the changeless nature of mind. As we recognize changelessness, all labels, appearances, and delusions naturally disappear. We perceive that the mind is only mental projection. Then, through the power of meditation on mind, freed thus of the veneer of dualistic grasping, we abide in the space of the great dharmakaya of unchangeable empty pure presence, released into the sphere of permanent happiness.

Great scientists have invented machines to fly in the sky, ships to cruise the seas, microscopes to see very tiny things, and many other wonders. People think that in this way these scientists have achieved greatness. But this planet earth (much less other planets) has itself not even been completely explored, which is something scientists themselves freely admit. They may investigate a given phenomenon thoroughly, but there are infinitely many things in this universe to explore, and it is impossible to examine them all.

In the past, the buddhas and bodhisattvas could fly in the sky. They could also foretell the future: for example, the great Pema Lingpa predicted some five hundred years ago the advent of Mahatma Gandhi. These accomplishments give proof that they understood the nature of all experience. In the nineteenth century, when Tibet was not known for having any modern technology, Ju Mipham Rinpoche invented a small bomb and displayed its potential to some of his disciples. He told them that if it was made bigger, it could be of some small usefulness, but that some people would likely misuse it, and grave consequences would ensue. So he stopped its development. As Mipham Rinpoche said, scientists may have provided us all with good food and easy transportation and other benefits, but when we ponder seriously the deadly weapons that were produced by some ignorant nations, we cannot enjoy that food or even sleep well at night. Once, when the extraordinary scholar Gendun Chophel was on the way to Lhasa, the capital of Tibet, he surprised many people by inventing a small wooden boat that could travel over the water by itself. He told people that if they were to construct the same boat according to a much larger and better design, then they would be able to travel across the great ocean.

Seeing that the root of all suffering is the mind's delusion, the noble beings of the past, though quite capable of scientific invention, chose instead to focus their efforts first in cutting the roots of disturbing emotions, and then in exemplifying the path of Shakyamuni Buddha.

These days the United States is like a small pure-land with many advanced technologies and facilities—yet many Americans have mental problems. Mental problems create more suffering than does physical disease. As Ju Mipham says in his *Traditional Shastra,*

> The suffering of hunger is great,
> But the endless suffering of mind is greater.

Stories of people committing suicide by starving themselves are very rare. People will always try to feed themselves and save themselves from hunger. Mental suffering can be temporarily relieved by consuming good food, drinking alcohol, or singing and dancing. But that is not an ultimate solution, so we hear of many cases of suicide. If the root cause of suffering, the root of mind, is not severed, no matter what method we employ, we will not be free of suffering and the binds of delusion. Even if we are born in a pure-land, we will not enjoy happiness. *The Amitabha Sutra* says, "Those bodhisattvas and bodhisattvanis who are born in the pure-land of Sukhavati have no ego, no sense of 'I' and 'you.' They are male and female buddha-deities."

As the peerless yogin Milarepa sang,

> Knowing one's mind as the dharmakaya,
> That is better than meeting the Buddha.

Knowing the nature of mind and its natural perfection is far better than meeting a buddha personally. To repeat a famous line, in *The Treasury of the Dharmadhatu*, Longchenpa says, "Simple recognition of the nature of being is called 'buddha.'" The very moment the nature of mind is seen as primal awareness, we understand that the word "buddha" refers to nothing beyond that recognition.

1.34 Illustrating that all things arise out of the basis of mind

The question, "Is everything rooted in mind?" has been addressed at length in earlier sections. Here I will discuss this in brief. All happiness and suffering arise from mind. Different beings perceive external appearances according to their own envisionment—water can be seen as a drink or a place of residence and so on.

The ground of being is the luminous mind, but a buddha's pure envisionment and the impure envisionment of ordinary beings are determined differently by karma. Everything emerges from the power of the mind as magical illusion. To that some people may respond, "Well, how can so much variety arise out of a single base?" The answer is that it is like the way that all trees, vegetation, minerals, and precious stones appear out of the one earth beneath our feet. Further, modern scientists believe that all things in the world are composed of atomic particles; surely all of samsara and nirvana are composed of luminous mind in a similar way. An even closer parallel is the variety of images of individual's faces that can appear on the single surface of a mirror. In a real sense, the nature of external phenomena and mind is one: the nature of mind is nowhere to be seen in any direction, nor is it limited to any one place or any particular conceptual imposition.

If we investigate this external world, we find neither unity nor multiplicity. If it is a unity, it is not a plurality; if it is a plurality, it is not a unity. Since it is not one or the other, it remains in emptiness. This emptiness is not like a sky-flower or the son of a barren woman because external objects are undeniably visible. They are seen just like the reflection of the moon in water: it is visible, but when we come to look for it in the container, no moon can be found. If we do not investigate conventional appearances, they seem to exist; but with investigation, since neither the external object nor the internal mind can be found to have any substantial existence whatsoever, we can say that neither has any existence.

If mind and external objects have no substantial existence, some people might wonder how suffering can arise from them. What is the use of meditation if nothing has any inherent existence? Quite so. Ignorant of this absence of any substantial existence in either external phenomena or in beings residing in the world, we conceive of a substantial "I" or ego and the notion of others "out there"; attachment and aversion then arise from perceived good and bad. This starts us down the long river of suffering. When we understand perfectly that there is nothing substantial anywhere, suffering will cease to arise. Consider a dream in which we are being eaten by a ferocious tiger or are falling over a steep precipice. If we knew at the time of suffering that we were dreaming, then, certain of being deceived, we would automatically find release from our terror.

Dream fantasies are sometimes happy—they are not always sad. Not only in dreams but also in movies—which we know to have been made by professionals—the audience still cries during sad scenes and laughs at comic ones. Why do we laugh and cry even though we know that the movie is a fiction? The happiness and sadness ensues from attachment to appearances; if we have a strong conviction of appearances as insubstantial, no such feelings will arise. If we are unable to detach our minds from the movie as we watch it, how then under duress from an aggregation of past imprints can we detach our minds in real life? From beginningless samsara we have been attached to things through different activities, and, like a potter's wheel after he or she has ceased spinning it, the wheel of life continues under its own momentum.

At present, during a meditation session, is it possible that our habitual grasping at objects could be abandoned suddenly? Some students, having met a great guru, come to know the truth of unreality, and, practicing for months and even years, receive great benefit in this life. They develop strong faith in the teaching and completely change their manner of conduct, just like turning their clothes inside out. Such a yogin or yogini is observed to be more polite, more kindly, in short, to be a person with many good qualities. There are some people, it is true, who, though they have received teaching and done meditation and so forth, claim that they have not been helped in any way. But consider the case of a doctor who prescribes medicine for HIV/AIDS or TB, with the instruction to take it every day for several months or years. If the patient takes it for only a few days and then argues that it was no help, that premature judgment is invalid. If the medicine had been taken for a sufficient length of time, surely it would have healed the patient. If we take instruction from a reliable lama, not for the sake of association with some famous teaching, but in order to train the mind until we attain the final accomplishment, we should strive in hearing, reflection, and meditation.

1.35 With a Full Understanding of the Inseparability of Appearances and Emptiness, Vision Is Naturally Suffused by Infinite Purity

Once we are certain that all phenomena are unreal mental projections, we no longer have to venture outside to other places to look for a pure-land realm. The place that we are in, here and now, appears as a pure-land paradise. During the Cultural Revolution in the 1960s, Minling Chung Rinpoche was given the duty of cleaning up excrement around the Barkor.

A woman took that duty upon herself to pay reverence to the Rinpoche, but one day Rinpoche asked the woman to refrain from doing that work for him, as he could do it for himself. She told Rinpoche that the smell was obnoxious. Rinpoche said, "To you it may smell bad, but to me it is a sweet aroma." In the period leading up to death, realized beings may see impure things as pure. Just before death, as ordinary appearances vanish into spaciousness, they see appearances as the Glorious Copper-Colored Mountain pure-land. When they go beyond, tents of rainbow light and other auspicious signs may be seen. Those watching may be inspired thereby. There are many stories to be told in this regard.

Buddhas themselves are visibly saturated with purity, while others, like Shakyamuni's disciple Sariputra and fortunate beings with just a little obscuration, have pure vision. Once when Vimalamitra came to Tibet, he saw king Trisong Deutsen as Avalokiteshvara seated on a turquoise throne, wearing the crown of the five buddha-families. Vimalamitra looked up into the sky, uttering OM AH HUNG SWAHA while snapping his fingers five times. The buddhas of the five families appeared, and the king and his subjects all saw them clearly and obtained steadfast faith. All fortunate beings like them enjoy pure vision.

Again, once, while Marpa Lotsawa was seated on his throne deeply absorbed in meditation, his disciple Marpa Golok came to see him, and in place of Marpa Lotsawa, he saw the real Vajradhara on the throne. Later, when he asked Marpa about it, Marpa replied, "It was a coincidence that, when I was meditating upon my personal deity Vajradhara, your defilements diminished, and you saw that vision." To obtain that pure vision, it is necessary to have diminished obscuration; then, with faith, there is confidence in the illusions of emptiness and appearance in union.

Once, when Do Khyentse Yeshe Dorje was giving an empowerment at Menyag Lhagang, everyone saw the lama as Avalokiteshvara seated on the throne with one thousand arms and eyes. Doubtless the lucky people who saw him had diminished defilements and obscurations.

1.36 A finger pointing directly at pure presence

If we put all of this in a nutshell, no matter what the quality of the view, whether we are happy or sad, whether appearances are fearful or pleasant, whether mind is active or passive, we should not tilt our mind toward any antidote. Whatever appears, look nakedly at the essence of the appearance as it arises, and, without modifying it in any way, just let it be. Then pure presence in all its radiance arises from within.

In his *Lifeblood of the Mountain Retreat*, Dudjom Rinpoche says,

> Whatever the sensory field, whatever the object, gaze at it like a child enrapt before an altar in a temple. Don't clutch the sensory specifics; hold to the freshness. Let it be in its own place without contriving anything about it, without changing its shape or complexion and without adulterating it with any conceptual fixations. Then all appearances will arise as the naked primal awareness of clarity and emptiness in pure presence.

In *The Chariot of Omniscience*, Jigme Lingpa says,

> Objective appearance in pure presence does not crystallize, and since pure presence cannot mingle with the object, the perceptual dualism of samsara is like a drawing in water, and there is Saraha smiling serenely, the renouncing and the antidote reflexively released. Without revealing any attachment or rejection to the pure presence that thereby does not slip into the objective field, there is Phadampa Sangye, shining, in the space of liberation of samsara and nirvana.

The five sensory stimuli—forms, sounds, smells, tastes, and tactile objects—do not crystallize in the five doors of perception, and whatever arises is allowed to arise just as it is. When the consciousness (pure presence) is not mixed up with the objective aspect of form and so on, when it does not slip into the object, the nature of dualistic samsara vanishes, just as a drawing in water vanishes as it is drawn. What is abandoned has no material attribute, and its antidote has no attribute, and in that moment of arising, grandfather Saraha, laughing, found the space of reflexive liberation.

When, on the basis of the lama's instruction, we realize the profound import of the view and recognize the nature of mind as pure presence, bright and nonconceptualized, we will have experienced it and thus will have no need to either describe it to others or discuss its ontological status. With an inner conviction that what we call "our mind," "the subjective knower abiding in nonthought," and so on, is meaningless, we will find born within us a deep abiding confidence that in itself is sufficient. Concerning the production of this profound confidence, we cannot realize the natural state of mind by any other means than reliance upon a rigzin-lama's blessing and oral instruction.

In the sutras of the Approach with Signs, which contain the highest Mahayana view, many profound truths are established by direct perception and inferential logic, but in the end they do not go beyond the intellect. Although we mouth the words "empty" and "beyond conceptual elaboration," such words remain mere semantic expressions because the mind cannot conceive them. There is no release from our dualistic bonds. If the nature of the mind is not seen directly in nondual vision, however it is expressed, dualisms can be neither transcended nor resolved. When we are holding a burning coal in our hand, unless we drop it, we cannot prevent the pain, no matter how much we cry. In the sutras of the Approach with Signs, in the Madhyamaka Prasangika school, and in the outer, inner, and supreme yoga-tantra schools—in all approaches below the level of the secret precept class of Dzogchen Atiyoga—propositions that tend to crystallize reality are resolved successively and gradually because in those schools nondual perception is not recognized as a valid means of proof. Due to the existence of higher and lower approaches and faster and slower paths, there is a gradation in the profundity of blessing. In *The Treasury of the Dharmadhatu*, Longchenpa says,

> Until we realize—experientially—the field of self-sprung sameness,
> We may verbally obsess with the term "nonduality"
> And speculate confidently about what is nonreferential,
> But such egregious thinking is dark and ignorant.

In Dzogchen, first, at the feet of a rigzin-lama, we are introduced to the actual experience of primal awareness. In light of this, all speculative concepts and assumptions belonging to the Approach with Signs surely vanish, and we "see" without any conceptual elaboration. If we fail to experience it directly, though perhaps wise in the dialectics of Dzogchen, we are not even close to the natural state of being, and we do not deserve the name "Dzogchen yogin." As Drubchen Pema Dewai Gyelpo says in *The Rampant Lion*,

> If the authentic nature of being is not known,
> Caught by the spirit of fundamentalism,
> The pains of bigoted sectarianism well up,
> And we are trapped in a net of karmic proclivities
> Of ignorant dualistic appearances.

In *The Heart-Essence of Vimalamitra*, Longchenpa says,

> It is taught by the Lama Vimalamitra, that buddha will never be attained on the paths of the nine graduated approaches by engaging in their view, meditation, and conduct. Why not? Because in the views of the nine approaches, there is only intellectual conjecture that is sometimes convincing and sometimes not, but which can never induce the naked essence.

In the same source, Longchenpa quotes the rigzin Garab Dorje saying,

> A view based on speculative thought brings suffering;
> Meditation derived from it creates a foggy mind;
> Activity based on it brings weariness;
> And any hope of result is total delusion.

Below the secret precept class of Dzogchen Atiyoga, each successive lower approach views the one beneath it as inadequate, inasmuch as each depends upon speculative thought. Most especially, the sutras of the Approach with Signs, which teach speculative deductive logic as being the leader, assume that the nature of mind cannot be realized directly in the spaciousness of pure presence. In the Approach with Signs, regardless of the profundity of the mind's meditation, there is only mere replacement of one dualistic concept by another. This method does not engage the reality of Dzogchen's natural state or the natural perfection of mind. However high it flies, a bird must always land; if there is no crucial realization of self-arising/self-releasing mind, then any effort is eventually only a cause of fatigue. As Drubchen Pema Dewai Gyelpo says in *The Rampant Lion*,

> Without realizing the crux of self-arising/self-releasing,
> Reification, with its heavy suffering, causes fatigue;
> If we do not understand primordial reflexive release,
> There is no liberation from samsara's rebirths.

1.37 Reasons for the necessity to seek a rigzin-lama to introduce pure presence

To receive a good introduction to the completely liberating view of Dzogchen, we need to serve a rigzin-lama, a Dzogchen yogin.

In the tantra *The Compendium of Pure Presence*, it is said,

> Without consulting wise teachers,
> A Buddha cannot appear;
> Without a teacher no Buddha has ever appeared—
> It would be contrary to prophecy.

After completing his studies of sutra and tantra at Samye, Longchen Rabjampa, the crown jewel of the scholars and sages of the Land of Snow, a second buddha, was known as the Samye Savant, with knowledge equivalent to all the Six Ornaments and Two Excellencies of India. He was an incomparable genius free of all bias. But the bodhisattva Tara told him in a vision that his lineal lama was the mahasiddha Kumaraja. Immediately Longchenpa stood up and went to find him and, once there, requested the heart-essence [*nying-tik*] teaching and received many transmissions.

The great Naropa was a famous pandita at the Vikramashila Academy in India, and there he saw a vision of the Dakini who told him, "You are now an expert in words; go and see the mahasiddha Tilopa and train yourself experientially in the natural perfection of reality." And Naropa went to serve Tilopa.

The hermit lord Dewai Gyelpo spent many years in retreat and became accomplished in the creative and fulfillment stages, and he exhibited many signs as clear as a rainbow on a summer's day. But he was left with some attachments, however, and later on, when he ran into Traktung Dudjom Lingpa, the latter shouted at him, "Now tell us the signs of your experience!" And with the chaff of conceptually elaborated signs all dissolving into space, the mind of the lama and the disciple become inseparable. Relying upon that experience, Dewai Gyelpo gained realization. To find the natural state of mind that is the great perfection, there is no other way than through a lama. Furthermore, we need to depend upon such a one with faith, pure vision, and devotion. If we recognize our lama as buddha, then we will receive the blessings of buddha; if we recognize our lama as a yogin, then we will receive the blessings of a yogin; and if we see our lama as an ordinary human being, then we will receive no blessings at all. As the sutras say,

> Whoever has yearning aspiration
> Sits in front of buddha.

And as the tantras say,

> The lama is the Buddha;
> The lama is the Dharma;
> The lama is the Sangha;
> He is the incomparable creator,
> The Heruka, the great and glorious guru.

Real blessings will only come from a rigzin-lama. As is said, "The rigzin-lama's followers receive the accomplishment." Moreover, in *The Aspiration of Ground, Path, and Fruit*, Ju Mipham says, "Through the power of the lama's precept, may I see!"

If we understand the Dzogchen view completely, powerful kindness will arise in us toward those sentient beings of the six realms continuously plagued by suffering who have not understood as much as we have because of the curse of their attachment to samsara's bewildering deceptive illusions as something substantial and real. As Shantarakshita says in *The Ornament of the Middle Way*,

> Toward those who have not understood,
> Compassion arises.

Such loving-kindness arises effortlessly. Just as a mother instinctively becomes anxious when her toddler runs in play hither and thither across a flat roof without balustrades, so the yogin who understands that all phenomena are mental delusion feels a patient love for people engaged in subduing enemies, caring for kith and kin, accumulating wealth and improving reputation—in short, for all the people who are bound in an environment of pain by the concretization of their delusions. With this understanding, bearing in mind the delusiveness of karmic result, we can nondelusively see karmic cause and effect working in specific cases, and strong confidence will arise in us. This is proof of correct view, or buddha-potential manifest. If, at the very center of mind, we lack a clear understanding of the view free of all bias, we are then ignorant of karmic cause and effect and without compassion for sentient beings, and we will wander like a blind man left in the middle of a large field, not knowing where to go. Ignorant of the view and thus bewildered, even if we walk the path of liberation and enact the conduct of the six perfections, we will remain ordinary beings.

In the context of the sutras, no matter what effort is applied to prove through logic and scriptural authority the reality of emptiness—the emptiness that is profoundly liberating and free of all conceptual elaboration—we cannot go beyond deductive hypotheses and speculative concepts. When the sutric mind investigates phenomena and discovers nonexistence, it takes it to be nothingness; when it discovers the absence of nonexistence, it takes that to be a constant. When it holds both existence and nonexistence together, it cannot conceive of both existent objects and nonexistent objects simultaneously. If the unity of existence and nonexistence is emphasized, the sutric mind tends to conceive of black and white threads wound together, and it can go no further. Such beginners, who understand reality only through intellectual analysis, conceive of it as categorized, nominal, absolute—a factor of deductive logic. But then just as a picture of the moon can introduce us to the moon, and just as its reflection in water can orient us toward its presence in the sky, so too we may connect to basic pure presence by applying the logic of the four extremes. Through the view of deductive logic practiced for a long time with correct reasoning, gradually we understand that the moon's reflection in water is illusion, an understanding that eliminates the extreme notion that it exists. Second, it removes the extreme notion of its nonexistence. Third, it removes the extreme notion of both its existence and nonexistence, and then fourth, it removes the extreme notion of its neither existing nor not-existing. Gradually, having removed the four extreme notions and free at last of conceptual elaboration, we can enter into the mind of buddha. This is not the same as the direct approach of Dzogchen.

On the sutric path, pure presence is not mentioned as existent, now, in the minds of sentient beings, except as the seed of buddha. If pure presence is taught as manifest here and now in the minds of sentient beings, then, due to the inadequacies of the sutric view, the result is the accumulation of the negative karma of wrong view. In the sutric tradition, when the bodhisattva Manjushri taught the twenty different kinds of emptiness, many sravakas' heads burst open, and some died vomiting blood. In Dzogchen, right from the beginning, all elements of experience are introduced as pure presence. This pure presence is primordially free of conceptual elaboration and is the contemplation of the minds of all the buddhas. Putting any effort into purifying it or adulterating it by concepts tends to conceal its nature and is counterproductive. We need to abandon all effort, along with deductive reasoning and speculative concepts, and for this, first, we need to receive instruction from a lama. Applying his instruction, we will understand that there is no other possible way.

If we have single-pointed devotion to the idea of the lama as buddha, and we seek the instructions that induce the vision of the pure presence of Dzogchen, the rigzin-lama skillfully introduces pure presence to us through signs, words, experiences, and so forth. For instance, Lama Tsangpa Drubchen introduced pure presence to Kyilkhor Rinpoche while they were herding yaks. The lama gave his student personal instructions on Dzogchen all day long, and then as the evening drew in, when lama and student were sitting on a rock, all of a sudden the lama shouted "Move back!" and Kyilkhor Rinpoche pushed himself bodily back on the rock. "No! No! Not like that!" whispered the lama, and understanding that pure presence should be distinguished from dualistic perception, he experienced naked pure presence clearly. "Today we have killed the real enemy, which is grasping," said the lama happily. "Now go to a place of deep seclusion, perfect the practice, and accomplish buddha in this lifetime."

Here is a similar story. Before Drubwang Pema Dewai Gyelpo met Dudjom Lingpa, because he retained a little attachment to the accomplishment that he had gained from his practice, he thought of displaying it to the lama. Immediately upon meeting him, the lama caught Drubwang by the throat and slipped his knife up and down in its sheath with his right hand so that Drubwang could hear what he was doing, and asked him loudly to tell him his realization. Instantly Drubwang's sense of accomplishment vanished, and he clearly saw naked pure presence.

The way accomplished lamas give introduction is unpredictable. Sometimes it is given through discursive teaching, and sometimes it is given playfully. There are many ways of introducing pure presence. Longchenpa in his commentary upon *The Treasury of the Dharmadhatu*, describes the introduction to pure presence as either without words or by one of six different contrived methods. Check out those details!

In short, putting aside the lower path's deductive reasoning and rational fabrications, we should rely solely upon introduction to the view as the naked experience of pure presence that is the natural state of mind. To facilitate that, first we need to establish all our experience of samsara and nirvana as baseless and rootless subjective envisionment. Then, without modifying the immediate awareness of our original condition, we can be introduced to the ground of being that is without dualistic perception and that is primordially pure and free of any conceptual elaboration. This introduction is not a part of the Approach with Signs and is also absent in the lower tantra approaches. It is the unique special supreme Dzogchen teaching.

This is the way that the famous fourth Dzogchen Rinpoche, Mingyur Namkhai Dorje, was introduced to the view that led to his attainment of the consummate level of reality, higher than the sky. At the age of twenty-five, he sought full ordination and studied all the five fields of cultural knowledge. Then he began to administer his 280 monasteries, and his sanctity and knowledge spread far and wide. In order to seek empowerments, transmissions, and explanations, he went with fifty monk attendants to Dokhok to see Do Drubchen Jigme Trinle Woser, who was a heart-son of the rigzin

Jigme Lingpa. When he met Do Drubchen, the lama gave him a skull cup full of pure alcohol and told him to drink it. As an ordained bhikshu, he was forbidden to drink alcohol, but ordered by the lama to imbibe, he had no choice, and without hesitation he consumed it in a single draft. Instantly, he was intoxicated. When he returned to his entourage, some high lamas and tulkus were critical of his drinking alcohol, but they thought that, after all, it was only a temporary lapse. When they found that Rinpoche was still not sober the next day, they were surprised, and even more surprised when they realized that, through that single skull cup of alcohol, Rinpoche was to be intoxicated for the rest of his life. He saw all the phenomena of samsara and nirvana and the path from one to the other as magical illusory envisionment and mental projection. Sometimes when he was called from his room, he simply walked into the wall, showing the front half of his body on the outside wall. This was seen by many people. He had unlimited psychic powers, had no attachment whatsoever to the appearances of this world, and had gone beyond to the Dzogchen place where reality is consummate.

When rigzin-lama and fortunate disciple meet, an understanding of the nature of things is not left to deductive logic but is experienced as pure presence itself. That is the supreme uniqueness of this path. The omniscient Jigme Lingpa said in *The Chariot of Omniscience*, "To accomplish pure presence as dharmakaya, there is nothing to prove. Here is effortless transference into the great primal awareness that is ultimate freedom."

The accomplishment cannot be attained by reason. It is inexpressible and cannot be presented logically. In *Ascertaining the Three Vows*, Ngari Panchen says,

> Only through the blessing of the rigzin-lama!
> Any other method is ignorance!

Like a finger pointing at the moon, the method is symbolic. We cannot define the method exactly, as in Do Drubchen's introducing Mingyur Namkha Dorje to pure presence.

The teaching of Dzogchen and the character of a rigzin-lama are beyond definition. As can be inferred from the examples above, do not presume that a significant encounter can be met with easily. Such lamas are as rare as a blue moon. The disciple must be super sharp in mind and have a strong karmic link with the lama. Just like an astrologer's student who intuits the key points of reckoning and has no need to compute each and every calculation, there is no use in making a disciple strive long and hard when simply by being shown the method he or she can easily and quickly become an expert. Consider someone who may have forgotten a past conversation but with a single simple reminder recollects it clearly. Likewise, through a lama's precept or by means of a single sign or symbol, we can recall pure presence and verify it. That is known as "the path of clear light" or "pure presence as process." Resting loosely in this pure presence, we will gain confidence, and signs of accomplishment will appear gradually or instantaneously. Finally, the basic pure presence that is unconditioned and pure presence as process mingle into one another, like a child nestling into the lap of its mother.

1.38 The Potential of Pure Being and Primal Awareness is Already Manifest in Basic Pure Presence

All the visions of samsara and nirvana are present in the space of pure presence. If we do not manifest the potential that resides in the ground, path, and fruition of intrinsic presence, it is like having an audience with the king but remaining ignorant of his palace, subjects, wealth, power, and fame. Thereby we will underestimate his power at the very moment when it is vital to know it. We may know the essence of intrinsic awareness, but what of the essence of pure presence, the three dimensions of being, and the five modes of awareness? Is it necessary to strive to accomplish what was apparently absent before, or do those aspects arise spontaneously? Of course they arise spontaneously! In primal awareness the ground, path, and fruition, and view, meditation, and conduct are all, already, primordially complete. If we are searching for manifest buddha-potential somewhere else, it is like having a lake in front of us and looking for some water behind us, or like keeping an elephant in its stable and searching for her footprints in the jungle.

Basic pure presence is the source of all the buddhas of past, present, and future, the treasury of pure being and primal awareness, and the chariot to traverse the path and the stages: it is a grand mansion replete with uncountable entryways to fully manifest buddha-potential. In this primal awareness, the buddhas' dharmakaya, sambhogakaya, and nirmanakaya are timelessly and unconditionally accomplished. If we look into the obverse side of pure presence, its essence, free of all conceptual elaboration, is the dharmakaya; its nature, unmodified and unadulterated clear light, is the sambhogakaya; and its expression of compassion, uncrystallizing and unconfined, is the nirmanakaya. To take the crystal as an illustration: its transparency is its aspect of emptiness, the dharmakaya; its radiance is its aspect of clarity, the sambhogakaya; and, as the basis of the appearance of an uncrystallizing multiplicity, it is the nirmanakaya.

In the tantra *The Supreme Source* it is said,

> In my all-creating bodhi-nature
> As effortless spontaneity,
> Lies the heart of buddha, the trikaya:
> My uncontrived nature, the dharmakaya,
> My uncontrived essence, the sambhogakaya,
> My manifest compassion, the nirmanakaya.
> These three are not to be discovered as results,
> Rather, they are me, the creator himself,
> Myself as whatever appears, all phenomena,
> My nature, essence, compassion unmodified,
> Since as reality I show the three dimensions of being.

And further,

> The five dimensions are my envisionment
> With pure-lands, and reality is completed.

1.39 Dispelling doubt about the unconditioned potentiality of pure presence

When we say, "The three dimensions of being and fivefold awareness are intrinsically and spontaneously completed in the spaciousness of pure presence," narrow-minded people who are biased against Dzogchen teaching and like to denigrate it say, "It is absurd to suggest that we ordinary sentient beings possess the pure being and primal awareness of the buddhas." This denigration is like saying that, when it is covered by a thick cloud, the sun does not exist. We fortunate people, engaged in Dzogchen, do not argue with such fools, nor should we be intimidated by such talk. If the potential for buddha is not already there, if the awareness of pure presence is not actually incipient, when in the future we become buddha, how can it possibly manifest?

In *The Supreme Tantra*, Lord Maitreya says, "Unconditioned and spontaneously manifest." In *The Secret Core*, it is said,

> In the causal Approach with Signs,
> Sentient beings are taken as the basis of buddha;
> In the resultant, tantric approach,
> Mind's nature becomes familiar as buddha.

And in the *Hevajra Tantra*, it is said,

> All sentient beings are buddha
> Yet covered by adventitious filth;
> Clean the filth and buddha actually appears.

With knowledge of that affirmation from the definitive transmission, we must agree that buddha-potential is not manifest without the purification of adventitious impurities. Clearly, we need to remove the clouds that cover the face of the sun before the rays of the sun will shine upon us.

However, the manifest buddha-potential that is the five buddha-families is completed perfectly in the primal awareness of intrinsic presence. Akshobhya Vajra represents the dimension of pure presence that remains unchanging and unchangeable in all appearances. Amitabha represents the dimension of pure presence that is immutable in time and space and that has no center or circumference. Vairochana represents the dimension of radiance in the utterly immaculate all-embracing, all-suffusing spaciousness, free of conceptual elaboration. Ratnasambhava represents the wish-fulfilling dimension of supreme and ordinary accomplishment attained through nothing existent, yet everywhere apparent. Amoghasiddhi represents the dimension where all-embracing buddha activity is accomplished effortlessly and primordially. These five buddha-family dimensions cannot be separated from the creativity of the primal awareness of pure presence. Similarly, considering a single ritual from the oral or revealed teaching, right from the refuge prayer to the final auspicious prayer, one pure presence is complete. If we need to know the twenty-one unadulterated potentialities and so forth, all the potential fulfilled, we can browse through the texts of Longchenpa and *The Intrinsic Nature of Being* of Dudjom Rinpoche and so forth.

If we wonder whether intrinsic presence and buddha-nature are mentioned in the sutras of the Approach with Signs besides the supreme tantra, the answer is "Yes!" In *The King of Samadhi Sutra*, it is said, "Buddha-nature embraces all beings," while the *Gandavyuha Sutra* says,

> Although in the mundane world
> Everything conceivable may burn,
> The sky will not perish
> Nor will intrinsic awareness.

This point of great profundity, the nature of mind as pure presence, should be kept secret from unworthy recipients, just as a mother refuses her breast to an infant who needs medicine. The sutra *Awareness of the Moment of Death* provides this story:

"O Noble sons! said the Buddha. There was once a woman with a sick child in great pain, and she called a doctor who put solid medicine into the child's mouth, telling the mother not to give milk until the medicine had dissolved. To deter the infant from her breasts, she smeared some bad-smelling ointment on them, at the same time telling the baby boy that it was poison and he should not suckle. Then, when the infant was thirsty, he begged for milk; but when he tried to suckle, the bad smell deterred him, and he cried. After the medicine had dissolved, the mother washed her breasts and offered them to the infant to drink. But thinking that there was poison on the breasts, the child would not drink. Then she told the infant that before, when he tried to suckle, the medicine had not dissolved and that she was afraid that he might die if he mixed her milk with it. Now, however, that the medicine had dissolved, he could drink. And the infant slowly suckled the milk.

"Noble sons! In order to tame the disciples' minds, just as the doctor gave the sick child medicine to dissolve in its mouth, so I gave them meditation instruction only on the egolessness of the body-mind. This mellowed the worldly view of the bhikshus by demonstrating three things: the superiority of the authentic world beyond, the falsity of the worldly ego, and that through familiarization with egolessness, the body is purified.

"Bhikshus, you must meditate on selflessness! Thereby you will abandon clinging to a self or an ego. When such clinging is abandoned completely, you will attain nirvana! Like the mother smearing bad-smelling ointment on her breasts, I instruct you to meditate on all phenomena as insubstantial, without self. Like the mother washing away the smell and telling her son that earlier, when the medicine had not yet dissolved, she could not let him suckle, but now he could drink, so too in order to divert the mind of the world into the teaching, I taught absence of self. But now I teach the existence of buddha-nature. Bhikshus! Don't be afraid, like the infant, but rather, like the infant after he had examined her breasts, drink the milk! You, bhikshus, should now assume that we all possess buddha-nature, and, after investigating it, meditate upon it and cultivate it with diligence."

Buddha-nature is not something that is newly generated through cause and effect, for it is spontaneously present in all sentient beings. The potential of pure being and primal awareness likewise does not need to be conscientiously generated, for it arises naturally, just as heat arises from fire and light from the sun.

The paths of sutra and tantra are similar in realization, but different in method. According to the sutras, to attain buddha, even brilliant individuals need to accumulate merit for three countless eons. Those tantrikas who believe themselves on the path of primal awareness and those on the path of the inner and outer yoga-tantra may accomplish buddha in sixteen or seven lifetimes, or in a minimum of three lifetimes. But from the point of view of Dzogchen, such yogins and yoginis are not really on the path of primal awareness because their views are not yet free of subtle apprehending marks, not yet released from time, and their meditation is still sullied by subtle goals that inhibit their encounter with the natural face of the dharmakaya. For these reasons, they cannot transcend the meditation. They may realize that their conduct is like a reflection in water, but since it contains the snake-knots of judgmentalism, such conduct cannot remove those deficiencies. In the view of the Dzogchen yogins and yoginis of Cutting Through and Direct Crossing, through which buddha is gained in one lifetime, they have not gone beyond the path of the intellect.

The nature of Dzogchen is such that nothing arising in consciousness is rejected, nothing is accepted, and everything is treated impartially. Whatever is perceived, nothing at all is done to it; thereby all experience whatsoever is known as nondual. Here, all views have been utterly forsaken and completely released in the matrix of luminous mind, self-arisen primal awareness. Unmoving from that space we remain in nonconceptual meditation. The propensities of rejection or acceptance are intrinsically released and what is called "ultimate, decisive conduct" arises, which, in short, is free from any focus, elaboration, or effort.

1.40 How to make the five poisons into the path itself

Turning the five poisons into the path is the actual path of primal awareness. The manner of engagement is not to reject desire, anger, sloth, pride, jealousy, and so on, but rather to nurture the five poisons as reflexively released pure presence.

Recall and relive the harm that an enemy has previously inflicted upon us, such as stealing from us, injuring us, or embarrassing and shaming us, and let hatred toward him rise intensely from the heart. As that hatred arises, look deeply into it and see where—not why but where—it comes from, where it resides (in the upper or lower part of the body, for example), and, finally, where it goes. Look whether the hatred has color and shape, and what that color or shape may be. When you see it is as primordially empty, selfless envisionment, do not abandon it because it becomes mirror-like awareness.

Imagine being with an attractive lover, drinking wine and eating meat, wearing designer clothes and jewels; imagine wanting to ride horses or travel in cars and aircraft and allow desire to arise. When desire arises, gaze at it nakedly, looking at where it comes from, in which part of the body it resides, and, finally, where it goes. See whether it has color and shape, and, if so, what are those colors and shapes, and so on. When you see it with detachment as primordially empty envisionment, do not abandon it because it becomes discriminating awareness.

When we are sleepy, in decline, in a state of dullness, gloom, and depression—in short, when mind is not clear but is imperceptive and bewildered, like a frozen computer—let sloth arise. As it arises, gaze at it carefully: look at the owner of the sloth, see where it comes from, in which part of the body it resides, and, finally, where it goes. See whether it has color or shape or any attributes at all. When seen with detachment as primordially empty envisionment, if we do not abandon it, it becomes awareness of vast spaciousness.

Then think of race, status, wealth, bone structure, powers of voice, and so forth, and let pride arise. When pride has arisen, gaze at the pride-holder nakedly: see where it comes from, in which part of the body it resides, and, finally, where it goes. See whether it has color, shape, or any other attribute. When we see that it is primordially empty self-envisionment, do not abandon it, and it becomes awareness of sameness.

Think of someone whose wealth, knowledge, fame, privilege, opportunity, and so forth, is greater than ours. Let our jealousy of him or her grow. When jealousy has arisen, just look at it fixedly, look at the owner of the jealousy, where does it come from, where does it presently reside in the body, and, finally, where does it go. See whether it has color, shape, or attribute. When we see that it is primordially empty envisionment, if we do not abandon it, it becomes the all-accomplishing awareness.

If we can realize the nature of the emotions, they become the various modes of awareness. On the flip side of the errant thoughts that arise with emotion we discover empty awareness, and what a joy that is! If we search for it, however, we cannot find it, and we become pathetically hopeless. We must first understand that all the five emotional poisons are baseless, rootless, and empty. Later, knowing this, when we are engaged on the path, during the gaps between sessions of meditation, no matter what thoughts and emotions arise, we remain at ease with them, without any need to examine their nature, origin, place of abiding, or place of departure, or to examine their shape, color, or attribute: the emotions and accompanying thoughts will effortlessly disappear by themselves.

In this meditation, both the introduction of the view and the maturation of meditation are completed. For beginners on the Dzogchen path, this sequence of examination, fixation, and establishment and of introduction and maturation is very profound. Later, no matter what emotional poison emerges, we can automatically recognize its nature as it arises and releases simultaneously, again and again. Then in our own experience, we can clearly see the inexpressible pure presence as the dharmakaya. There is no higher view or meditation than this. In *The Treasury of the Dharmadhatu*, Longchenpa says,

> View and meditation are primordially released,
> Liberated in nondiscrimination;
> Conduct and character are primordially released,
> Liberated in the All-Good;
> The goal is primordially released,
> Liberated in the absence of hope and fear.

When Padmasambhava left Tibet for the island of Ngayab Ling in the southwest, the king, ministers, and people of Tibet saw him off on a Gungtang hill top. They prostrated to him and wailing with grief requested him not to go to Ngayab but to stay with them, to be the object of prayer of the king, ministers, and people. He left them anyway saying, "All experience is ephemeral, and it is natural that all composite things eventually decay. I have been here long enough, and there is no place in Tibet that I have not visited and blessed. Yeshe Tsogyel and Bairotsana are staying behind, and they are not different from me. In the mountains, cliffs, and remote places of Tibet, I have hidden treasure texts for the benefit of fortunate people of the future." Having relieved the sorrow of the people in this way, before leaving he sang this song:

> I go to the land of mirrorlike awareness,
> And in those fields of the land of clear light
> There will be no hatred for enemies,
> Just pure presence and spaciousness inseparable,
> United like mother and son.
>
> I go to the land of awareness of sameness . . .

and so on, through the five modes of awareness.

In this last instruction given by Padmasambhava to his disciples, to

Dzogchen yogins and yoginis, the morning and evening sessions of ritual meditation sitting in the seven-point posture of Vairochana are implied. Body, speech, and mind should not wander into trifling places. In short, yogins and yoginis should not go beyond the norms of the view, such as the manner of sleeping, eating, walking, speaking, sitting, thinking, and so forth.

The land that Padmasambhava goes to is the land of the five modes of awareness of all buddhas. He goes to the place of the unchangeable mind of mirrorlike awareness, where there is no hatred for enemies because anger is reflexively released. In that clear light space, the mother of basic pure presence and the child of the pure presence as process are united, and right there is the primordial dharmakaya lord Samantabhadra. It is very important to know the manner of recognition of the five poisons as the five modes of awareness. Singing this song, Padmasambhava departed from Tibet, riding his horse King Balhati through the sky to Ngayab Ling.

Abiding in unmodified pure presence, these are the twenty-five aspects of the ultimate result according to Longchenpa's *The Treasury of the Dharmadhatu*:

> The reason that everything is perfect by simply letting it be
> Resides in the incorrigible master that is fivefold pristine awareness—
> Physical, energetic, mental, qualitative, and active perfection, each fivefold—
> And this is the original buddha, the spontaneity of the vast primordial matrix.
> Do not search elsewhere—buddha is already accomplished right here!

Since the essence of pure presence is unchangeable, it is the fivefold body of buddha: the changeless vajrakaya, the manifest bodhikaya, the dharmakaya, the sambhogakaya, and the nirmanakaya. Since the essence of pure presence is inexpressible, it is the fivefold buddha speech: the speech of bodhi-reality, the speech inseparable from the vajra, the speech of unborn meaning, the speech of meaningful symbol, and verbal speech. Since the essence of pure presence is free of conceptual elaboration, it is the fivefold buddha mind: the mind of intrinsic awareness, mind of mirrorlike awareness, mind of awareness of sameness, mind of discriminating awareness, and mind of bodhi-accomplishing awareness. Since the essence of pure presence accomplishes the nine wishes to completion, it possesses the manifest fivefold buddha-potential: it is the ground of every perfection and, more particularly, is the throne of the noble ones, pure and clear light, the boundless mansion, and a pure-land. Since the four perfectly appropriate activities are accomplished in the same purity as primal awareness in the essence of pure presence, immaculate reality contains five buddha-activities: pacification, enrichment, control, destruction, and spontaneity.

As the basis of all potential in intrinsic presence, every potentiality matures and manifests immediately, the external world expands, beings in the world multiply, and enjoyment of the five sensory pleasures increases. All these are like the envisionment of a magician's horses, elephants, and so forth, apparent yet not truly existent, an indisputable vision of emptiness free of all extremes.

To reveal that vision we need to have confidence in meditation. If we lack such confidence, we will not be able to remove the veil of dualistic delusion. What we call "meditation" is nothing but a confident view, keeping pure presence fixed leisurely within that view. When we have gained confidence in meditation, all the phenomena of samsara, nirvana, and the path from one to the other arise as forms of emptiness, apparent yet not truly existent. Those forms are the path, and traversing it there is neither hatred of an enemy nor love for a friend, neither hope for nirvana nor fear of samsara. Moreover, when our potential for such meditation is realized, both samsara and nirvana are bound together in the one cosmic seed, free of all conceptual elaboration, and whatever we have specified, focused on, imagined, referenced, or elaborated will gradually vanish, like mist dissipating in the sky. The meditation will become increasingly unchanging, the view of dharmakaya as empty pure presence will be revealed, and with this the obscurations of semen, ovum, and energy flows (that is, basic gender dualism), which are very fine dualisms of karmic propensity, are abandoned: here, it is as if dust, haze, and darkness were eliminated from the summer sky. And we arrive at the place where all experience is consummate and all intellection exhausted.

In *The Chariot of Omniscience*, Jigme Lingpa quotes this verse:

> The yogin freed, like the sun rising at dawn,
> The dharmakaya appears. Wah! Wah!

The body dissolves into its quantum-level constitution; mind vanishes into dharmakaya and buddha!

1.41 Until discursive thought dissolves in spaciousness, karmic repercussions must be considered

Until our pure presence is a constant, until we attain fearless confidence, we must attend to karmic causality, vows and samayas, accumulation of merit, abstention from vice, and so forth. As Padmasambhava famously said, quoted in *The Chronicles of Padmasambhava*, which were revealed by Orgyen Lingpa,

> My view is higher than the sky;
> My karma is finer than barley flour.

Pay attention to karmically effected events with the same care we reserve for protection of the eyes. But at the same time, such events should not be seen as real and true. Quoted in *The Samye Chronicles*, Padmasambhava again says,

> Maharaj! In my tantra it is the view that leads; but don't let your conduct bend toward the view. If you do let it stray, you take the black demonic sophistic view that may justify any wicked action by "emptiness." But on the other hand, don't let the view tend toward conduct because if you do, trapped by notions of concrete materialism and specific attributes, the occasion for liberation will never arise.

Due to his misconception of karmic cause and effect, Tarpa Nakpo was born in hell and then reborn as Rudra. For further details of this story, browse through the tantra *The Discourse of the General Assembly.* Tarpa Nakpo's fate was determined by his contempt for karmic repercussion in his confusion about the causal process. As Jowoje Atisha said in *The Lamp of the Path*,

> Until concepts are exhausted, there is karma;
> Believe in the repercussions of karma!

1.42 The benefits of hearing Dzogchen precepts

Dzogchen yogins and yoginis appear to be normal ordinary people, but inwardly their mind is buddha. In *The Tantra of Perfect Creativity*, it is said,

> Whoever abides in nonaction,
> Even though he has a demon's body,
> His mind is buddha.

If we can walk the Dzogchen path, we can gain enormous merit. We have received a human body, which is very rarely obtained. We have encountered a rigzin-lama, which is a very rare occurrence. We have met the Dzogchen teaching, which is extremely fortunate. It is as if a blind beggar found a jewel in the garbage. For countless lifetimes, we have wasted our time in trifling matters, yet this present human body has not emerged from nowhere without causes and conditions. It was obtained because of the accumulation of merit in previous lives. In this present form, we have met with a rigzin-lama, and we can hear, reflect, and meditate upon Dzogchen. This good fortune is greater than rebirth as Indra, king of the gods, or as Brahma, greater than rebirth as a celebrity millionaire, or an iconic American president, like John F. Kennedy, or a famous Nobel laureate, like Nelson Mandela.

Compared to rebirth as a Dzogchen yogin, such destinies are nothing. Whatever wealth we possess, however famous we may be in this world, in the end it is all suffering because samsara is marked by change, and change implies suffering. In this way, our every activity is suffused with it. If we but observe and consider, we will become convinced of this. Of the sickness and disease of body and mind that we endure—we will not speak of that. Even the fame and wealth that we take to be happiness lasts only for a very short time. Due to strong emotional affliction, some dominate others in competition. No matter how much wealth we possess, we anxiously want more, worried by enemies and thieves and provoked by the suffering of failing to reach the status of richer people. In heaven, for example, after spending a life span of five hundred years enjoying the pleasures of the senses in every manner possible, a god knows, through his power of foreknowledge, a week before his death, when he will die, what manner of death he will endure, and how he will suffer in his next life. It is said that his suffering will be one hundred times greater than the pleasure he enjoyed in heaven. The more possessions or fame we have, the more we will suffer. That is a fact.

To repeat what Sri Saraha sang,

> Contentment is the ultimate wealth;
> Detachment is the final happiness.

Supreme happiness and pleasure is contentment and freedom from attachment. Contentment is a certain degree of satisfaction. The freedom from attachment implies knowing that whatever appears to exist is unstable, unpredictable, and untrue and that all things are mere conceptual labels and mental delusion. To realize these two, there is no better method than dependence upon the Dzogchen view and meditation. To accomplish Dzogchen, in the beginning, we should approach it through reason to attain a logical view; in the middle, we should practice meditation; and, at the end, we accomplish the result. All three phases—beginning, middle, and end—are important. At the beginning, even though we cannot eliminate the inclination to gain fame, amass wealth, subdue enemies, and care for friends, we should reject these inclinations as much as possible. In the middle phase, in an isolated place, if at all possible, or in a quiet room without disturbance by traffic or radio, try to meditate morning and evening. In the final stage, we reach the level of Dzogchen called "all reality consummate."

If we cannot attain the vision all at once, we need to familiarize ourselves gradually with Dzogchen view and meditation. This will be beneficial in this life and also in the next life, and we will eventually become free from samsaric wandering.

In this present age of raw competition in business and trade, even though we might not be able to train frequently, as our time schedule allows, we should remember to sit down daily for meditation. Whatever anxiety we incur, due to sickness, conflict, aggression, or loss of profit, and so on, through the power of this training we will not become so attached to external objects: thereby suffering is alleviated. The more the mind is concentrated, the fewer mistakes will occur in any task. There is no better advice than this to benefit this life and the next.

As Longchenpa says in his *Collected Fragments*,

> At the beginning, let go of worldly concerns;
> In the middle, retreat to a place of seclusion;
> At the end, arrive at consummation.
> This advice is favorable to this life and the next.

2. Meditation as the Path

2.1 First, conviction in the view is essential

We receive instruction from a rigzin-lama. Then, with experience of the essence of the empty pure presence of the dharmakaya, which is the view free of all conceptual limitations, immaculate and certain conviction naturally arises. We cultivate and deepen this by training in meditation. If we lack experience in the Dzogchen view, if we lack realization of our own nature, then conduct will not be perfect, and no matter how much effort we apply, it will only make us tired. The measure of conviction is indicated in this anecdote about Dzogchen Shenga Rinpoche, who, when asked by a disciple, "What about the view, Uncle?" replied, "My view? If Guru Rinpoche came in the door right now, I'd say, 'Welcome! How are you?' That shows the view!" Shenga Rinpoche meant no disrespect; he meant rather that only personal experience provides complete assurance in the Dzogchen view. Similarly, Sri Saraha sang,

> In front, behind, in the ten directions,
> In whatever is seen, there lies the suchness;
> Today the lord in me has eradicated delusion.
> I never need ask anything of anyone again!

Saraha says that he has now gained certainty in the reality of all experience of samsara and nirvana, free of conceptual limitations. With absolute certitude, meditation and conduct will emerge effortlessly from the view. In his *Beacon of Certainty*, Ju Mipham says,

> What is the perfect way of being?
> Certitude in seeing!
> Conviction in the view
> Facilitates conduct and meditation.

Meditation is nothing more than sustaining the essence of the view, and the view, as mentioned earlier, is direct awareness of appearances or consciousness that does not crystallize into this or that. Pure presence itself does not slip into the object, and all positive and negative attachments vanish by themselves into the spaciousness of the dharmadhatu. That is not the method of the Approach with Signs, wherein each object is neutralized separately with an antidote.

2.2 The Reason for Meditation

If the view itself is meditation, what need do we have for meditation? The perfected view becomes perfect meditation only in an ideal world. After introduction to the view, until the view has entered the matrix of the here and now or until we attain confidence in it, we need to meditate. Dudjom Rinpoche quotes Longchenpa, in *The Dakini's Heart-Essence*, saying,

> We may realize the timelessly liberating view, but if we are not constant in meditation in that view, it is not possible to turn back the delusory appearances of samsara. It is vital to familiarize ourselves with the natural state of pure presence.

In the actual praxis of Dzogchen, view, meditation, and conduct are not distinct. In *The Three Incisive Precepts*, Patrul Rinpoche says, "View, meditation, and action are not to be distinguished." That is true, but for the student on the graduated path, the view, meditation, conduct, and result should be taught separately. So long as we are plagued by dualistic concepts, like the viewer of a painting who sees in three dimensions what the artist had painted in two, we must distinguish between view and meditation. For this reason, yogins and yoginis should strive in their meditation in a secluded place.

Now I will explain the meditation that is required at that time. Ordinary meditation—mundane meditation—is the basis and practice of all religions. But with regard to Dzogchen meditation, it is impossible to talk about it without having experienced it—it would be like trying to talk about delicious food without ever having tasted it. We may have received excellent instruction, but without an understanding gained in habitual Dzogchen meditation such instruction is of no use. When someone is suffering from severe sickness and the doctor, instead of giving medicine, gives a long story about the medicine—how it is made, what it's composed of—we will know that he is a learned doctor. But unless the medicine is given to the sick person and heals him, the story about the medicine is a joke. Unless we actually meditate, the stories of this and that teaching are of no use when we face the suffering of death, the bardo, and rebirth. So meditation practice is essential. Meditation means familiarization with mind. In Sanskrit it is called *dhyana,* the technical meaning of which is to focus the mind on one locus without distraction from any other, so that attention rests on a single point. If we think that Dzogchen meditation is performed in the rational mind and for that reason cannot go beyond that mind, we make the false assumption that meditation is performed by anything or anyone at all.

In general we distinguish three types of meditation: first, the concentration that is like a child's play; second, the concentration that thoroughly differentiates meanings; and third, the concentration that is the prerogative of the tathagatas. The children's meditation is what many religions talk about these days, the type of concentration that Buddhists regard as the cause of birth in the formless realms of the gods. Meditation on selflessness as practiced by the lower Buddhist approaches [*sravakas* and *pratyekabuddhas*] for the purpose of liberation is known as the concentration that thoroughly differentiates meanings. The meditation upon the selflessness of all experience free of conceptual elaboration practiced by bodhisattvas for the purpose of attaining buddha is the concentration that is the virtue of the tathagatas. More on this topic is contained in other texts, so I will stop writing about it here.

2.3 Disposition of meditation

Let me now give a Dzogchen pith instruction, or secret precept: the method of maintaining the view is called "meditation." When we are convinced that all experience of phenomena is apparent yet not truly existent, like magical illusion, then as each separate emotion arises, it is free of the need of a separate dose of emptiness as an antidote because neither the affliction nor the antidote have ever existed. Whatever appears, however, should remain loosely in perception just as it is; sustaining that disposition is called "meditation."

If someone asks, "Why in Dzogchen is meditation called 'nonmeditation'?" the answer comes that all phenomena are seen as space. But how can we "hold" space as an object of focus? Space has no specific characteristic, so there is nothing to meditate upon. The nature of mind is primordially unborn and free of any conceptual elaboration, so nothing can arise there upon which to meditate. Here no effort is made to distinguish any difference between the object of meditation and the mind that is meditating—what difference could be found since there is no meditation and no one who meditates? This disposition of mind in its natural state is called "nonmeditation" in Dzogchen.

What is the meaning of "in its natural state"? When mind is disturbed by thoughts, its nature is unclear in the same way that a pail of dirty water is unclear after it has been stirred: the bottom of the pail is then imperceptible. When mind is kept unmodified in its natural state, like a pellucid pail of undisturbed water, the nature of mind is pure presence. As the reality or "suchness" of all phenomena is ascertained in the view, there is now no need of any scrutiny or investigation of the nature of mind, and therefore simply to abide in the natural state of whatever appears is labeled "meditation." This nonmeditation that is the meditational disposition of Dzogchen is the crux of practice. When we stay in nonmeditation without drifting away, all the points of reference of our internal discussion vanish, and the bright pure presence of self-arising primal awareness dawns spontaneously.

Some may say that this is a mind-constructed meditation because it does not go beyond mental experience. But the temporal mind of the ordinary being who is the meditator is not the meditating mind—the "meditator" is self-arising primal awareness free of all conceptual elaboration. Even though the ear-sense is engaged and mind perceives sound, this sound is in itself an utterly unelaborated empty echo; likewise, even though in meditation it is the mind that is engaged, this meditation is free of all elaboration.

But, then, on the other hand, as Ju Mipham says in his *Reply to Refutation*,

> The inexpressible nature of being is experienced and understood as a mere general idea by ordinary beings who possess conviction. In the sutras it is called "the patience that is in total accord with buddha-dharma in experience." In the tantras it is called "illustrative primal awareness." In reality, in short, it is the mind that is in accord with the ultimate absolute.

With certainty in unelaborated reality, meditating on the gradual path, ordinary beginners first produce a subtle realization consonant with reality and finally unite with the real primal awareness, or the natural state of unelaborated reality. As the great Rongzompa says, that type of meditation is conventional meditation. If we appear to be meditating well but cannot get any direct experience, the fine view that gives no result is like a child who at birth has neither friends to care for him nor enemies to hate him. Until he becomes older, he needs to be nurtured with food, clothing, education, and so forth. If he is not cared for, he will die immediately. Depending upon his nurture, the boy will mature. Likewise, according to the quality of the meditation based on a fine view, the result will be good, medium, or bad.

Some claim that they practice Dzogchen, but when happiness and suffering arise in them, the requisite equanimity does not arise. That is the fault of lack of familiarity with the view. If we can practice the view continuously for months and years, like a perennially flowing river, eventually no matter what situation arises, like joy, misery, or fear, it just vanishes, released immediately upon its arising. We will experience every situation vanishing as it arises, and an ineffable sense of pleasure, clarity, and brightness will manifest, along with a powerful inner certainty that transcends negative and positive. Even when we are dying, we will feel no regret. Such are the accomplishments of a little meditation. Even if we have only confidence in the view, we will be free of fear in life and death.

Until we are able to abide from the first moment in the view and maintain equanimity in the flow, in the second moment dualistic thoughts will arise, and suffering and fear will follow us continuously. Whatever happiness or suffering arises, we should have the confidence of liberation right in the moment, and the key point here is to hang loose in that moment of release. If this is lacking, then the meditation is ineffective. It is very important that we sustain our nonmeditation until we get strong and unchangeable pure presence. If we practice at the juncture of unification of view and meditation, we will not find suffering, fear, or any untoward situation even if we were to look for it.

Longchenpa says in *The Treasury of Natural Perfection*,

> We may recognize the nature of mind,
> But if we do not familiarize ourselves with it,
> It is like having an infant son kidnapped.

In the first moment, we may recognize the nature of mind as indicated in the view, but if we lack sound experiential familiarity with it, in the second moment the enemy "dualistic thought" will steal away the mind. We will then suffer just as we would suffer if our infant son, left unattended on a battlefield, were to be kidnapped by the enemy and mercilessly tortured. If we have been introduced to the view and cannot meditate properly, no benefit is gained. Rather than reading many books on Dzogchen, it is better to do a single session of meditation. Meditation must thus be emphasized. Just like a great musician who, though able to mesmerize a large audience, gets no joy from it, if those who read or hear the teaching do not realize it, they will get no benefit in this or the next life. Just as a great cruise liner may take many people across the ocean but itself can never land on the other shore, so those who teach Dzogchen to others but have no experience of meditation will remain as ordinary people. Just as the sight and sound of water does not quench our thirst, so teaching without meditation is unfulfilling. Just because we have heard and understood innumerable expositions of the profound teaching does not mean we have yet reached the place of reflexive liberation.

"Meditation practice" means, primarily, familiarizing oneself with the view. Whatever we do, whether good or bad, if we have practiced it diligently, we can do it without difficulty. At the Olympic Games, for example, we can see amazing things done by athletes in the high jump and in gymnastics. These great feats are due to constant practice. Likewise, if we can train the mind, we can master it in rest and in movement. This mind training is called "meditation." All beauty and ugliness and all happiness and sadness are just products of mind. It is vital to train the mind!

2.4. Without meditation, even trivial events create severe suffering

Whatever our misfortune, serious or trivial, we should include all personal misery in the process of our meditation. We tend to fall under the influence of pain and suffering—we let them push us around. Consider the pain derived from losing our business, the sadness of divorce, the pain of lost opportunities or that of lost status. Think of the anxiety when we live in fear of violence from enemies, of our worry about disobedient children, or simply whenever things fail to happen in accord with our desire. If we encounter suffering, we may seek relief in the use of alcohol or drugs, or we may engage in gambling to forget it. Such escapism is like pouring cold water into boiling water while it is still on the stove—though it immediately cools the pot down, unless we turn down the heat, the entire thing will return to the boil. An antidote may give us some small relief, but more suffering is always around the corner. What we think of as a solution can often become the cause of a greater problem. A hare trapped inside a net struggles to free herself, but the more she struggles, the tighter she draws the net, until finally she is sufficiently desperate to gnaw off her own limbs. The more we think about a solution, often the worse the problem becomes.

Once when a flock of geese was flying through the sky, at one particular place the leader warned them all to be quiet because of the danger of hunters. One goose told another goose and that goose told a third goose and soon the entire flock was repeating the warning. The noise was heard all over the area where the hunters waited, and they were able to shoot down many of the geese. So, childlike people bring suffering upon themselves by trying to eliminate it. Yet however much we try to forget it, suffering rears its head again. When we cannot sleep at night and we think that we are thinking too much, the more we think like that, the longer we lie awake! This "thinking of not thinking" itself is the gross thought that keeps us awake. Likewise, ordinary beings are unskillful in their treatment of suffering, and wishing to change suffering into happiness, they take to alcohol and become mad, or perhaps commit suicide to get rid of their suffering.

In May 21, 2007, in the Nepal daily newspaper *Kantipur* a headline read, "After Killing His Lover He Killed Himself." The story went like this. Pukar and Prabina were lovers. Pukar's love for Prabina was so strong that he could not live without her. They were both well educated, and Pukar had recently graduated from a hotel-management course after studying for a year and a half in Singapore. When he returned to Nepal, he obtained a good job in a foreign business and also a visa for Canada. But the girl's parents objected to her affair with Pukar, so they married her off to a man in the nearby city of Pokhara. When Pukar heard of this marriage, he was distraught and bewildered. He phoned Prabina and told her that since they lacked the karma to be together, there was no point in staying friends. He wanted his letters and gifts returned and suggested a place that they could meet—the Salagiri forest. He had something to share with her, he said. She agreed to meet him and keep the assignation secret. Pukar was so depressed that he got drunk while waiting for her in the forest, and in his distress decided that if his beloved could not belong to him that she should not belong to anyone else. When she arrived, he took her by the neck, then shot and killed her. Then, driven by fear, he ran some three kilometers away from that place and shot himself to death.

If we examine these lovers' emotions carefully, we cannot find them anywhere since they are not based anywhere in particular. Consider a dream in which your only son suffers from sickness, receives treatment, the treatment fails, and he dies. In this situation, immense emotional pain arises for you, the parent. If you take the illusion of the dream as true and cling to it, you will suffer. To save yourself from such fear and suffering, you have to know a dream as a dream or awaken from your sleep. When you are awake, the suffering disappears from the bed. In the same way, if you experience such suffering in love affairs, it is because you regard illusions as truly existing.

How can there be suffering in delusion? We all feel what arises in us just now as real suffering, and we make the same mistake in the dream. Consider Pel Dorje, a man who lives in Yangkar, which is close to my monastery. After finishing his work one day, he returned to his house, ate dinner, and before his family had finished their food, lay down by the hearth and slept. Suddenly he woke up, shouted that rocks were falling, and ran outside. His father and two sisters tried to catch him but failed, and he ran twenty feet to a fearful pit full of rocks and nettles, and without hesitation, jumped into it. The people pulled him out still alive. Later, when we asked him what had happened, he said that he had mistaken his dream for waking experience.

The fear and anxiety of dream can be more intense than waking experience. Pel Dorje's family still lives in fear that the same thing might occur to him again. If we speak from the perspective of the dharma, we could say that his disease is a strong attachment to dualistic appearances—even dream appearances—as substantial and true.

When chicken-hearted people travel at dusk through a place known to be infested with snakes and catch a glimpse of a short length of rope on the road, they may become very nervous, believing that the rope is a snake, and may even think they see it move. Due to their strong tendency to believe in the substantiality of appearances, they make mistakes in perception and are deluded. After September 11, when terrorists attacked the World Trade Center in New York, many Americans were not able to forget it, and the incident remained in their memories for months upon months. Many were plagued by insomnia because of this incapacity to let it go. Whenever they heard the sound of planes or vehicles with a loud noise, remembering 9/11, they became apprehensive. Similarly, in Pakistan, after suffering a strong earthquake, people talked quietly for many months because loud sounds triggered their fears of a repetition of the earthquake. When they heard loud noises, they clung to each other. This behavior is due to the strong imprint of traumatic incidents upon the mind. We sentient beings are attached to traumatic events not only in the present but throughout beginningless samsara. This attachment cannot be abandoned easily. But, as in the case of illness, no matter how serious it is, if we encounter a good doctor who prescribes effective medicine, gradually we can recover. Likewise, if we meet a rigzin-lama who can guide us with the profound teaching of Dzogchen, in a short time our attachment to dualistic delusion as substantial and true will dissolve. Day by day delusion will vanish, and intrinsic awareness will become clearer and clearer to us. Finally, delusion vanishes entirely, and we attain buddha in pure presence.

So whether it is daytime or nighttime, we need to realize that suffering arises only because we cling to delusion as reality. If we can understand that what we cling to as truth is actually delusion, without an atom of substantiality, that it is self-envisioned illusion, we can thoroughly excise the notion that there is an objective field of suffering "out there" and a subject who suffers "in here." Through this understanding, we can relax, and, in the spaciousness of pure presence, where there is no way to conceptualize a place of suffering, we can increase our confidence.

A few years ago, in the area around Koltri in Nepal, there was a great famine. A man lived there with his wife and five children amid the severe suffering of near-starvation. The man, trying to save his family, felt enormous responsibility for them. After a few weeks, unable to earn enough to feed them, he went to another place in order to work and to earn money. He worked hard in his new job, and, after some weeks, set out for his home carrying thirty kilos of rice; but the rice was stolen as he slept during the night. He was utterly distraught when he woke up the next morning and found the rice gone. He was so distraught that he bought some poison, and when he reached home, he told his family that they were going to feast that night. He cooked rice gruel and put the poison in it and gave a bowl of it to each of them; finally, he drank a bowl himself. All seven of them died. He had believed that the best way of avoiding suffering was to poison himself and his family. The man had no bad intention, but he was simply supremely unskillful. Had he moved to a suitable place, he might have been able to beg for food and save the lives of his family. From the president down to the lowest person on the street, we can all make such mistakes. We can all cite examples of events designed to eliminate suffering that actually multiplied them. Such unskillful people are seen by the noble ones as the real fools among fools.

2.5 Meditation removes the attachment that is the root of suffering

If we want to counteract suffering in this life, in the bardo, and in the next life, there is no better way—in fact, no other way—than the path of Shakyamuni Buddha. Buddha taught many methods—Theravada, Mahayana, outer tantra, and inner tantra—to remove suffering. Here we are looking at Dzogchen, where what is to be abandoned and what is to be adopted are identical in the one taste of pure cognition. In the Approach with Signs, each particular emotion has its own antidote: the antidote to desire is meditation on disgust, for example, while the antidote to hatred is meditation on loving-kindness, the antidote to sloth is breathing meditation, and so on. But in Dzogchen, whatever fear or suffering occurs, whatever arises in mind, is known as subjective envisionment because not a single atom anywhere has any substantial existence. For that reason, the meditation precept "hang loosely in pure presence" takes precedence. The implication of "hanging loosely" is that because appearances are not blocked or rejected in any way in the nature of mind, the objective field is allowed to appear just as it is. Hanging loosely in pure presence, free of objectified appearances, and abiding such that the very complexion of our experience is transformed—this is meditation. Prolonged, it is excellent meditation.

Some think that during actual meditation, appearances, being delusion, should be stopped. They can, however, only be impeded, not stopped. Just as a dam constructed across a river for generating power brings destruction to the environment, so it is with appearances. We should not obstruct appearances at all because they are the creativity of pure presence and the doorway to primal awareness. If they are obstructed, later, when buddha could be attained, primal awareness as a multiplicity has no basis out of which to arise.

If we cannot stay relaxed in pure presence for any length of time, we should instead do short sessions of meditation repeatedly. Now do not think that "meditation" is merely following Vairochana's seven points; just this is not meditation at all and refers only to the optimal bodily posture that supports meditation. On the other hand, if we think correct bodily posture is not necessary, we are mistaken. "Short sessions of meditation" does not mean sitting in the posture and then releasing the posture again and again, or sitting and then rising from the posture repeatedly. The meaning is that in one session, sitting in the posture of the seven points of Vairochana, we should let the mind hang loosely. When stormy thoughts arise and obstruct our meditation, we should recall the original view of pure presence that is free of conceptual elaboration. Thus our meditation consists of sometimes being aware of the mind's digressions and sometimes resting in its nature, alternately, or according to our necessity. Through repetition of this process, the meditation is strengthened, and we can abide in pure presence for a longer time each day. If we can rest in pure presence, we no longer need to watch the mind, as that phase of practice has been completed.

Through such meditation, no matter what kind of suffering arises, the experience is like meeting an old acquaintance in the middle of the market place. Whatever painful thoughts arise, in their very appearing, they are known through familiarization to be baseless and rootless, and thus left alone, they arise and just vanish by themselves. So no matter how great the suffering, when we experience it in the timeless moment of pure presence, it turns into happiness. We have no need to confirm this with anyone else, for we experience it ourselves. Further, we should look into the nature of mind not just when we suffer but also when we are very happy. When happiness is seen as a concrete thing, then attachment gradually increases, and in this way, in turn it becomes the root of suffering.

2.6. The cause of manifest suffering is hope and fear

Hope for fame, wealth, and pleasure, and fear of robbers, thieves, and disease—this is our lot as ordinary beings. So long as there is hope of happiness or fear of pain, suffering is not eliminated. We accumulate wealth for our own benefit in this life and look for fame, health, and so forth. We are always attached to these things, and if we already possess them, we try to hold on to them. If we do not possess them, we are constantly thinking about how to obtain them, scheming and plotting. When we have what we want, we fear losing it, so with lots of hard work we protect it and in the process risk offending others.

Consider the *Mahabharata* epic of the Hindus. This story is so long that it can be narrated for months on end. It is one of the longest and best stories in the world, containing both worldly and religious advice. It provides moral instruction and advice on manners, respect for elders and spouses, and on the raising of children. It gives very good advice based on truth. In short it is the story of a conflict between truth and falsehood, where the truth is reality and falsehood is delusion. It shows how to win such a war, and since the war is waged on behalf of reality, it is a virtuous war. Attachment to reality—the nature of mind—is noble attachment, but in buddha-dharma, it is taught that the root of suffering is attachment. Whether the *Mahabharata* shows noble attachment to the body and primal awareness of reality, or the ignoble attachment of subduing enemies and cherishing kith and kin, the truth is that both are attachments and hence the very root of suffering.

As it is said in the *Avatamsaka Sutra*,

> Wherever an objective is reified,
> It becomes a bone of contention for demons.

So long as there is an objective to focus upon or become attached to, there can never be any attainment of the happiness of liberation. This has been emphasized in the sutras and tantras. In the war of the *Mahabharata*, attachment to truth and dharma caused the death of many thousands of people, both kings and subjects. In the *Vinaya* of Bhagawan Buddha, it is said,

> Whatever doctrine creates desire directly or indirectly cannot become the cause of freedom from desire. Know that such a doctrine is not the Buddha's teaching, nor his discipline, nor his exposition.

Whatever we may call it, if it is an attachment, it does not go beyond the circle of suffering. If it is a pure event, on the other hand, it will benefit both self and others. Take compassion, for instance, which brings benefit to all beings and is the root of peace and the heart of buddha: if we have attachment to it and assert any kind of control, such compassion will certainly neither provide much benefit to the world nor become a support for the attainment of buddha. Like gift-wrapped dog vomit, it is outwardly attractive but inwardly utterly revolting. It is important that compassion not be stained by attachment.

In *Entry into the Middle Way*, Chandrakirti says,

> Compassionate mind, nondual perception,
> And luminous mind create bodhisattvas.

Objectless compassion inseparable from insight into emptiness is attainment of the bodhisattva level. When compassion is tainted by attachment, it cannot become a support for the realization of buddha. Attachment to one's nation, country, fellow citizens, and so on, inevitably leads to perennial sufferings in this life and the next.

It is vital to train in nonattachment. In the *Vinaya*, the Bhagawan Buddha says,

> If any person in anger destroys or burns a symbol of my mind such as a stupa, a symbol of my speech such as a scripture, a symbol of my body such as a temple, in that event no disciple

> of mine should fight that person or abuse him or protect those things with anger.

And in *Entering the Way of the Bodhisattva*, Shantideva says,

> Don't show anger to those
> Who destroy images, stupas, or scriptures,
> As they are not harming the Buddha or anyone else.

Any happiness there is in the world ultimately turns to pain. Why? Consider the two sides of a coin: just because what we desire is to be seen on the front does not mean that dislike won't soon appear on the back. Likewise, hope and fear are a single coin, one entity with two faces—on the other side of a moment in which we hope for more happiness will be our fear of more suffering. Until attachment is eliminated, we can be certain of having both hope and fear. As long as there is hope and fear, the delusions of samsara will be perpetuated and there will be constant suffering. Thus attachment is the nature of both hope and fear: looking at the ultimate emptiness of the self-envisioned magical illusion of hope and fear, we should hang loosely in the flow.

It is not enough merely to look into the space of happiness or sadness; it is important to have pure presence constant in that flow. If the power of meditation is not constant, it is impossible to remain long in the place of nondual perception. Thoughts that arise intermittently will break the continuity, and radiating out from this, like ripples on a pond, the poisonous taste of emotion will arise to obstruct the meditation. As gross thoughts increase, ripples become rough waves that intensify the emotion. Until subtle emotions are left behind, we cannot eradicate suffering, so it is crucially important to sustain the state of meditation. When we gain strong familiarity by staying in that space for a long time, then no matter what thoughts arise, whether gross or subtle, they will not be able to dislodge us: upon recognizing the first thought, whatever thought it may be, in that very moment, we realize it to be the play of the spontaneous creativity of dharmakaya. Like a wave falling back into the ocean, the thought vanishes into the dharmakaya. In that space of naked empty pure presence that is the view, always cherishing thoughts of the five poisonous emotions and all the movements of body, speech, and mind, and the acts of eating, sleeping, moving, and sitting, we are known as the yogins and yoginis who stand guard over the shifting dharmakaya display. This is the supreme method of sustaining the essence of meditation. According to Dzogchen teaching, this is unadulterated by any kind of focus; it is called "the great meditation that is nonmeditation."

2.7 A short explanation of how to sustain the primal awareness of intrinsic presence

In his *Wish-Fulfilling Treasury*, Longchenpa says,

> Sit cross-legged upon a comfortable cushion, take refuge, and generate a compassionate attitude. Then, when the mind focuses loosely on any single perception, without any idea in mind, without any thought, distraction free, radiant and shining, abide there without concentration or diffusion for an instant. Without externalizing any object or thinking any thought, material objects and the immaterial grasping mind are now no longer dualized. The mind that meditates is neither affirming nor negating; what is in front of the mind is said to be absent, for there is nothing established there. Each separate nonreferential perception is equal in the immaculate primal awareness of intrinsic presence.
>
> During informal contemplation between meditation sessions, recognize appearances as apparent yet nonexistent, like magical illusion, and perform dedication and aspiration prayers for the sake of the six illusory classes of sentient beings, all of whom have been our parents. During informal contemplation between sessions, without even a whit of desire, attachment, or clinging to the illusory appearances of this life, perform prostration and circumambulation, read texts, make tsatsa [clay images], water offerings, and so on.

2.8 The place of meditation

The place of meditation is solitary. Physically, we should retire to a secluded place, away from entertaining distractions, and mentally, we should be in a place free of discursive thought. Physical seclusion implies an isolated place free of the mundane affairs and frivolous entertainment of the big city, free of the pollution and roar of traffic and people. In the city, there is no time to rest, and we are wafted along like a piece of paper driven by the wind; time goes so fast that we have no time even to sit and eat comfortably. The dissatisfaction generated in the city is caused by attachment to external objects. So, like earlier generations of yogins, in *Entering the Way of the Bodhisattva*, Shantideva says,

> Desire brings sadness;
> Joy arises in seclusion.
> Conflict and emotion are absent
> In quiet forests glades;
> In blessed moonlight in a cool sandal forest,
> With a beautiful simple retreat house,
> The forest trees silently tossing their heads,
> Sweet breezes blow to benefit others.

We need somewhere free of people and traffic, with some flowers growing round about, streams bubbling by, a spacious view, and a pond nearby, perhaps a place with sandalwood trees, birds flying freely, and animals roaming leisurely. From time to time the sound of musical instruments like flutes, lutes, and guitars may be heard. A cave on top of a mountain or in its lap, preferably a natural cave, is best. If this ideal place of seclusion is impossible to find, go to a place where there is no chance of attachment to friends or hatred toward enemies, where there is no noise from neighbors, dogs, vehicles, or anything else, and no disturbance to our meditation from frivolous activities. If we find such a place that supports our practice, accomplishment will arise much more easily; if our practice is uninterrupted, we will attain true accomplishment. Such a place is difficult to find these days. Everyone is busy pursuing happiness in external, material things. If it is impossible to go into secluded retreat, just leave work aside for one hour in the morning or evening when there is no noise and devote it to a daily meditation practice.

Beginners will not gain any advantage if external conditions are not supportive. The mind will be distracted and diverted in a second. Like a stampeding horse in a market place, the mind runs to frivolity and noise and cannot stay still for a moment, and there can be no meditation. So practice calmly in a secluded place and meditate well. Gradually we will be able to assimilate more and more noise until finally when our meditation is perfect, we can sit in any noisy environment and be like Jetsun Milarepa, who sings in his *Songbook*,

> When I move in a crowded market place,
> No matter what appears, I look at the nature of mind;
> When I stay all alone,
> I rest in naked empty pure presence.

When in a crowd, whatever subtle or gross emotion arises, our attention needs to be instantaneous in recognition of it, just as it arises, so that it can be integrated into the matrix of meditation. In that way whatever appears is absorbed into meditation, and there is no need to search for isolation and seclusion. But for beginners, it is best if they find solitude in a forest, or if not there at least in a quiet room where they can meditate morning and evening.

The main supports to accomplishment of samadhi are freedom from entertainment and freedom from discursive thoughts: these freedoms are best optimized in a place of solitude. As Longchenpa says in his *Collected Fragments*,

> Mountains covered with forests are a pleasure,
> And in valleys of herbs and flowers with waterfalls,
> May I transcend the activities of this lifetime
> And attain supreme liberation.

2.9 The disposition of the body

First, take a comfortable seat, sit cross-legged, hands in meditation posture, spine straight like an arrow, shoulders held back like a vulture's wings, neck slightly hooked, tongue held against the palate, and eyes dropped to the nose. If we can apply these seven instructions of Vairochana in our meditation, then with a straight spine our energy channels become straight. If the energy channels are straight, then the movements of energy within the body are quieted, and with energy pacified, the mind is luminescent.

2.10 How to sustain pure presence in brief

The pure presence that was introduced in the section on view is itself the meditation. Wherever a single perception falls, let it hang loosely but firmly, without modifying it in any way, and it rests in naked empty pure presence. If we are unable to abide in this due to the sudden arising of thought, we should just hang loosely in the thought. Then that creativity, like a wave falling back into the ocean, is released into its ground, and thus buddha is attained in alpha-purity. We should engage diligently and one-pointedly in this practice until we become confident, and then, our creativity optimized, we attain constancy.

2.11 How to sustain pure presence in general

Generally speaking, in both the sutrayana and tantrayana, accomplishment on any path depends upon shamata meditation. Whether on the common path of supersensory awareness and miracles, the uncommon path of emptiness and compassion, the development and completion stages of visualization and recitation, and channels, energy, and seed-essence, or the path of the two phases of Dzogchen—all rely on shamata.

Shantideva says in *Entering the Bodhisattva Way*,

> Knowing that shamata subsumes vipasyana,
> Emotional afflictions are completely eliminated.
> First, seek shamata.

In *Applying the Mahayana Method*, Rongzompa says,

> For those who are unable to remain in the natural state that is the great perfection, we teach the mode of striving. Even though they practice that graduated, progressive mode, their view is still based in Dzogchen.

Dzogchen is the ultimate teaching, as it heals all the diseases that afflict us. On the many paths that require effort, the highway to liberation teaches the concentration that includes the eight volitional antidotes that alleviate the five faults, which I discuss next.

2.12 The five faults that hinder concentration

The five faults that hinder concentration are laziness, forgetfulness of instruction, sinking and agitation, failing to apply antidotes, and overintensive application of antidotes.

Laziness: When it is time to meditate, we feel tired in body and mind and decide to procrastinate. The dualistic mind that always lingers on external objects fools us by its very structure. Meditation contradicts its purpose, so when meditation comes to mind, lethargy is the response. Lack of interest in meditation is laziness.

Forgetting the instructions: When we cannot remember the instructions about posture, and shamata and vipasyana that were taught by the lama, we are at a loss as to how to meditate. This is forgetting the instructions, and together with laziness, it obstructs meditation at the outset.

Sinking and agitation: These two obstruct meditation in its process. "Sinking" means that the mind is losing energy and feeling sleepy and dull because it is engulfed by the murkiness of consciousness. "Agitation" describes that state in which the mind, like a drifting feather, will not stay in the place where we put it.

Failing to apply antidotes: If we forget to apply the antidotes to sinking and agitation and fall under their influence, we cannot engage in concentration.

Overintensive application of antidotes: Here, even though the mind is free of sinking and agitation and we remain in concentration, the antidote is now applied too intensively and concentration is obscured.

Among these five the first two, laziness and forgetting the instructions, obstruct engagement of concentration at the outset. Sinking and agitation are obstructions in the process. Failure to recall antidotes and repetitive recalling of the method are obstructions that prevent development of concentration. These five faults should be abandoned.

2.13 The Eight Volitional Antidotes to the Five Faults

The eight antidotes are faith, aspiration, effort, pliancy, recollection, attention, motivation, and equanimity. Faith implies trust; aspiration is the will to strive; effort is exertion; pliancy is mental flexibility: these four are the antidotes to laziness. To induce concentration, trusting faith creates aspiration and will; with effort, pliancy is attained, and laziness is overcome. The fifth, recollection, overcomes forgetfulness. The sixth, attention, which can be thought of as inner concentration, is an antidote to sinking and agitation. The seventh, motivation, can also overcome sinking and agitation, in this case by the application of intentionality and volition. The eighth, equanimity, alleviates sinking and agitation by effortlessly preventing the composition of thought.

Avoiding the five faults and depending upon the eight antidotes, we train the creativity of shamata. If creativity is not trained, even the most brilliant mind in the realm of aspiration cannot produce a supreme single-minded wish. In order to generate that aspiration, we need to train our mind in the nine stages of mental stillness. These nine stages are resting, continual resting, repeated resting, fully resting, taming, pacifying, fully pacifying, one-pointedness, and settling in equanimity. By hearing the instruction on the disposition of mind, the faults that obstruct concentration disappear and the qualities that facilitate it—faith and aspiration—naturally arise.

Intense effort in concentration and so on gets rid of the five faults. Thereafter, no matter what object is envisaged, whether in the development or completion phase—or even in the empty pure presence of the dharmakaya—resting within that object is the first stage, which is called "resting."

When the mind will not stay still even for an instant, moving around like lightning, use mental constructs to create effort and persevere in the training. The ability to sustain fixation upon the object of previous focus is the second stage, "continual resting."

Beginners will face difficulty maintaining continuity during practice of these first two methods, so keep in the stream through alertness and vigilance. When mind wavers and moves like a shooting star, distracted elsewhere from the object of focus, remember to guide it repeatedly, like guiding a jet of water. This is "repeated resting," the third stage.

As recollection grows stronger than previously, just abiding in the object before us, regardless of how clear it is, mind will become a little more stable. Then, through increasing one-pointedness, mind focuses on the object alone. This is "fully resting," the fourth stage.

Out of that concentration, some conceptual elaboration will naturally arise, and like a bee that does not stay long in one flower, drinking nectar quickly and moving on, we can gain motivation and inspiration in that process, and those movements of thought that previously were intolerable now fall under control. This is "taming," the fifth stage.

Now, while abiding in the object with attentiveness, we find that sinking and agitation may arise. By the application to each of its own specific antidote, the various thoughts will vanish into themselves, assuaged. If indeed we can achieve that, the faults of sinking and agitation will vanish, like the sediment in a limpid pool of water once it has been left to settle. This is the sixth stage, "pacifying," which is like a person who is relaxed and attentive in a state of equanimity.

Then as thought diminishes, a little concentration increases, and the emotions generated by the thoughts are cleared, just as muddy water clears when the mud settles. Distractions no longer occurring, the mind is "fully pacified." This is the seventh stage.

Through exertion, progress is faster, and now, effortlessly, conceptual obstacles no longer arise, and we rest in one-pointed focus. This is "volition" or "one-pointedness," the eighth stage.

With that volition there is no need of effort in order to progress exponentially, and we achieve "equanimity" automatically. This is the ninth stage, and it is also known as the "single-pointed aspiration of the realm of desire," which is achieved by familiarization with all of the nine stages.

2.14 In Unitary Shamata and Vipasyana, the Nine Mental States and the Five Mystical Experiences Are Correlated

Whether we wish to meditate through inseparable shamata and vipasyana in the ultimate Dzogchen manner, or whether we seek the five supersensory powers and temporary happiness in the realms of the gods or men, first, in order to become fit for the task, we need to cultivate the mind, just as we need to cultivate a field to prepare it for crops. If we train in shamata at the beginning, we prepare for the pure presence of Dzogchen. The well-known Dudjom Pure Vision training (*Dudjom nangjang*), in which the syllable "A" is fixed upon, is a preliminary shamata practice for Dzogchen. As the great Rongzompa says in *Applying the Mahayana Method*,

> For those who are unable to remain in the natural state that is the great perfection, we teach the mode of striving. Even though they practice that graduated, progressive mode, their view is still based in Dzogchen. Since the great bliss of the luminous mind is the root of all experience, it has the power to cure every sickness that afflicts us.

As it is said in the tantra *Meditation upon the Luminous Mind*,

> Founded in Kuntuzangmo, everything is necessarily virtue; all Kuntuzangpo's behavior, even devilish conduct, thus ultimately vanishes. Thus all action founded in Kuntuzangmo, even devilish action, is bodhisattva action.
>
> There are many methods of changing the mind provided by the paramitas and the yoga-tantras, such as the concentrated absorption free of the six faults that removes the ten veils on the path of liberation; the samadhi of the eight impulsions that voids the five faults, which is also on the path of liberation; the technique of aggregates [*skandha*], elements [*dhatu*], and sensory fields [*ayatana*], and the concentration of grasping, establishing, stopping, opening up, and eliminating that is also on the path of liberation; the concentrated absorption of recitation that prevails over the six obstacles that are difficult to overcome and is also on the path of liberation; and the samadhi of visualization of body, mind, and deity that is also on the path of liberation. There are so many methods of concentrated absorption like that.

Here we stay with the Dzogchen view, meditating on shamata and vipasyana combined with the nine stages of the resting mind, and the order of appearance of the nine stages of the resting mind is correlated with the five mystical experiences.

At any rate, when we practice shamata, the five mystical experiences—fluctuation, attainment, familiarization, continuity, and completion—appear one after the other. The experience of fluctuation is like a high waterfall; the experience of attainment is like a cataract in a narrow valley; the experience of familiarization is like the river flowing sedately across a plain; the experience of continuity is like a gentle breeze blowing over a small lake; the experience of completion is like an ocean free from waves. We need to continue with shamata meditation until these five mystical experiences have occurred.

Furthermore, when we practice the single-pointed meditation of the aspiring mind, if the nine stages of resting mind and the appearance of the five mystical experiences are correlated, they arise in the following way. During the first three dispositions, while meditating on the stages of resting, continual resting, and repeated resting, strong thoughts arise like a high waterfall. Many bright thoughts arise here, seemingly more than before the start of meditation practice, but that is a delusion because earlier, the thoughts were not examined, recalled, or focused upon, and for that reason alone, we were not aware of them. During meditation according to shamata instruction, however, we actually become aware of such thoughts, and it seems therefore that there are more of them. Through this ongoing recognition, thoughts will gradually become clearer and eventually will disappear. When thoughts arise and are not recognized, it is like what happened to Chonga the fool.

Once Chonga, the idiot, was lost, and he did not return to his house until a month later. The people asked him where he had gone. He replied that some Khampa traders had taken him to Lhasa. Everyone believed him. One day a man asked him what he had seen in Lhasa. He replied that he did not know exactly, but that Grandfather Jamyang was there. Grandfather Jamyang, however, lived near Mount Kailash, so the people assumed that he had been to Mount Kailash.

Chonga had seen thousands of people, but he had not registered his perceptions. It was not that he had not had the perceptions. In premeditation experience, although thoughts arise uninterruptedly, they are unexamined and unnoticed and hence do not rise to the level of consciousness, as in the case of Chonga the fool on his tour. Now, by virtue of the meditation precepts, the thoughts that arise are recognized, and their nature is understood, so that slowly, through meditation, they will disappear.

During the fourth disposition, fully resting, and the fifth, taming, what earlier were gross thoughts become more pacific, like a cataract in a narrow valley. There is the continuity of many subtle thoughts here, many busy whirls and swirls of thought, becoming more dense. It is understood that the falls in a cramped gorge are slower than high falls.

The experiences of the sixth disposition, pacification, and the seventh, thorough pacification, are like a broad river running across a plain. From far away, it appears that the river is not moving. When we get closer, we can see its slow, dignified progress. Likewise, from above, we may think the mind is resting, but looking more closely, we can see many subtle fluctuations. At this time, the crux is to apply increased effort.

During the eighth disposition, one-pointedness, the experience of firmness is like a fresh breeze over a small lake, the mind abiding in the object of focus, and—if effort is sufficient—abiding continuously. This is attentiveness. Like a stone dropped into a pond making ripples in concentric circles that eventually become imperceptible, in this experience, the rising of thought becomes so subtle that we do not quite catch it, even though we are paying attention.

During the ninth disposition, at attainment and resting in equanimity, we gain the experience of completion, which is like a mountain, unmoving and unyielding. If that type of single-pointed aspiring mind is accomplished, the mind becomes effortlessly familiarized. All the stages are accomplished automatically, and if the mind is kept without thought in its own place and all appearances cease, we have the experience of mind mixed with space. Later, desire and anger and other emotions become reduced and finally vanish altogether. Experiences of bliss, clarity, and no-thought arise, and even sleep seems to be mixed with concentration, and most dreams seem pure.

If the nine dispositions of mind and familiarization with the five experiences are completed outside the Dzogchen context, then we do not go beyond the worldly path. It is best first to develop perfect shamata and then find Dzogchen. A good field will yield a good harvest, no matter what we sow.

After accomplishing this single-pointed mind, if we then train in the development and completion stages, we can easily accomplish both. Moreover, whether we enter the Dzogchen path of Cutting Through to alpha-purity or Direct Crossing in spontaneity, we are blessed with supreme good fortune.

Consider Polo Khen Rinpoche, the emanation of the rigzin Garab Dorje, who practiced a shamata retreat for three years. Afterward he trained in Dzogchen and accomplished a unique result, as has been told to me personally by my lama Khen Rinpoche Dawai Wozer. He reiterated that neophytes should practice shamata if they wish to accomplish the Dzogchen teaching.

Furthermore in the tantra *The Secret Core: Illusory Display*, it is said,

> A mad elephant-like mind,
> Tamed into equipoise,
> Then following tantra, mantra, and mudra,
> Achieves a miraculous accomplishment.

2.15 The simple, quintessential disposition

People who are not interested in elaborate methods or who are unable to practice them can use this instruction from *The Super-Refined Oral Precepts* of Pema Lingpa, which is eminently portable and extremely potent in its blessings.

> Then the Dakini Yeshe Tsogyel requested her master Padmasambhava to give her simple instructions that condense the teaching into a single precept that is easy to practice. The Guru replied, "Listen, you beautiful, devoted, and joyful being! There are all kinds of instructions on posture, but just sit relaxed and at ease—that's the main point. There are many precepts concerning speech and energy, like binding the breath and reciting mantras, but just stay silent like a mute—that's the main thing.

> There are many key points of mind to follow, like fixating the mind, relaxing, radiating and absorbing light, concentrating, and many more, but just stay free and easy without trying to change anything, just resting naturally—that's the main thing.

Let the body rest like a corpse, without movement; keep silent like a mute; leave the mind alone without changing anything. Leave pure presence alone, unmodified, just as it is. Relax, at ease, and hang loosely in the natural state.

That is the best disposition of body, speech, and mind. There is simply no better method than that, and anyway it is a simplification of what has been explained in detail in previous sections. People today are more happy and competent in this type of disposition. Whatever may be our practice, however, whether short or extensive, to completely understand the Dzogchen view is the crux.

In *The Words of My Perfect Teacher*, it is said,

> Meditation without instruction—
> Climbing a rock without fingers!

Seek an introduction to the Dzogchen view from a rigzin-lama and consider it well. Then enter meditation—that is the crux.

2.16 The method of practicing the essential pure presence in sessions

There is no view other than what has been explained above in the section on view. During the time of actual meditation in seclusion or in a quiet room, sit upon a comfortable cushion in the ideal body position. Then recite the refuge prayer and aspiration to a compassionate attitude like this:

> In the supreme Buddha, Dharma, and Sangha,
> I take refuge until I attain enlightenment;
> May I achieve buddha for all sentient beings
> Through the merit of generosity and other virtues.

Here we need heartfelt faith in the three jewels—Buddha, Dharma, and Sangha—and we should repeat the refuge verses three times. Then, with the intention of attaining buddha not just for ourselves but for all sentient beings everywhere, all of whom have been our parents at some juncture, we generate a compassionate attitude. Then we should visualize the root guru in the form of Padmasambhava seated in front of us, and while in a state of deep devotion induced by his blessing of mind bestowed on us and all sentient beings, recite the following prayer three or seven times:

> HUNG! On the northwest border of Orgyen,
> Born in the pollen bed of a lotus flower,
> With miraculous supreme accomplishment,
> You are known as Padmasambhava, the lotus-born:
> Surrounded by a retinue of dakinis,
> We follow after you,
> Please come here to bless us.
> GURU PADMA SIDDHI HUNG.

After reciting the Seven-Line Prayer, repeat the mantra OM AH HUNG VAJRA GURU PADMA SIDDHI HUNG one hundred or three hundred times. Finally, we receive the blessing of the guru's body, speech, and mind by means of rays of white, red, and blue light flowing from the syllables OM AH HUNG in his three secret places to our own. Then the guru melts into light and dissolves into us, and his mind becomes inseparable from our own, like water being poured into water. In that space, without modification, in a relaxed manner, sustain the view. Alternatively, at this time we can pray to our guru and Padmasambhava as one, letting the mind stay easy and relaxed, looking at the luminosity of pure presence. Then, when a thought suddenly arises, we can use either method, and relax into it, just as it is. With neither affirmation nor rejection, whatever arises in the objective field or as a thought form does not crystallize, is not pursued, and is left unmodified. It is naked pure presence, shining and vivid, with neither projection nor absorption; thus, slowly, pure presence recognizes itself, and we rest in the stillness of the stream of it.

Again, when thought arises, look into its very essence as before and let it rest in its natural state, without accepting or rejecting it as good or bad, without desire or aversion, and so forth. Do not follow thought or suppress it like ordinary worldly people, or like monks of the lower approaches who count it a sin if the thought is not cut or transformed in a meditative process. Do nothing whatsoever, abiding in the natural state.

When we sustain that practice for a long time—days, months, or years—gradually pure presence becomes a natural constant. External conditions cannot change it, and whatever thought arises does so as meditation and dissolves into itself. Then we come to have a natural trust in our meditation. We have no need to consult others because meditation comes automatically, and we know instinctively with total assurance that there is no other buddha than that.

At the end of the meditation session, we dedicate our merit to all sentient beings and make wish-fulfilling prayers.

> To all below the great Kunzang Dorje Chang,
> To all above our own gracious gurus,
> Whatever is requested by sentient beings,
> May I accomplish that all myself.

And we recite,

> Through this merit, seeing all like buddha,
> And thereby overcoming error and fault;
> Roiled by the waves of birth, old age, sickness, and death,
> Let all beings be released from the ocean of existence.

By embracing the three excellences (excellence of engagement with the generation of a compassionate attitude, excellence of the nonreferential main practice, and excellence of subsequent dedication), engaging in meditation in the morning and evening or during retreat, the merit will prove highly efficacious.

Quoting Longchenpa in *The Dakini's Heart-Essence*, Dudjom Rinpoche says,

> Not so much meditation but rather familiarization;
> If familiarization becomes the matrix, it is supreme meditation.

With constant meditation, one day meditation becomes the matrix. Insofar as there is nothing to meditate upon, and there cannot be any wavering from it even for an instant, nonmeditation is the ultimate meditation.

In *The Words of My Perfect Teacher*, Patrul Rinpoche quotes Guru Padmasambhava as saying,

> Buddha through meditation is the common path;
> Buddha through nonmeditation is unique to me.

If we practice accordingly, we hit the target.

2.17 The place of deviation into mystical experience

Mystical experiences are actual signs of meditation and its power. Mystical experiences follow from meditation just as smoke follows fire and shoots follow the germinating barley seed. When we rest loosely in the wonderful, naturally occurring pure presence, our awareness of the here and now is not as it was previously; bliss, clarity, and no-thought arise together with pure presence. If we do not abandon the identification of naked pure presence with mystical experience, then pure presence will always arise with attachment to bliss, clarity, and no-thought, and our meditation will never go beyond the three mundane worlds.

In the tantra *The Source of Sacred Samadhi*, it is said,

> Meditation may be stable,
> But if there is attachment to it,
> It is like a child's enjoyment,
> And it will not accomplish nirvana.

While we are bound to the mystical experiences of bliss, clarity, and no-thought, there can be no understanding of naked reality. However, under the influence of meditation, these experiences of bliss, clarity, and no-thought will gradually and surely arise. The reason for their arising is that basic intrinsic presence is the empty essence of the dharmakaya, the natural clarity of the sambhogakaya, and the all-pervading compassion of the nirmanakaya. Pure presence is our own natural perfection.

In our ignorance, delusion appears as a stain on the ground of being [*alaya*], on the ground consciousness [*alaya-vijnana*], and on ordinary consciousness [*vijnana*]. The ground of being holds the karmic propensities of the threefold world; the ground consciousness generates the six realms of the six classes of beings, (the world as container and sentient beings who are the elixir therein contained); and ordinary consciousness fixates on samsara by focusing upon specifics in the arena of physical enjoyment. During the time of practice, the ground of being veils the empty essence of the dharmakaya; the ground consciousness veils the clear nature of the sambhogakaya; and ordinary consciousness veils the all-pervading compassion of the nirmanakaya. In short, since the ground of being, ground consciousness, and ordinary consciousness are adulterated, pure presence is veiled, and the experience of bliss does not arise as intensely as before in mind and in the flow of consciousness. When the experience of bliss arises with a comfort that we cannot resist, we become irrevocably attached to it, and we are flung into the gods' realm of desire. Likewise the experience of clarity in cognition arises with brightness and is accompanied by the emergence of some slight psychic powers. If we become attached to this, we will be cast into the gods' realm of form. Likewise, insight can be bewildering—as we experience emptiness with no-thought like a kind of forgetfulness or unconsciousness, our subtle proclivities completely inactive, as in deep sleep, we may be propelled into the formless realm of the gods.

These mystical experiences are thick obstructions that block release from the threefold world of samsara, so do not fall under their influence for even a moment. Perceive them as big mistakes. No matter what experiences of bliss, clarity, or no-thought arise, perceive them as delusory signs of mystical realization and relax loosely in objectless pure presence: in this way, seize the citadel of the dharmakaya.

In a nutshell, the mystical experiences of bliss, clarity, and no-thought are a product of attachment to meditation. While there is attachment, there is no chance of seeing the face of the dharmakaya. We make progress only by terminating our attachment to mystical experience.

In *The Three Incisive Precepts*, Patrul Rinpoche says,

> Precipitous descent increases the ferocity of a mountain stream;
> Disruption improves the yogin's meditation.

The mountain stream in the upper valley is clean and pure as it falls fast over its rocky bottom, and the yogin's meditation is best when it destroys attachment to mystical experience. Dilgo Khyentse Rinpoche related this story:

When Deshag Phakmo Drupa came to see Nyamme Dakpo Rinpoche, he had some pride in thinking that he had long ago achieved the first level of meditation of the Sakya tradition of Path and Fruit. He shared his meditation experiences with Rinpoche, including his claim of reaching the first level. Rinpoche said nothing, but on the day of departure, Rinpoche asked him to come to his room. As he entered the room, Rinpoche was eating barley dough. "Did you really think that the experiences you told me about were first-level experiences?" he asked him "Yes, I did," he replied. "I am certain that I have reached the first level." "Did your lama confirm it?" asked Rinpoche. "Yes, my lama told me absolutely that I had attained it," replied Phakmo Drupa. Rinpoche picked up a hunk of barley dough and said, "Between this dough of mine and your first level—I prefer this dough," and he broke wind. After this, Phakmo Drupa lost his pride, his view of the nature of reality focused, and uncontrived devotion toward Rinpoche as the actual buddha arose within him. Like Phakmo Drupa, yogin-meditators obtain all kinds of mystical experiences, external or internal, on different levels. As they are purified upon their arising, the certainty of reality becomes more profound until finally it is realized as what we call Dzogchen.

So, in short, until we attain buddha, we are not able to abandon the attachment to the very fine subtle karmic propensities of dualistic perception. The weak points are the points of attachment, the places of deviation from the naked pure presence. All such attachments need to be abandoned. As Sri Saraha sang,

> Where there is attachment, let it go!
> Just letting go, we are entirely free.
> What else can anyone wish to know?

Every yogin or yogini is inclined toward attachment to their own accomplishment. When others pay us compliments and honor us or when we gain some little fame, we identify with that famous person and attachment to our name arises. If the yogin or yogini cannot undo the attachment instantly in a reflexive release, obstacles will be encountered, and a lower rebirth will ensue. We know such things happen from stories of past great masters who tell their students that favorable conditions are less conducive to attainment than unfavorable ones. When we encounter unfavorable conditions such as sickness, war, conflict, or slander, we are able to recognize them, and in a state of confidence, we can allow our envisionment to self-release. Favorable conditions, on the other hand, incline us toward attachment. The beautiful wife, fine children, wealth, fame, honor, and international recognition with prestigious awards constitute such conditions that lead to attachment to external objects. If we practice buddha-dharma, our dreams may be realized, and sometimes there are actual signs of accomplishment in dreams. Sometimes those dreams are the creation of devils, even those in which we hear the lama giving transmission. Our thoughts are equivocal, and since our body-minds are not the same as previously, and since various mystical experiences such as bliss, clarity, and no-thought arise—some pure and others impure—we cannot distinguish between accomplishment and the miasma of the devil's antics.

In short, whether favorable or unfavorable thoughts arise, if we are free of attachment, understanding thoughts as illusion, they will release themselves by themselves. The crucial point is that misfortune provides good fortune, and unfavorable conditions are actually more easily dealt with than favorable conditions. But for ordinary yogins and yoginis, it is more difficult to take favorable conditions as the path than unfavorable ones. The story of the yogin Surya Vajra, told in the Dudjom Lingpa's *Cutting Instruction*, illustrates how favorable conditions can rebound upon us. When Surya Vajra was about to attain accomplishment, devils conspiring to obstruct him bewitched the people of his town, especially the beautiful women. Here is how it went.

Once in the great kingdom of Magadha a man called "Surya Vajra" abandoned his family and assiduously practiced the Dharma. When his commitment was seen by the devils [*maras*], they conspired to harm him. The devil of form offered to show the yogin his own fearfulness and thereby disturb him. The devil of formlessness offered to obstruct him by entering into his mind and letting him experience the heights and depths of happiness and sadness. The devil of pride offered to obstruct him by inducing equivocating thought. Finally, the devil of happiness made his offer, saying that the devil of form could show Surya Vajra fear, but Surya Vajra's oral instruction upon selflessness could assuage that fear and the yogin would gain accomplishment. Fear would actually be the cause of his accomplishment, and he would go beyond their sphere of influence. So fear was of no use. He went on to say that if the devil of formlessness entered the yogin's heart and induced various feelings of suffering and happiness, all of them would be easily recognized and provide means of release into the space of freedom from rebirth. So likewise such obstacles should be classified as favorable conditions. To the devil of pride, he said that the equivocal thoughts that he could induce would be countered by the oral instruction of taking misfortune as advantage, so that also would not work. He assured the three of them that their plans were bound to fail because they consisted of the provision of unfavorable conditions, which are easy to overcome. On the other hand, if they befriended him and provided favorable conditions, he would come under their control forever. Asking for their help in this, he promised to enslave Surya Vajra by inducing a state of enchantment, and he laughed uproariously. The great siddha Luhipa happened to witness this conference of the devils and reported it to Surya Vajra, who was grateful, saying that to be forewarned was to be forearmed. Luhipa left him with the warning that his weakness lay in his openness to the temptations of pleasure.

Then with Surya Vajra diligently continuing his meditation night and day, the devil of happiness began his agenda by bewitching the townspeople, in particular its beautiful women. One night in a dream they entered Surya Vajra's mandala, and this particular devil came forward in the guise of his personal deity. The demon assured the yogin that he had now gained supreme siddhi and that tomorrow he would possess all the common siddhis. Finally, the devil told him that henceforth he was free of the kind of obstacles raised by devils and that he need not meditate so much, as he had now attained all real knowledge. Instantly Surya Vajra was transported to bliss.

Next day some people came and made an offering of fine food and wealth, which confirmed in his mind what his personal deity had told him in the dream. A few days later a beautiful woman approached him with rice for him to eat and white cloth for him to wear and supplicated him for secret instruction. Surya Vajra was doubtful that women were included in the rewards of accomplishment that his dream indicated. But he accepted her as his consort anyway, sure that he would be free of both attachment to her and sexual pleasure. But over time his relationship with her became so deep that he could not bear to be apart from her love and care. He could not leave her alone. She visited him often, but despite this people still came regularly to pay him respect and make offerings.

One day it occurred to him that perhaps he should abandon his meditation and become a householder, but he was undecided. So he approached Guru Luhipa and shared with him his intentions. Luhipa immediately told him that he certainly had been possessed by devils: the transformation of his conduct already clearly indicated this. The guru advised him strongly that he would be saved if he dissolved his attachment to the woman, but if he failed to do this, he would fall back into samsara and remain trapped there. Surya Vajra believed what Luhipa had told him, but realizing that he could not break his attachment to the woman, he ignored the guru's advice and committed himself to the life of a householder. All his disciples and admirers then abandoned him, chiding him for his loss of commitment, and when his decision was reported at court, the king ordered him to be cast out. Surya Vajra had now lost all his religious beatitude and became the poorest among the poor of that town.

At the beginning the yogin was deceived by his dream experience and became entangled in attachments. In the middle he did not realize that his woman was a gross delusion, and at the end, diverted from Dzogchen praxis by real attachment, he fell into endless samsara. So whatever thoughts appear in real time or in dream must be released loosely into pure presence. If we are tempted and trapped in those ideas, we will be inveigled into the mystical experiences of bliss, clarity, and no-thought and find no release from the three realms of samsara. If we can sustain this—the release upon the arising of mystical envisionment—there is no need to regard discursive thinking as a fault. We can then look at it this way: the more thoughts, the more dharmakaya.

The extent to which we can cut ourselves free from experiences of bliss, clarity, and no-thought is the extent to which we gain confidence in our practice. With confidence there will be no attachment to friends or hatred toward enemies and no need to choose between samsara or nirvana. Whatever thought arises vanishes immediately, like writing on water. Later, not only does attachment to the experiences of bliss, clarity, and no-thought disappear, but also whatever arises becomes the food of naked empty pure presence, and nonmeditation becomes the meditation of the great yogin-meditator. Since there is then no point of reference, there can be no wavering even for an instant from the naked pure presence. Since the function of removing the obstructing experiences of bliss, clarity, and no-thought is an autonomous reaction, no matter what we encounter—sleep, food, walking, sitting, happiness, pain, misfortune, sickness, harm from an enemy, and so on—we recognize it as a part of the universal lie of appearances. If faults of attachment arise, if we relax into the offending cognitions, they dissolve like the morning mist under the warming sun. If obstacles are removed this way, naked pure presence is revealed like grain falling out of its husk, and this is to be highly cherished.

Regarding subconscious thoughts that arise during meditation, very subtle thoughts that are unsensed—when they go unrecognized, they will arise one after another and gradually engulf us in delusion, eventually appearing as gross thoughts that accumulate the karma of desire, hatred, and ignorance. These subconscious thoughts—thoughts that remain unrecognized—are like water running on the ground under green grass. We need no extraneous antidote to counteract them, however, because if we simply rest in naked pure presence, they are released.

Further, when strong aversion is generated and immediately recognized as pure presence, the anger inherent within it is reflexively released. But in the following moment, subtle anger arises like a snake quaking, unable to rise after being cut in two. If at that moment we target the pure presence fiercely, and then just hang loosely, the subconscious emotion dissolves into itself. The rigzin's instruction on dealing with subconscious thought is an imperative for the great meditator.

Just by training on this path both gross and subtle attachments to bliss, clarity, and no-thought are exhausted, basic pure presence is revealed, and buddha is realized. Delusory samsaric appearances, which had risen from the ground of being, the ground consciousness, and ordinary consciousness, now rest in their own place, utterly pure, and buddha-nature, in essence empty, in nature clear, and in compassion all-embracing, is spontaneously accomplished.

2.18 The distinction between mind and pure presence

In his commentary upon *The Treasury of the Dharmadhatu*, Longchenpa says,

> When pure presence is separated from mind, it is separated from the mind's delusion, and there is no other possible result than buddha. Its essence is buddha, and since it is now free of defilement, it manifests as buddha. When pure presence is bound up with mind, it is called "sentient being." When it is separated from mind, it is called "buddha."

It is very important to differentiate between the primal awareness that is pure presence and mind. Mind is structured by dualistic perception, just as water is frozen like stone by intense cold, and since there is no heat therein, it will not return to liquid until the end of the eon, just like the icecap on a mountain. Primal awareness, on the other hand, is not structured by dualistic perception, and its inexpressible nature of transparent, pellucid, clear, pure presence is like water in a pail, naturally free of turbidity, through which the bottom of the pail is clearly visible. In brief, so long as our experience is that of an objective field and a mind that perceives it, we are to be called "sentient beings." In abiding in naked empty pure presence, untainted by dualistic concepts, however, there is only pure presence, primal awareness. Again in his commentary to *The Treasury of the Dharmadhatu*, Longchenpa says,

> Ordinary unmodified consciousness, which grasps at objects, not realizing them to be uncrystallizing pure presence, is known as samsaric consciousness. Abiding in naked pure presence, uncontaminated by hope or fear, fully radiant, and without wavering from that realization—that is to be understood as the nondual mind of buddha.

So be wise in your differentiation.

2.19 The rigzin-lama's personal instruction inspires meditation

In the tradition of buddhas past, before requesting teaching, disciples checked the authenticity of the lama. If they found genuine quality, they requested and received the Dzogchen teaching, from the preliminaries right up to the maturing empowerments, explanations of the method of liberation, and the supporting oral transmission. We should regard that rigzin-lama as no other than the Buddha himself, and not as an ordinary being.

In the tantras it is said,

> The lama is the Buddha,
> The lama is the Dharma,
> And the lama is the Sangha.
> The lama is the universal creator.
> The lama is Sri Vajradhara.

The rigzin-lama should be respected as the lord of all mandalas and the principal deity of each. He must examine the disciples to discover whether they could keep the tantric samayas intact. If they are ready, he starts their mind training with the four discursive meditations that turn the intellect back upon itself (meditations on precious human body, impermanence, karmic cause and effect, and karmic retribution) and eventually leads them to the actuality of Dzogchen. He guides them as if they were blind, providing each and every explanation, allowing them to do the training. Sometimes when they go astray, he chides them, and when they are successful, he praises them, and thus he checks their practical experience.

Unique to the Cutting Through phase of Dudjom Rinpoche's *The Intrinsic Nature of Being* is a tradition of instruction and training lasting six months. These days, due to conditions in our times, this tradition is no longer followed; rather, the students read the text cursorily and receive only a superficial understanding of it. Taking what is superficial as a basis for practice, they fail to find the essence. Though the lama that we serve need not be famous, he should certainly practice what he preaches. It is very important that no matter what oral instruction we receive from that lama, we comprehend it completely; otherwise there will be a gap between the instruction and ourselves. There is no use in reading an instruction text as if it were a Sunday newspaper because it is then mere hearsay, imitating the lama as a monkey imitates a man, and there will be no fruit from the meditation. To find a real rigzin-lama is vital.

When the lama identifies mistakes in our practice, we need to rectify those errors, just as we straighten out what is crooked, bind what is cracked, or mend what is broken. If we follow his instructions on removing obstacles, our practice will produce results.

The rigzin Kunzang Sherab had four heart-sons—Shugang Badang, Jangang Aphen, Tsangda Dorjethar, and Serwa Yeshe Senge—to whom he taught Dzogchen, guiding them in their practice for a long time. One day he took them to the bank of the Drichu River at Derge and asked them to sit cross-legged on the bank with him. That evening the river had risen so much that there was fear of floods in the village, and the lama finally left his seat and ran away. Three others followed suit, leaving only Shugang Badang still sitting unmoving. Recognizing all experience as a great lie, he sat on the bank of the river with pure presence unwavering from its own natural state and not a single hair of his body was harmed: great assurance in his practice emerged within him. The lama praised Shugang Bhadang highly and scolded the other three disciples, showing them the crux of Dzogchen and asking them to be like Shugang Bhadang. It was not that the lama ran away from the flood out of fear, but rather he fled in order to check his disciples' reactions.

These days some of us Dzogchen teachers just pretend to know Dzogchen, but nonetheless we propagate it, as a practical experience, throughout the world. But when we face difficulties like sickness, pain, conflict, and so on, we suffer like ordinary beings. Some of us go mad, or if not mad perhaps we make offering to the gods and demons: this shows the inherent fault of failing to assimilate the benefit of practice. Just as past masters would say, "He may have entered the dogma of Dzogchen, but he has not encountered the personal Dzogchen"—we may have received the teaching, but we have yet to assimilate it. In short, only if our praxis can be described as abiding in our own unmodified, uncontrived mind can we say that we have assimilated Dzogchen. At that point we will have constant recognition of naked pure presence unadulterated by the mystical experience of bliss, clarity, and no-thought.

Think about our enemies and look with pure presence; examine the attachment to our near and dear and look with pure presence. In the advent of negative situations, look with pure presence. In this way we will discover the "heat," or effectiveness, of our practice, and we will discover whether external circumstances can still harm us, and we will gain confidence accordingly. That confidence is the product of our practice. If we grow immune to misfortune now, then later, in the bardo, we can remain indifferent to the visions and gain release.

Here is an instruction for a session of formal contemplation: while pure presence is still, we gain the aspect of clarity; when pure presence is clear, we gain looseness; and when pure presence is dynamic, we gain release. That is realized through the instruction of the lama.

In brief, detached from its still, clear, and dynamic aspects, the naked reality of pure presence in the view alone clears away all obstruction. When we have attachment to the stillness, the formless realm is created, when we have attachment to the clarity, the realm of form is created, and when we are attached to the dynamic, the realm of desire is created. These three are the obstructions that bind us in the three realms. If we are free of attachment to these three, then dharmakaya, sambhogakaya, and nirmanakaya arise respectively.

After we rise from formal contemplation, our ongoing state is called "informal contemplation." During formal contemplation, "the knower" and "the known" are both free of all conceptual references and are lost in the one intrinsic presence. When we come out of it, our experience is fully purged of every conceptual mark and is like the middle of the sky, apparent yet nonexistent: we see all the appearances of samsara and nirvana as nonexistent, naturally arising forms of empty appearance, and in this we are supremely confident.

3. Conduct

3.1 An explanation of conduct

The field of our objective projections does not crystallize in the face of pure presence. So long as we abide in the formal contemplation in which the delusory discursive thinking of dualistic perception dissolves in spaciousness, pure presence will not become lost in the objective field. When we cease formal contemplation, then in informal contemplation, whatever arises in the physical, energetic, or mental aspects of sitting, walking, eating, or sleeping is automatically self-released as it arises. Automatic self-release is the natural propensity of informal contemplation, and "the conduct of inseparable meditative equipoise and postattainment" is its corollary. In Dzogchen there is no specific form of conduct separate from the practice of view and meditation. If conduct is other than practice of view and meditation, it is erroneous conduct. The practice of view and meditation is free of all conceptual elaboration, so it is impossible for conduct to become anything concrete or specific or for it to take on the forms of spiritual materialism. However, that being so, do not make the mistake of mixing up view, meditation, and conduct, or confusing one with another.

Formal and informal contemplation are similar in that no matter what arises, good thought or bad, everything reflexively releases, like a design that is drawn in water dissolving as it is written. Whether at rest or in motion, all thought is released instantaneously so that there is no continuity or connection with the next instant. This implosion into a pristine, relaxed space is the natural propensity of informal contemplation. No matter what thought occurs—happy or sad, fearful or hopeful—we let it resolve itself into its own nature, like a wave falling back into the ocean. At this level, where the thought itself, without rejection, becomes the meditation, we know all experience as enchanting illusion. In the empty pure presence of the dharmakaya, the innate creativity of uncrystallizing compassion commingled with loving-kindness naturally arises in the mindstream, and that too is the natural propensity of informal contemplation. By sustaining informal contemplation and attaining buddha, the unique quality therein is the inseparability of formal and informal contemplation: that is due to this manner of practicing informal contemplation.

These days some meditators claim that even though they engage in practice, it does not improve their mind-set. Some claim that meditation itself does not help in any way. This is due to the absence of this crucial aspect of conduct whereby we abide in formal contemplation in the unelaborated space of intrinsic awareness. Reflexive release of whatever arises in informal meditation is the central element necessary for long stays in formal contemplation. As for beginners, their thoughts create blockages from one moment to the next.

It is surely true that, for ordinary people, thoughts run continuously, like ripples on a pond, and if each is to be caught and rejected one by one, then even though we practice for an eon, they cannot be eradicated. Whatever thoughts arise, let them arise, and when they have arisen, do not cling to them, but let them disappear, like a drawing in water. Letting the thought disappear into its own pure presence is the Dzogchen mode.

3.2 The Sin of Ignorance of the Continuity of Reflexively Liberating Thought

When we face the vicissitudes of happiness and suffering in business, farming, politics, domestic life, and so on, when we lose the momentum of selfish aspiration, it is enough to look into the nature of suffering and relax. It is not necessary to destroy thoughts or obstruct them. We do not need to try to destroy or to forget the thought of a heavy loss in business, for example. When we are depressed about it, our friends may come to console us, telling us that there is no need to worry because the neighbor has a much greater loss. In that way, they try to calm us down. Or when we grieve at the loss of an only child, our friends might console us by narrating the incident of such and such a person having lost all three of his or her children all at once in the river and so on. This method of providing consolation is considered to be effective in human society. But it provides only temporary relief, not a permanent solution. When our best-intentioned consoling friends leave us, many more thoughts arise, and if we watch carefully, we will see that there are even more thoughts than before the consolation. We will think, for example, of people who have never had business losses before or of people who have never lost a child. So we start to worry again. Unable to see the nature of mind or its suffering, we are simply transported to another place, where another set of thoughts replaces the previous set. Such an exchange of thoughts provides no benefit.

When during the time of Shakyamuni Buddha, a woman lost her beloved only son, she was so sad that she stopped eating and was about to die. Her friends tried hard to console her, but all in vain, so they asked her to visit the Buddha, who perhaps could bring her son back to life. She was revivified by this idea and went to see the Buddha. She paid homage to him and weeping asked him to bring her son back to life. Buddha agreed to do so for her on the condition that she brought him fire from a house in which no one had ever died. So the grieving woman went from house to house throughout the kingdom but could find none that had not seen death; realizing that she was not alone in her desolation, that everyone without exception knows death, her sadness decreased. Then she went back to the Buddha and told him that she could not find such a fire, and the Buddha taught her about the impermanence of both the world and the beings in it. She was consoled by his teaching, and her life was saved.

3.3 The Preeminence of the Mode of Simultaneous Arising and Releasing of Thought

When we can see the nature of reality, or the nature of mind, at the very moment of the appearance of happiness or sadness, we understand it to be unreal, just like a magical illusion or a dream. If we sustain that insight, mingling formal contemplation and informal contemplation, then intrinsic awareness of ultimate buddha, which itself is the inseparability of formal contemplation and informal contemplation, will abide unchangeably.

In some non-Buddhist schools, the purpose of meditation is to extinguish consciousness of the five senses of the body, which is like putting thoughts in prison. Staying in that state for a long time is thought by them to be meditation. It is considered to be an antidote to suffering, but it provides only temporary relief, or as mentioned before, it provides merely a change in the kind of suffering. It does not eradicate pain. We may shake off the leaves of a poison tree and lop off its branches, but unless the root is severed, the tree will grow back again. So it is with thoughts.

Some people think that we suffer because of previous karma or because it is the will of God, and they endure it. Stopping up the five doors of the senses may temporarily block gross thoughts, but not for long, and it can never be permanent. In *Entering the Way of the Bodhisattva*, Shantideva says,

> What is momentarily blocked is released again,
> Like an unconscious trance.

The gods reside in unconscious trance or samadhi for a thousand years, but after the power of the samadhi is exhausted and the discursive thoughts of the five poisonous emotions arise again, they are reborn into samsara. Such samadhi is not permanent happiness. That path is not relevant to those yearning for liberation and omniscience. Like AIDS patients who take medicine to reduce their fever and vitamins to strengthen their immune system but who need to address the root of the disease if they are to be cured, yogins and yoginis may exchange one set of thoughts for another, more congenial one, but their suffering will not be eradicated.

Those who think that stopping thought is meditation will be reborn merely in the realm of the unconscious gods and will attain neither liberation nor omniscience. Those who stop thoughts and meditate on the nature of a still mind find it very difficult to apply the antidote to emotions. Consider the life of the fallen yogin Surya Vajra who after meditating for many years finally seemed to have achieved his goal only to lose it through attachment to a phantom woman. A Hindu yogin may sit in the Joyous Samadhi for many years only to awaken from it and indulge in hatred and plunder of neighboring kingdoms, as we can read in *The Extraordinary Exalted Praise* of Totshun Drubje. When a strong intention to achieve attainment on our own path results in failure to eradicate emotional afflictions, it probably indicates that stopping thoughts or exchanging one set of thoughts for another is not an effective antidote to suffering. Whatever suffering arises is, in Dzogchen nonmeditation, released in its own shoes, like a snake uncoiling itself, without the need of extraneous assistance.

3.4 Meditation experience arises naturally in the mindstream

The crucial manner of release, like a snake uncoiling its knots, is not something to be achieved in a handful of energetic meditation sessions. We need to relax into it in order to come to experience it as a constant. In that way it becomes familiar, and there is no need for any purposeful or fruitful application of antidotes because the counteraction is applied automatically, just as a potter who applies a strong push to the wheel does not need to apply force again before the pot is complete. Once we are accustomed to such an automatic process of release, whatever thoughts of happiness or sorrow arise simply dissolve by themselves, and, unaffected by them, we experience confidence arising automatically. When strong hatred or pain arises adventitiously and we recognize the immediate release of the thought, a laugh or some other extraordinary expression of joy may suddenly escape us.

Whether significant or trivial, no matter what activity we perform in samsara, there is nothing that is not mixed with suffering. All experience is of the nature of all-pervasive suffering since it is derived from impulsive habit. Take the dream birth of a son. First, we are happy at his birth; later, we worry about his health; and at the end, there is the grievous suffering of his death. If we think about it closely, these three aspects are all unreal, although in the dream we perceived them to be real, and we did actually suffer. Dreamers who dreamt the experience never moved from their bed for a moment, so there was no way they could have experienced the suffering, yet until they awoke, they felt that the experience was real. When we are in dreamland and we understand that we are asleep and that we are dreaming, then even though the dream continues, the suffering dissolves like mist in sky. In *The Thirty-Seven Practices of the Bodhisattva*, Ngulchu Tokme says,

> All suffering is like a son's death in a dream,
> And we are sick of believing delusion to be true!
> When we encounter untoward circumstances,
> The bodhisattva sees them all as illusion.

No matter what happy, sad, or neutral thoughts arise, for ordinary beings, the manner in which they appear is the same. But for the yogin who is relaxed in the nature of mind, the manner of release is special since, for such a one, arising and release occur simultaneously. Just like a drawing on water, appearances vanish. This is a crucial point of practice.

3.5 When conduct consists of simultaneous arising and releasing, it is free of karma and its effects

In the yoga of crucial simultaneous arising and release, the mere arising of desire and anger does not generate bad karma. To take a single thought as an example—the thought has gone as soon as it arises. Until it is created, it exists only in the future. In the present, it has no time to rest, and since the object, agent, and action have no time to interact in the timeless present, karma cannot be accumulated. Karma can be accumulated only in the continuity of thought, and because in Dzogchen yoga, thoughts are released as they arise, thus inhibiting continuity, no karma is accumulated and suffering does not arise. No aggregation of circumstances can establish itself in the first moment, so no continuity is possible and no result is possible.

Whatever appears in the daytime did not first appear in a dream, but if we have a strong impression of a beautiful object again and again in the daytime, it may arise in a dream. If we are not attached to the beautiful object even for a moment, then there is little possibility of its arising in the dream. It is the repeated attachment to it that makes a continuity of it and that causes it to arise in a dream. Likewise, consider a seed for which the conditions of its germination last only a second; there is only a very small chance of its producing a shoot. If the seed is planted and lasting conditions obtain, then the seed will most probably germinate and shoot. Surely it is true that a single watering of a seed will not engender growth. Whatever thought arises, if it is released in the moment, even though emotional affliction may arise as in ordinary beings, because of the difference that immediate release makes, we are not touched by karma. In his *Treasury of the Dharmadhatu*, Longchenpa says,

> Arising, abiding and release in an uninterrupted flow—
> No break in the arising and dissolving—
> In an unbroken stream, cause and effect are inseparable.
> Because there is no causality, the abyss of samsara is crossed,
> And if the abyss is traversed, how can there be any downfall?

When in the first moment of arising, thought releases itself and there is sameness, there is neither the chance nor the possibility of either karma or causality. We neither judge a negative thought as sin and abandon it purposefully nor judge a positive one as meritorious and cultivate it. Attachment to positive thoughts may be virtuous attachment, but it casts a shadow over natural perfection. It is a critical point that we are released into the naked emptiness of pure presence without abandoning the bad thoughts or cultivating the good.

Kyabje Dudjom Rinpoche says in his commentary on the *Heart-Essence of the Dakini*,

> Generally, the informal contemplation has two kinds of meditator, the real and nominal meditators. The real informal contemplation between sessions allows only an unelaborated formal contemplation to take place so that later the meditator will arrive at the crucial place of buddha where formal contemplation and informal contemplation between sessions are identical.
>
> When the nominal between-session meditator arises from formal contemplation, his experience is the ordinary activity of body, speech, and mind lacking the arising/liberating function. His experience consists of the perception of material objects in a concrete sensory field.

The nominal informal contemplation is no antidote to the apprehension of things as concrete and substantial, so it cannot release us from emotional afflictions such as desire and lust.

These days many people with spiritual pride say that religious practice does not affect the mental life and that meditation cannot transform the mind. In *The Three Incisive Precepts*, Patrul Rinpoche says,

> Knowing meditation but not release,
> Isn't that the divine trance of the gods?

The mere ability to abide in formal contemplation free of mental elaboration does not necessarily take us into informal contemplation that is different from the ordinary activity of body, speech, and mind. If we are unable to mix the practice of unelaborated formal contemplation with informal contemplation, there will be no benefit.

If, on the other hand, we can integrate our experience of simultaneous arising and liberating and our experience of reflexive release and liberation into pure presence, and so on, with the happiness and sadness of body, speech, and mind, real benefit will emerge. If we cannot integrate the two, our meditation is like the concentration of child's play—bound by attachment. During formal contemplation, gross happiness and sadness will not arise, but when we get up from shamata, the joy or the pain will come as before. Just as we contain a heap of dust by sitting down slowly on it, but upon our getting up, the dust arises in clouds, in the concentrated absorption of child's play, gross thoughts are stopped for a while, and we seem to experience happiness, but when we arise from the concentration, we find that more gross thoughts intrude than before. This is why people say there is no benefit from meditation.

These days it is rare for informal contemplation practitioners to have certainty in the profound view. Due to this, their meditation is just like taking time out and that will not release anyone from the threefold world. When strong sufferings, acute pains, or misfortunes temporarily afflict our minds and sickness afflicts our bodies, it sometimes seems that we react like ordinary people. That occurs first because we are not recognizing the profound Dzogchen view of Cutting Through. Second, even though we are meditating, our meditation is based on a mere intellectual understanding of the alpha-purity free of all propositions, and therefore we do not abide in the essence of naked pure presence. Finally all effort is meaningless if we lack confidence in its reflexive function of arising and release during informal contemplation between sessions . During life, death, and the bardo, when we are tortured by intense fear, sickness, and sadness, and there is no help, to remember this instruction is the crux.

3.6 A categorical assertion that Dzogchen transcends cause and effect

In the informal contemplation phase, if the crucial function of release upon arising is recognized at all times and in every circumstance, then no matter what act of body, speech, or mind is performed, since it cannot go beyond the display of dharmakaya—the natural creativity of pure presence—karma is not accumulated. As the rigzin Garab Dorje said, "Dzogchen is beyond causality." For those who have doubt regarding that statement, consider these two aspects. First, during the actual engagement in formal contemplation that is free of any conceptual elaboration, because we cannot see even an iota of karmic relationship, we can assert that causality does not exist in the natural state of reality. It is said that no recognition nor any actor or action can ever be established in that state.

When Jampel Shenyen heard that the rigzin Garab Dorje was giving teaching beyond the law of karma, he was incensed and went out to challenge him with the intention of defeating him in debate. These two debated for many years and finally Jampel Shenyen admitted defeat and regretted his denigration of Garab Dorje. In contrition and in order to expiate his fault, he tried to cut out his tongue, but Garab Dorje stopped him, advising him that he should instead study and then teach the precepts beyond karmic cause and effect, predicting that all his sins would be purified thereby. Jampel Shenyen became devoted to Garab Dorje and finally asked him to accept him as his student, and they become guru and disciple.

The key point here is that while Dzogchen prevails, there is no causality—the great perfection is beyond causality. Moreover, while sustaining the view that is part and parcel of the natural informal contemplation, there is no karmic cause and effect to be seen. In instantaneous release upon inception, cause and effect are inseparable, so there can be no perception of causality. In *The Treasury of the Dharmadhatu*, Longchenpa says,

> If we examine our authentic nature, nothing can be said to
> exist therein;

Likewise, taking authenticity as the path, becoming one with it,
Knowing it only in a moment of unimaged, nonconceptual vision,
Consumed by it, we are completely, transparently naked.

Without any base or support in this supermatrix,
Afflictive emotion, karma, and habitual propensities
Create magical, illusory, apparitional games,
And since we need freedom in it, let causality be resolved.

Whether we are in formal contemplation free of all conceptual elaboration or in the informal contemplation sustaining reflexive release of whatever arises, beyond all causal propositions, causality cannot be recognized. That is the first aspect for consideration.

The second point is that Dzogchen transcends karmic causality only in the state of pure presence. When pure presence goes outside the natural condition or wanders during the mundane informal contemplation phase, karmic causality is inevitable and must be heeded. That is discussed below.

3.7 So long as dualistic perception obtains, heed karma and its effects

The straight answer to the question whether Dzogchen yogins and yoginis should follow the laws of karma in all situations is "Yes!" When we leave the state of basic pure presence or formal contemplation and enter what is called "informal contemplation," we should follow the laws of karma as nondeceptive, without any disavowal. We should never denigrate causality even conventionally. On the level of definitive meaning, causality cannot be held as a truly existing process; immaculately transcending the two extremes of permanent and impermanent, it becomes the sovereign of all gradual approaches.

In the *Treasury of the Dharmadhatu*, Longchenpa says,

Creativity projects display into another dimension,
Where it appears as the multifarious variety of the universe.
Never say categorically that there is no cause and effect.
The complex conditions that arise from interdependence
    are incalculable;

> The states of samsaric delusion and nirvanic joy are incalculable;
> A mass of causes and conditions constitutes a sublime
> synchronicity.

When contemplation and real informal contemplation are broken, we enter the state called "nominal informal contemplation."

Due to the flickering of dualistic thought that seems to possess concrete attributes, increasingly subtle karmic causes and effects should be taken into account. In *The Chronicles of Padmasambhava*, discovered by Orgyen Lingpa, Padmasambhava says,

> My view is higher than the sky.
> My karma is finer than barley flour.

The meaning here is that every single trivial action is determined by previous action and that every present action will have its repercussion in the future.

Also in *The Chronicles of Padmasambhava*, it is related—as in *The Legend of the Great Stupa of Boudhanath*—that in a past life Padmasambhava, king Trisong Deutsen, and the bodhisattva abbot Shantarakshita were three brothers who constructed the Boudhanath Stupa in the Kathmandu Valley. After they had built the dome of the stupa, they prayed in front of it, and by the power of each of the brother's prayers, the first was born as Padmasambhava, the second as king Trisong Deutsen, and the third as the bodhisattva Shantarakshita. When they met in Tibet, buddha-dharma flourished in that demonic land. This was by virtue of the merit that they had accumulated by constructing the great stupa and making such strong aspirations.

When the Buddha had a headache and his disciples asked the reason, the Buddha told them that once he had been the son of a fisherman in the Sakya kingdom. One day his father caught two big fish and bound the line to a pillar, leaving the fish to flounder on the hot sand, and he had laughed at their suffering. "Now, even though I have become enlightened, due to the residual karma of that laughter, I have a headache," said the Buddha. "Furthermore, if I had not become enlightened, at this very moment the Licchavis would be plundering the Sakya kingdom." Karmic causality is beyond the intellect to comprehend or calculate. It is impossible to explain it here. Until the thoughts of sentient beings cease, karmic causality will prevail. In *The Wish-Fulfilling Treasury*, Longchenpa says,

> The mind sets the pattern,
> And mind accumulates karma,
> Mind projects appearances,
> And mind applies labels.
> Strive to subdue delusive mind.

Those who enter the natural state of Dzogchen are not themselves affected by karma and can therefore explain the particular karmas of the conventional world, disciples, and ordinary beings. They can become the teacher of the inevitable repercussions of karma, wise in describing the stages, paths, and cause and effect.

It was during the first turning of the wheel that the Buddha, our teacher, taught karmic cause and effect, giving us provisional instruction in the presentation of the four noble truths. Some may think that the provisional teaching is not even conventionally true and that the Buddha was actually deceiving his disciples, but that is a seriously wrong-headed way of thinking. Until mental concepts and mental events vanish into spaciousness or disappear in the natural state of Dzogchen, the mind is not exhausted. Until the mind is exhausted, the five poisonous emotions that depend upon it will inevitably arise. Sentient beings in their environments will be created continuously, like pots flying off a potter's wheel: good karmic effects will eventuate in the upper realms of samsara, the realms of the gods, titans, and men, and bad karmic effects in the lower realms, those of the hells, hungry ghosts, and animals. For that reason, so long as there is a mind, we are tied to samsara, where the laws of karma are established. So long as beings exist, it is certain that causes gave them birth and their present actions produce effects. In his *Ornament of the Middle Way*, the abbot Shantarakshita said,

> Depending upon causes before and before that,
> After and after that, effects will arise.

Just now we need to train in both the formal and informal contemplation of Dzogchen and dissolve all the conceptual elaborations of mind.

Then one day the mind that grasps at all phantoms will be completely exhausted, and when light-forms of primal awareness arise, there will be no causal interference, in the same way that the sky remains unaffected when we throw colored powders into it. Since there is utterly no desire for, or hatred toward, material objects any more, and there is no attachment to causation or to samsara or nirvana, we develop strong trust in the inevitability of relativistic moral laws and become wise in showing them to others.

Some contemporary teachers of Dzogchen, without differentiating between formal and informal contemplation, state categorically that karmic cause and effect does not operate in Dzogchen and that that is the special characteristic of it. This is not only self-deluding but destroys the seeds of faith in others. Be careful of those who would lead us astray. Again, I repeat the famous lines of Longchenpa in *The Treasury of the Dharmadhatu*,

> Creativity projects display into another dimension,
> Where it appears as the multifarious variety of the universe.
> Never say categorically that there is no cause and effect.

Jowoje Atisha said,

> Karma exists until thought is exhausted.
> You can depend upon the maturation of your karma!

Until thoughts are exhausted, until we are free of all mental and sensory elaboration, and so long as there is dualistic perception, there is karma. From that karma sentient beings and their projected environments are established, and thereby all the various sufferings of the six realms, high and low, are inevitably endured. That is certain. Until the dualistic grasping of mind is either quickly exhausted through Dzogchen nonmeditation, or very slowly exhausted on the sutric path of Approach with Signs, which may take three countless eons, in short, until the mind is free of concepts, the abuse of karmic causality is a damnable risk.

Longchenpa says in *The Treasury of the Dharmadhatu*,

> If we vacillate, losing that essential space,
> The intellectual mind at work becomes samsara itself,

> Involving the causal concatenation that precludes resolution,
> And, inevitably, confused beings fall lower and lower.
> In the supreme secret that is Dzogchen, on the other hand,
> We never stray from intrinsic spaciousness,
> And its creative expressions naturally fall back into their source:
> This vision implies resting in immutable sameness.

So long as pure presence abides in the dharmakaya, we are untouched by karmic cause and effect because in that space there is no opportunity for the movement of dualistic thought. When we waver from pure presence, the speculative concepts that are the function of the dualistic mind tie us to samsara, and in that dualistic condition, samsara and nirvana, cause and effect, are established, and we cannot go beyond it. Unable to transcend cause and effect, clinging to things as substantially true, we are caught in the trap of samsara, and mistaken in that way, we go down to the lower realms and suffer accordingly. For that reason the supreme secret of Dzogchen yogins and yoginis is that they are never separated from the space free of conceptual elaboration. No matter what positive or negative thought arises, right from the moment of its appearance, they hang loosely, without rejecting or accepting it, in the primordially released ground of the dharmakaya. That is unwavering mind abiding in the magnificent sameness of reality, uninfluenced by karmic cause and effect, where they cannot be harmed by karmic retribution, and no matter what concepts arise, however they arise, they are all released in the matrix of the dharmakaya.

Only Dzogchen yogins and yoginis with such an understanding can boast of freedom from karma. Just as when we fall sick, we need a doctor to heal us, or when attacked by an enemy, we need to fight, or when we suffer some great loss and thus endure some acute pain—as long as we are at the mercy of circumstances, we should never say that there is no karmic cause and effect, or even consider the possibility of its absence, because we cannot hide it from ourselves. In *Entry into the Middle Way*, Chandrakirti said, "Take karmic cause and effect for granted!" Just a single erroneous thought about the validity of karmic cause and effect will bring endless negative karma. So it is imperative that we trust in the conventional law of karma and follow correctly the rejection of vice and the cultivation of virtue.

3.8 The evidence of the accomplishment of unchangeable self-beneficial pure presence is equanimity in the face of the eight worldly obsessions

In brief, although it is difficult to evaluate one's own mind, still, we cannot keep the mind secret from ourselves. Also we cannot judge the worth of our training. If our pure presence is constant, or if genuine emptiness and compassion are generated, then the evidence of that is an absence of hope regarding the four positive mundane obsessions and an absence of fear in the face of the four negative mundane obsessions. The four enjoyable mundane obsessions are taking pleasure in profit, sensory pleasure, good reputation, and praise, and the four abhorrent mundane obsessions are the loss that leads to poverty, the pain from illness and robbery, the notoriety produced by false accusation, and the blame in public for our faults or public criticism in general.

3.9 The evidence of the accomplishment of unchangeable altruistic pure presence is spontaneous compassion and reliance on the laws of karma and their results

Since beings of the six realms have not understood the nature of pure presence, internally due to dualistic perception as the cause and externally due to the five sensual pleasures as condition, so all beings from beginningless time cling to "I" and "mine," and, as in a nightmare, they suffer. For them we have compassion. Every single one of them has been a parent who cared for us lovingly. They all wish for happiness, but they are unable to find the cause of it. With all their heart, they want to avoid suffering, but they always create it for themselves and are tormented by it. They are like a crowd of the blind left in the middle of a field without any help. Compassion for them is a natural response, like a mother's instant response to her baby's cries, as if she were caught by a naked electric wire. A yogin or yogini who has realized emptiness naturally feels compassion toward confused beings from the bottom of the heart.

In his *Ketaka Commentary*, Ju Mipham has:

> In those who have realized emptiness, strenuous impulsion toward equanimity in the face of the eight worldly obsessions and effortless compassion for others arise simultaneously in the mindstream.

And in the *Ornament of the Middle Way*, the abbot Shantarakshita said,

> Toward those beings who have not understood,
> Immense compassion arises.

Then the individual who has attained the immaculate view gains immeasurably more trust in karmic cause and effect than before. The lama who shows us the natural perfection of mind is regarded as the real buddha. Compassion arises naturally for those beings who have not understood the nature of mind and that compassion is uncontrived, unfabricated, and arises together with every perception.

Furthermore, we manifest potential that we were not even aware of possessing earlier. Our reasoning is more clear, and common clairvoyance and the ability to perform miracles and so forth increase like the waxing moon and creep up on us without our being aware of it. At that time we do not need confirmation from anyone else as to whether our view is genuine or not. We can be quite sure of it ourselves. We will have lost any pride and haughtiness that we might have had on the path to nirvana. From then onward whatever acts of body, speech, and mind we perform are all naturally correct. Not a whit of any sort of desire or hatred arises toward anything, and if some gross thought of desire or hatred arises all of a sudden, it is immediately one with luminous mind, like a wave mixing again with the ocean. All thoughts will dissolve in the dharmakaya.

Remember what Sri Saraha sang,

> The ultimate wealth is contentment;
> Detachment is the ultimate pleasure.

If we are not satisfied with the wealth and reputation that we possess presently, then our dissatisfaction will be limitless. Even if we have a mountain of food in front of us, still we will feel hunger, and if we have a lake of water, still we will feel thirsty. From history we know that some rulers spent their entire lives in expanding their empire and power—Adolf Hitler, for example—but still they were not satisfied.

If we become attached to beautiful things, we will suffer either directly or indirectly. Desire and hatred are the cause of suffering right from the beginning. Unless desire and hatred can be released, there is suffering; in the same way fire, unless released, will burn the hand that holds it. Suffering ensues from attachment to our jewels, our money, and of course to our favorite child. Shakyamuni Buddha abandoned everything—his kingdom, subjects, wife, and son—and renounced the world. This was an object lesson to show that we need to abandon desire and anger, for surely he did not renounce without good reason. Likewise, Atisha, who was the son of an emperor of Bengal, abandoned all his pleasures and renounced the mundane world.

In short, it is very important that no matter what we do in body, speech, and mind, we should be free of attachment. Even regarding the activities to which we are not attached, when suddenly some happiness or suffering arises in them, be aware of it immediately and without modifying anything in any way, hang loosely in that perception, letting the mind settle into its own place, like a huge wave returning again to the ocean.

All good or bad thoughts that arise, whether happy or sad, are all creativity. Creativity is essentially pure presence and the authentic characteristic of self-arising and reflexively released conduct. We need to engage in that training of arising and liberating wherein thoughts have no previous or subsequent phase. When we have such praxis, we need not conscientiously abandon bad thoughts or cultivate good thoughts. If we realize that whatever thoughts arise are all released right from the instant of their arising, we know that such thoughts are the food of naked empty pure presence—the creativity of the dharmakaya. Even though there is no object of meditation, we are not distracted for even a second, and we are called a "meditation practitioner," although there is no meditation. Since there is nothing for us to do—we are simply looking at the essence of the thought as it arises and falls—there is no better way or easier meditation than this.

Likewise even though the way emotional affliction arises in yogins and yoginis is similar to that in ordinary beings, the manner of liberation is unique to Dzogchen yogins and yoginis. There is no need, however, to stress its superiority.

3.10 Practitioners of the lower approaches are bound by strenuous effort

Nothing that is taught in the sutras and tantras—the emptiness free of conceptual elaboration, the creative stage, fulfillment stage, the fulfillment stage with signs, energy control and yoga, and so on—goes beyond eliminating, modifying, or transforming thought. When we actually look at those lower-approach meditators, all of whom make distinctions between antidotes and what is to be rejected, we see that, from the perspective of effortless Dzogchen, they are all afflicted by the sickness of subtle striving.

No matter how profound the stages and paths of these lesser approaches, during the main practice of meditation on the view, some thoughts are sent off only to be welcomed anew, or one set of thoughts is exchanged for another. There can be no going beyond this subtle dualistic clinging to thoughts. Longchenpa, in *The Heart-Essence of Vimalamitra*, quoting the rigzin Garab Dorje, says, "Intellectual control of meditation that opens upon the view is so fatiguing!" If only our thoughts were naturally released instantaneously as they arise, like a drawing written in water, then informal contemplation itself would become the antidote to our most subtle proclivities toward dualistic perception. Conduct assimilated on the path of practice during the present period of training, which sustains the reflexive release of whatever arises during informal contemplation, is the condition of buddha—the complete identity of formal and informal contemplation.

3.11 Conduct is characterized by the three modes of release

The natural praxis of Dzogchen is to be sustained over a long period. When the first thought arises for beginner yogins and yoginis, they recognize it, just like meeting their long-lost friend. The mere arising of a thought, whether happy or sad, good or bad, occasions the recognition that it is the creativity of pure presence, that it is a subjective illusion, and that it is released as it stands. In the middle of the practice, when meditation has improved somewhat, the thought releases itself like a snake uncoiling. Whatever happiness or suffering arises in mind simultaneously releases into the matrix of pure presence, where hope does not arise with joy or fear with sorrow. Finally, when the meditation is complete, neither benefit nor detriment arises with a thought, like a thief entering an empty house—whatever negative situation arises can no longer disturb us, can have no effect upon us, and we act like children gazing at wall paintings.

Consider Serwa Gomchen, a close disciple of Yukhok Chadrel Choying Rangdol, who stayed in retreat his whole life engaged in the praxis of Dzogchen. He had five brothers, and all of them were very rich and famous in the locality. There were twenty-five people in his family including wives and children. They were a very powerful family, and in using their power, they were so envied and loathed by the local people that the people decided one day in a secret meeting to kill them all. The people would not be happy if even a single one of them remained alive, or so they said. And so it was that one night, when the entire family was gathered in their house, the people set it ablaze, and the locals waited around the blazing fire with guns, letting none of the family escape—all were killed. The next day one of the relatives of the dead family went to see Serwa Gomchen in the mountains and told him what had happened, weeping the whole time. The Gomchen enunciated the syllable "A" once, and then pretending not to have heard properly, he asked him to repeat the story. When he had heard the story again, he said, "Now a termite's nest has been destroyed!" He stayed totally relaxed, without grief or anger, and never mentioned it again. Dzogchen yogins and yoginis are that kind of person.

If we ordinary human beings are able to, we fight our enemies physically, if not, we challenge them in court. If we cannot fight them openly, we perform ritual magic and invoke the gods or naga serpents to harm them. In that way, when we face misfortune, the imperative of remaining in the Dzogchen view is forgotten, and we cannot remember even a single word of its precepts. This is because we have been unable to build confidence in the view or to sustain the meditation. If only we could make the habitual activity of body, speech, and mind into equanimous conduct, then, even though we remain ordinary beings, we would not suffer acute pain or unbearable suffering at the occurrence of any small personal reverse of fortune. There are many stories of past masters who illustrate indifference in the face of what would be for us intolerable suffering.

If we can become yogins and yoginis who no longer discriminate between good and bad, or between samsara and nirvana, then we will be released from the abyss of hope and fear. At this stage all karmic causality is constantly resolved in the basic spaciousness of alpha-purity, and there is no fault in saying that there is no karmic cause and effect. But while we are yet caught in the net of hope and fear, proud to be a Dzogchen yogin or yogini, presumptuous regarding our status, saying that there is no karmic cause and effect, acting instinctively and impulsively, doing whatever we like in body, speech, and mind, then by the force of inevitable circumstances, we will be reborn into the limitless lower realms and suffer for eons.

3.12 The Perspectives of Both Sutra and Tantra Agree in Rejecting Gross Emotivity

In short, in both sutra and tantra, gross emotion is to be abandoned. In the *Vinaya* it is said by the Buddha,

> Whatever teaching is the cause of desire, directly or indirectly, and whatever teaching is not the cause of separation from desire, that is not buddha-dharma, and it is not the discipline, and I am not its teacher. I teach what frees from desire and frees from the cause of desire and that is the vinaya.

Whether it is the sutra or the tantra approach, however it is said, it should be an antidote to desire, hatred, and ignorance. If it is not an antidote to emotion, no matter how high or deep it is, it is a false teaching. There are many skillful means or profoundly different methods in sutra and tantra to tackle emotional afflictions. If there were not, then there would be no necessity to differentiate between sutra and tantra. Concerning the manner of abandoning emotivity, in his commentary upon *Finding Comfort and Ease in Meditation*, Longchenpa says,

> In brief, reject emotivity through one's personal vows, purify it in luminous mind, and take tantra as the path: these three are one in the task of abandoning emotional affliction, just as avoiding swallowing poison, treating poison with medicine, and transmuting it by mantra are the specifics of avoiding death by poison.

Thereby, no matter what physical or vocal acts yogins and yoginis perform, they do not permit their emotivity to grow overtly gross. Avoidance, neutralization, and transmutation act as automatic antidotes to gross emotion. Such practice can define the conduct of yogins and yoginis. If we fail to transcend desire, hatred, and ignorance, no matter what method we use, we will be left with ordinary gross emotivity, samsaric karma will accumulate, and suffering will follow us like running water. So avoid boasting of high conduct and profound view and follow the *Vinaya*:

> Trust in karma and the maturation of karma and guard your vows like your eyeballs. If you do not, you will burn in the lower realms.

If we have any attachment to the experience of samsara or nirvana, suffering inevitably follows; if we are detached from those experiences, then happiness will result. This is established not only by those who have deep experience of meditation but also by our own ordinary experience. In his *Collected Fragments*, Patrul Rinpoche says,

> What we cling to, abandon,
> For attachment is the work of the devil;
> With confidence that objects of attachment are illusion,
> That all and everything is play—ganachakra feasting!

Regardless of whether attachment is to something good or something bad, if it is attachment, it is the cause of suffering. If only we could engage wealth, fame, and a youthful body without desire or attachment, we would be able to experience total temporal happiness. We would then not accumulate negative karma, and, recognizing everything as the creativity of pure presence, we would experience all sense pleasures as the play of the primordial unborn space of Samantabhadri's great happiness. In this way, we practice the yoga of constant enjoyment in the feast offering of primal awareness.

For yogins and yoginis who have confidence in the yoga of constant enjoyment, every single action of their body, speech, and mind is an offering at the feast, and there is no need to strive for the accumulation of merit or develop view, meditation, conduct, or fruition. As Jigme Lingpa says in *The Chariot of Wisdom*,

> Thoughts released into pure presence, the artificialities of view, meditation, conduct, and fruit all crumbling, regular ritual and daily religious devotions ceasing to be a burden, free of all conceptual elaboration, inseparable from luminous mind, reality is all-embracing.

This type of nonattachment to the view, meditation, and conduct is difficult for the beginner, but it is very important to carry the release of whatever arises—all the nonattached movements of body, speech, and mind—into the bed of the dharmakaya. That can be called "excellent conduct."

It is obvious that attachment to the eight worldly obsessions must be abandoned, but attachment to the vows of self discipline, the vows of a bodhisattva, and the commitments of a tantrika should also be forsaken. The latter are positive attachments and should not be rejected by ordinary people, but since such attachment is an obstruction to buddha, even such noble attachment must be cast off by Dzogchen yogins and yoginis.

Impure samsaric experience in which nonexistent illusory appearances are believed to have substantial existence and the peaceful visions of nirvana labeled immaculate: these two are mutually dependent and therefore exist as nothing other than mentally imputed experience. The word "father" is given meaning by a son, and the word "son" is validated by "father"; in the same way "the noble attachment to experience of nirvana" and "the ignoble attachment to experience of samsara" are mutually dependent in the intellect. When thoughts naturally remain in the matrix of pure presence, which is quite free of conceptual elaboration, they disappear, like mist dissolving in the sky. In that the concepts of samsara and nirvana vanish in natural, genuine, intrinsic presence, the duality of samsara and nirvana is resolved.

3.13 Infusing conduct with the six perfections

In *The Three Incisive Precepts*, Patrul Rinpoche says, "Bodhisattvas engage in socially beneficial conduct;" accordingly, Dzogchen yogins and yoginis, engaging in the informal contemplation phase of the arising and liberating of magical illusion, train themselves on the path of the six perfections but with nonattachment as the principle. Bodhisattva conduct is the training, but the Dzogchen view is fundamental and crucial.

Then, since there is no reification of anything inside or outside, there is no break in the continuity of the perfection of generosity. Since the hankering after worldly pleasures is doused, leaving no taint of vicious thoughts, there is no break in the continuity of the perfection of moral discipline. Since the egoism of Rudra is no longer affective, without anger there is no break in the continuity of the perfection of patience. In the reality of the pure presence of the dharmakaya, mind is naturally endowed with projective energy, so there is no break in the continuity of the perfection of perseverance. With freedom from the oscillation between the polarities of dualistic hope and fear, there is no break in the continuity of the perfection of concentration. Since there is no point of reference in homogenized samsara and nirvana, there is no break in the continuity of the perfection of insight [*prajña*].

Concerning the benefit of making offerings to pure-lands with an attitude of detachment, consider this story. Once in the kingdom of Varanasi a mother gave birth to a baby girl, whom she then wrapped in white cloth. When the child grew up and matured into a very beautiful girl, many kings, ministers, and wealthy men sought her hand in marriage to their sons. The girl was reluctant to commit to the life of a householder and refused all proposals of marriage. Instead, she approached the Buddha Shakyamuni, asked for ordination as a nun, and was ordained. Within only a short period after her ordination, she achieved the level of an arhat. When Ananda asked Shakyamuni the cause of her attainment, he narrated the following story:

Once, during the eon of the Buddha Sokyab, there lived a very poor couple. Every day when the Buddha taught the dharma, the king, the nobility, and the wealthy townspeople would make grand offerings to him and listen to his teaching, but the poor couple had not a mite to offer. Their sole possession was a single piece of cloth that they used as clothes in the daytime and as a blanket at night. Whoever remained behind during the day would sit covered with grass to hide his or her nakedness. One day, a group of monks wandering in town spoke of the great benefit of giving to the Buddha with generosity, and the woman heard it. Inspired by it, weeping, she asked a monk how she could make offerings to the Buddha, given her pathetic condition. The monk replied, "You make your offering to the Buddha according to your capacity. Buddha has no judgmental thought about the offerings made to him. Merit will accrue according to the gift." "I may be poor in this life," thought the woman, but if only I can accumulate merit now, I need not be so poor in the next life." And she was determined to give generously however she could. She asked the monks to wait for her, and she went to her husband to discuss it with him, telling him of the benefits of generosity and encouraging his own sense of giving. He reminded her that he had nothing hidden away and that the only thing they possessed was the cloth. They agreed to give the cloth to the Buddha and subsequently gave it to the monks. Later, in the evening, when the assembly made offerings of gold, silver, pearls, brocade, and so on, to the Buddha, the monks made an offering of the filthy piece of cloth, full of lice and nits. Buddha requested them to bring the cloth to him, and he joyfully placed it under his feet. Asked by the king for the reason, the Buddha replied, "Among the offerings of the day, the cloth of this poor couple is the best. They gave it with pure faith and without attachment or concern for name or fame. Through the power of this couple's generosity, they will take rebirth in rich families for eighty lives, and from the moment of their birth, they will be covered with white cloth. At the end of their eightieth life, they will hear the Buddha Shakyamuni's teaching, and they will attain arhatship." So impressed were the king and queen that they gave the couple each a set of clothes, and food to eat, and they became rich in that very lifetime.

The root of that couple's huge benefit was the absence of any attachment to their offering and the complete absence of expectation of any reward, particularly in terms of reputation. The generosity was pure, and within their lifetime they could see some result. Moreover, their final achievement of arhatship through the merit of generosity was due to the power of absolute nonattachment in the event of giving, with no selfish thought of any personal benefit, and quite without attachment to the gift as a material object.

Generosity, moral discipline, meditative patience, constant perseverance, equanimous concentration, insight into the empty selflessness inherent in every thought—the merit of these is the unfailing cause of the attainment of the most excellent and the very highest quality of buddha, and so we train in it.

3.14 Addiction to wealth leads to suffering

Once in the kingdom of Sravasti, India, there was a poor man called "Nyepa." He had few needs and was content with what he had. One day, by the grace of the gods, he found a precious stone. His first thought was that he would give the fortune that it represented to the poorest person in the village. Going from house to house in search of the poorest person, at last he discovered him at the palace of Selgyel, the king—for the king was the poorest of all relative to his desires, which were insatiable. Nyepa gave the stone to the king, because, as he said, the king was the poorest. But the king was unhappy with Nyepa and told him that there was no one more powerful, rich, or famous than him in the whole kingdom, so the stone should be given to someone else. Nyepa insisted that since no one in the kingdom had so little compared to his demands, it was therefore appropriate for the king to have the gem.

Nyepa and the king approached the Buddha for a pronouncement on the issue. King Selgyel narrated the entire incident and what he had said to Nyepa. The Buddha told the king exactly the same thing that Nyepa had told him. The ultimate poverty is insatiable desire, and the king's greed, being insatiable, determined that he should have the fortune. As the Buddha taught, the smaller the desire, the greater the contentment: this is crucial for this life and the next.

Consider rich people: most of them have great mental and physical hardship in accumulating their wealth, and most accumulated it without concern for their health. Their enjoyment is thereby impaired by disease or sickness, high blood pressure, or a liver problem. When the doctor tells them that they have only a short time to live, owing to the liver damage, they realize that they must leave their wealth behind, and their suffering knows no bounds. So it is. We may become rich, but look at the suffering it entails! We cannot sleep without sleeping tablets, for example, because day and night we are obsessed with increasing our wealth and protecting it. Is there any happiness or any benefit in wealth? A healthy body and mind provide much more happiness than the possession of wealth. Actually, the purpose of power and wealth is a healthy body and mind, and if sickness and stress for the sake of wealth and fame intervene, then its purpose is undone. Why, anyhow, accumulate wealth if it has to be spent on curing the sickness and recovering the lost peace of mind that its accumulation entails?

3.15 Everyone, high and low, has been a slave to attachment

It is human nature to lose our freedom through slavery to our attachments. Conversely, whosoever has no attachment is free. This is real freedom. There is no need to demonstrate in the street for political change or to litigate in court for human rights, as people do these days. What is crucial is the praxis of detachment.

In general, people have attachment to three things: money, reputation, and sex. Just look at the way we become slaves to these attachments. First, for the sake of money, we work hard day and night without resting, and our lives are fraught with tension and anxiety. Consider the way people live in big cities like New York. The speed of the traffic and the noise are overwhelming. If we examine the lifestyle closely, we find that a building bought with a down payment of six or seven hundred thousand dollars entails a payment of at least five thousand dollars a month for the following thirty years. The big car bought with a down payment is followed by regular payments of five hundred dollars a month for three years. If the monthly fee is not paid regularly, then the car will be confiscated by the company. So, without resting, the people have to work to earn large amounts of money. That makes them lose their nightly sleep and skip holiday breaks. How beautiful the external appearances, but how infinitely anxious the lifestyle! No sleep and not enough leisure to even appreciate the taste of food! Factories and businesses likewise—outer appearance is not in harmony with inner actuality.

Furthermore, although a family may eat at the same table in the same house, they don't eat at the same time. What the man eats, and when he eats, is not known by his wife. The times of the children's departure for school and their return home and the parents' departure for work and their arrival home are all different. When the children leave for school, the parents have already left home. When the parents return home late at night, the children are already fast asleep. Though they stay together in one house, they can meet only once a week. That is all because of money; it is money that so often creates the chasm between family members. Businesspeople and wage earners are all the slaves of money. Capitalism is basically money-slavery!

Second, through attachment to our reputation, we become a slave to it, and we cannot eat properly or sleep well. When life does not work out according to plan, some people commit suicide; there are many cases that could be recounted. Some die having climbed into a rocket for adventure; some die for the sake of name and fame trying to climb a mountain; some die deep down in the ocean where they dive for adventure. When someone becomes famous during his lifetime and after his death has his name carved brightly on a tall pillar, no doubt it gains attention for a few years. But after a decade or so, the person will be forgotten, and the pillar will be neglected; his name, carved upon the pillar, will be covered by moss, and weeds will obscure it. Even the statues of national heroes and heroines remain unattended, and bird droppings cover them. We can all see these things happening. Our heroes' and heroines' fame lasts for only a few years and then slowly fades away. To spend life looking for fame is to waste a precious human body as a meaningless slave to reputation. Also, consider the effect of divorce on reputation, or an abortion that must be kept secret to protect reputation. It is all meaningless. In *Entering the Way of the Bodhisattva*, the poet Shantideva says,

> Spending money to sate desire,
> Risking life for reputation,
> What is the point of that?
> Who will benefit at death?

Third, we all know the disasters that attachment to a spouse or consort has wrought throughout history. Consider the Mogul emperor Shah Jahan's madness when his queen Mumtaz Mahal died—he built the Taj Mahal. Even the great gurus suffered from this kind of attachment. The rishi Vyasa, who wrote the *Ramayana*, for example, was deeply attached to a woman of Varanasi named Kashi Koliti. Koliti's beauty was legendary, and it attracted many men. Vyasa fell under her spell and began an affair with her. Then one day the kingdom of Kashi was attacked by an enemy kingdom, and for defense the king ordered all the youth of the kingdom to dig pits about ten feet deep in a single day, find a stand-in to do the work, or pay a high fee to avoid so doing. Kashi Koliti could not afford the fine, so she searched for a substitute to do her digging for her, but she could find no one, and this made her sad. The rishi Vyasa, knowing her situation, asked her to bring him a spade and a shovel and said he would dig the pit for her. The task had to be finished before sunset, but the rishi was advanced in age, and, since it looked as if he'd not be able to complete it before the sun set, he stopped the sun in its tracks and continued with his work. The king and people of Kashi knew the time had come for sunset, but they could still see the sun in the sky. One other rishi knew the situation and guessed that it was Vyasa who had stopped the sun to accomplish his task. The king, his ministers, and all the people went to the place where the rishi Vyasa was digging, and the king paid homage to him and asked him to stop the work. The king's presence embarrassed Vyasa, so he ignored him. Rebuffed, the king found out whose work the rishi was doing and then went to see Kashi Koliti to ask her to release the rishi from his labors. Koliti sent three messengers, one after the other, to ask Vyasa to stop digging but to no avail, so she went herself, and kicking Vyasa in the head, scolded him for not heeding her messengers. Vyasa, happy that she had come to him herself, ceased his digging, and let the sun set. The moral of the tale: sexual attachment leads to sexual slavery. Look at the great rishi Vyasa who became the menial servant of the courtesan Kashi Koliti!

As the mahasiddha Saraha sings, "Wherever there is attachment, let it go!" If we wish for permanent happiness and freedom from suffering, we need to eliminate attachment—in such a way we will benefit this and future lives. If we cannot avoid attachment, looking for happiness outside while at the same time hoping for eternal happiness is like applying medicine on the skin when the disease is in the entrails.

It is important to realize that the Dzogchen view eradicates the affliction of attachment and other emotions that are the cause of suffering. If we cannot apply the Dzogchen teaching just now, we should at least walk the paths to contentment taught in the Mahayana and Vajrayana approaches; then, finally, we may engage in actual Dzogchen. If all we can do is practice the four common discursive meditations that turn the intellect back upon itself (that is, meditations on precious human body, impermanence, karmic cause and effect, and samsaric retribution) in this life, we will be more peaceful and happy. We will be free from covetousness, competition, aggression, enmity, and bad intention, and everybody will love us. We will have less sickness; when we are ill, we will recover quickly; and any serious chronic disease will not get worse. Some scientists, understanding the close relationship between body and mind, know that religious conviction can sometimes alleviate sickness. For these reasons, it is very important at all times to try to avoid both internal and external attachment.

3.16 The stupidity of suicide

These days people who are ignorant of Dzogchen and have no understanding of buddha-dharma regard suffering as real and solid. So everywhere in the world, especially in the West, some deranged individuals shoot randomly in schools, or in other public places, killing innocent people, and in the end often kill themselves. Such cases create anxiety in society, particularly, because governments are helpless to prevent such incidents. The phenomenon of random killing is caused by the frustration of an individual's personal desires and aspirations. Intense anger and hatred result, and repeated rejection and frustration may lead persons to attempt suicide by jumping off a bridge, setting themselves on fire, poisoning themselves, and so forth. But if they choose the way of random killing, in an instant, they terminate lives full of human resource and potential. The mass murder of so many innocent people, which creates sorrow and misery for so many more, is an act of great foolishness. Since the root of the act is jealousy and attachment, we must strive for nonattachment and reflexive release of any attachment as it arises.

These days some people maintain that, when their situation becomes insupportable and out of control, suicide will solve the problem. Such thinking is an attempt to escape from the suffering of past lives. About such people Sakya Pandita in his *Elegant Sayings* says,

> Although they desire only happiness,
> Fools pursue goals that bring only suffering;
> Those who are bewitched by devils
> Attempt suicide to end their pain.

People who have been bewitched by demons attempt suicide by jumping into fire or water or from a cliff top, says Sakya Pandita, adding that suicide is a grossly foolish act. People who commit suicide do not come only from the underprivileged classes. It occurs right across the social spectrum, including scholars, presidents, and famous performers, and even the wealthy. In general the cause of all these suicides is a strong attachment to belief in the real existence of happiness and suffering as externally based and in the true existence of friends and enemies.

When we cannot accomplish our aims and attain the objects of our desires, when frustration of our intentions becomes the rule, the possibility of committing suicide comes to mind. Though depression, pain, and anger are the root causes of suicide, in reality the heartfelt suffering or deep depression we endure is like the suffering that arises in a dream of the death of our beloved only son. If we compare the suffering found in waking and dreaming experience, we cannot find any difference between them. All suffering and happiness in their own nature are emptiness, but they appear in different ways. Just like a rainbow conjured by a magician, these are illusions that possess the mind and that have no true existence. So no matter what occurs in the mind, pleasure or pain, sickness or health, fame or ignominy, friend, enemy, or beloved partner, understand instantly that what we are experiencing is just an illusion without any true existence. When our relatives or parents die or we hear the story of a suicide, we need not give ourselves over to grief.

According to the Buddhist viewpoint, the karma of suicide is equal to killing the forty-two peaceful deities and fifty-eight wrathful deities that live in our bodies. Consequently, we have to suffer many eons in hell. Even though we are eventually released from hell, because of the previous action of suicide, we will tend to commit suicide many more times. In the great tantra *The Rampant Lion*, it is said,

> Whoever takes his own life
> Will suffer suicide
> In five hundred further lifetimes;
> And in this life, all kinds of suffering
> Will adventitiously occur.

In general, obtaining human birth in the human realm is very rare, and it is even more unusual to find a human birth with the possibility of hearing the buddha-dharma. In this human body it is possible to obtain liberation and buddhahood. As Shantideva said in *Entering the Way of the Bodhisattva*,

> Rely upon this human body as a boat
> To cross the great river of suffering;
> Such a boat will be difficult to find in the future.

To escape from the great ocean of birth, old age, sickness, and death, there is no better way than dependence upon the great boat of the human body. The act of putting an end to the precious human body due to adverse circumstances is very stupid. People who can satisfy their desires are very few in this world. Even people who have acquired name and fame have to protect their interests constantly, and they, least of all, attain peace. Actually no person like that is ever contented— it is much better to be satisfied and contented with just what we have.

3.17 With Detachment, the Mere Possession of Wealth and Fame Does No Harm

If we are famous or rich and yet have no attachment to anything, we will suffer neither physically nor mentally. At the beginning, suffering arises from the manner in which the wealth was accumulated, or from the way in which the fame was attained; in the middle, suffering arises from how these were protected and sustained; and at the end, suffering arises from ongoing attachment to them. Even if we possess universal wealth or fame, we will be free of suffering if we can practice nonattachment. If we are free of the root cause of suffering, which is attachment, then we can be like Indrabhuti, Dzogchen yogin and king, for whom it was possible to possess a vast kingdom full of innumerable subjects, enjoy constant sensual pleasure, and become buddha in one lifetime.

This depends on the praxis of Dzogchen and nonattachment to view and conduct. If we can sustain whatever appears as reflexive release, then we will not suffer in the process of accumulating and protecting wealth or fame. The root of this praxis is the nonattachment of pure presence to an object. If we possess such a technique, then we will have a happy family, harmony with friends, a liberal mind for every kind of situation, and intelligence enough for any task. Altruistic motivation and compassion for all beings arises in us naturally. This is reality. The sole cause of all the skillful means of the bodhisattva's way of life—the primal awareness of the nature and diversity of emanation, and the nature and manner of being of all of our experience—is the strong reflexively liberating conduct that is free of attachment and clinging.

Strong reflexively liberating conduct is the performance of the six perfections of wisdom by body, speech, and mind for the benefit of all sentient beings, with neither hope for return nor expectation of reward. There is no possibility of self-interested motivation in that conduct, for it is only for the benefit of other beings, in this life and the next. It is the nature of beings in samsara on the other hand to be self-interested and to act "altruistically" only out of that self-interest.

Once when I was in Hong Kong my patron took me to a famous restaurant for dinner. The manners of the staff in the restaurant were exemplary in courtesy from the moment we entered, on through the meal, and up to our departure. I was very impressed by their manners, and when we were leaving, I said as much to a monk who was in front of me. The monk waved toward the cash register and smilingly told me that every expression and gesture of courtesy had a price. Thinking that even such a beautiful enterprise was run on a system of quid pro quo and of expectation of reward, I was suddenly disgusted by the situation.

In the last century, I believe, families were more harmonious than they are today; there was more sharing and more courtesy among family members, and everyone had greater trust in karmic cause and effect. These days people are not so polite and benevolent, and their relationships are more self-centered in regard to the care of children, cooperation between friends, respect of children for their parents, and love between couples. "What is in it for me?" is what we think before we do anything for anybody. Our relationships thereby become simply exercises in diplomacy, which is good neither for ourselves nor others, because self-motivated love for friends, parents, children, and so forth, is not a firm and stable love. Generally, all phenomena are impermanent, and, furthermore, in this twenty-first century, every day things change drastically. If I am a person who believes in rebirth and wishes to have happiness in mind and body in this life, it is necessary for me to be benevolent. If I do not believe in rebirth, over the course of time it is impossible that my emotional afflictions—desire, hatred, and pride—will not increase. Due to this I begin to hate others and to create more suffering for everyone, myself included. If only we could all care for each other without self-interest, everything would be perfect!

3.18 Others are served best by an unselfish mind

If we have the pure intention of the compassionate luminous mind to benefit others, now or in the long run, without self-interest, it is of great benefit in this life and the next, and in this life we will be happy. As Ju Mipham says in his *Traditional Shastra*,

> A steward who is grossly selfish,
> Even if he becomes a leader
> Eventually falls, like water over a high cliff.

Even if selfish persons are appointed to a high position, due to their selfishness, they will fall so low that they will be treated as less than a human being. But again in the *Traditional Shastra*,

> A man with an altruistic mind,
> Who takes responsibility for others
> Even if at first he is a servant,
> Slowly rises up,
> Like a dragon flying up into the sky.

When we benefit others, even if we are like servants, gradually, more and more people regard us highly, and we can become leaders of men. This is the result of an altruistic mind and freedom from selfishness. So it is better to think how we can benefit others rather than how we can benefit from them. This will provide a good environment, and there will be harmony among parents, relatives, friends, countries, and so on. It can make this twenty-first-century world a happier place to live.

Consider this story of Upagupta from the *Vinaya*. There was once a woman in the city of Varanasi in India who was beautiful like a goddess, and her song and dance charmed everyone, including the king, nobles, and ministers. As time passed, she gained power and wealth, and the king and ministers happily obeyed her in her every whim. Due to her position as a courtesan, sometimes she had to sleep with them, but she herself was not interested in sex. One day, in front of the palace, she set eyes on the monk called "Upagupta" and became so attracted to him that she would watch him every day as he passed by the palace. Even though she tried for several days to attract his attention, she failed to draw even a glance. She tried many methods to pull his attention to her, but all were in vain. This only increased her interest. One day she waited for him at the crossroads, and when he came by, she invited him to visit her house for alms, but he refused her request. Her attachment grew in intensity until one day she lost control and touched him, again requesting that he visit her. The monk replied that though he had no need to visit her, he would come later. And they parted. Her attachment to him remained, but several years went by in which she was still fully engaged in her work, mesmerizing people with her dance and song. But one day she caught the dreaded disease of leprosy and, her mouth and nose being eaten away, very quickly lost her beauty. Finally her friends and relatives no longer visited her, and she found herself alone in the cremation ground, deprived of the last bit of her wealth, and there she remained. One night, when she was left with no food to eat or clothes to wear, she felt so thirsty that she cried out for water, but there was no one to hear her. She was tired of this life and so sad. Just then she heard someone approaching, a man who had come to give her water to drink, and she felt restored. She asked him who he was. "I am the monk Upagupta," came the reply. She asked him why he had not come to visit her in her youth but waited until this sad moment to see her. "In the past your beauty and charm attracted many friends, and you had no need of me," he replied. "Now there is no one to look after you, so I have come." She was touched by his affection and tears filled her eyes.

The monk Upagupta was not interested in her voice or her beauty, but later, when she was diseased, he came to visit her. The king, ministers, and others who were attached to her beauty shunned her when she lost it.

The moral of this story is that compassion and an altruistic mind free of self-interest is supreme, while self-motivated kindness generated by ego is self-destructive.

The compassionate luminous mind is without attachment and benefits all. If we are detached from the view and conduct, then steady love and compassion arise for all—for parents, relatives, friends, and whole countries—and there would be harmony in every direction.

Another story: once when a mother and daughter went to bathe in a river, they were both carried away by a sudden strong current. The daughter thought, "I don't mind dying if I could save my mother!" And the mother thought, "If I could only save my daughter, I don't mind dying!" Due to their good intentions, the gods praised them, and both of them were reborn in heaven.

Liberation and omniscience are the unfailing cause establishing the absence of self-interest that benefits others. It is impossible to attain that absence of self-interest without abiding in emptiness and sustaining the conduct of reflexive release. Ordinary beings cannot perform the conduct of the noble ones, whose actions are not mixed with self-interest. Whatever ordinary beings do, there is some self-interest involved, either directly or indirectly. Some act out of greed and some out of pride, and we can see this with our own eyes. If we have the Dzogchen view so that whatsoever appears is reflexively released, then mean or coarse emotions, such as hatred of enemies or desire for friends, will not arise. If we can meditate and practice the conduct of allowing thoughts to be liberated reflexively again and again, then subtle self-motivated thoughts will not arise later.

If we want to make some great beneficial difference to this world, first we have to sustain the conduct of reflexive release of whatever arises on the path of nondesire and nonattachment. Then to engage in the great wave of selfless action for the sake of others is a great joy.

3.19 When we know objects of attachment as delusion, the five sensory pleasures do us no harm

If at present we detach ourselves from our home, wealth, relatives, reputation, and so on, just by this detachment we will suffer less. Consider the Sahor king, Indrabhuti, who invited Padmasambhava from Sindu, adopted him as his son, and gave him royal power and five hundred beautiful princesses. Padmasambhava taught buddha-dharma to the people of Sahor, but one day, realizing that religion and politics do not mix, he decided to abandon the life of the palace. Sure that the king, his adoptive father, would object, he conceived a stratagem. In the middle of a crowded market place, he took off his clothes and, naked except for bone ornaments around his body, went dancing, holding a staff and a damaru. Coming close to a minister's son, whose reputation was particularly questionable, he pretended to trip, and his iron staff pierced the boy's body, killing him on the spot. This incident of murder was reported to the king, and in order that the law should be respected by the people in the future, he decided to punish Padmasambhava. The king knew his son well, but to pacify the people and ministers, he called a meeting to discuss how to punish him. At the meeting some suggested that he should receive capital punishment by impalement; some that he should be imprisoned; while others suggested exile. After the meeting, the king met Padmasambhava secretly and asked him which of the three punishments he preferred. Padmasambhava replied, "I have no attachment to the kingdom, so I do not fear banishment. There is neither birth nor death, so I can endure impalement. I have broken the law of the kingdom, and I prefer exile. Please don't worry, father. We have a karmic relation, and we will meet later."

Padmasambhava had no fear of horrible places infested with snakes, wild beasts, demons, and so forth, or any place of unbearable heat. Because he was fearless, he could be exiled without danger. Since birth and death are just labels, and they have no substantial existence, he was not afraid of dying.

I'll do whatever my father and mother prefer," he said. "But I would like to go to the cremation ground of Sosaling to practice tantra. I prefer to be exiled to a far-away kingdom."

The king told the assembly of ministers and people that he was going to expel Padmasambhava to the charnel ground of Sosaling. And so it came about. While he was there, he was accompanied by thousands of dakinis and performed great benefit to many men, half-men, and spirits.

Where did Padmasambhava's fearlessness of death and banishment come from? It arose from nonattachment to whatever arose and from the realization that all experience is like a drawing on water, a continuity of simultaneous self-arising and self-release.

Those great meditators and yogins unable to sustain the actions of body, speech, and mind as reflexively liberating nonreferential conduct are referred to by Patrul Rinpoche in his *The Three Incisive Precepts*,

> Knowing meditation but not release,
> Isn't that the divine trance of the gods?

When we engage in rigorous meditation with fixation of mind, we will be released from suffering for a while. But when we arise from that meditation, suffering will again follow us like a shadow. This is the fault of not knowing the manner of release.

Patrul Rinpoche says in his *Collected Fragments*,

> In short, resting completely in whatever arises, there is no need of any antidotal practice. Totally relaxed, gaze into whatever arises, and clear and pure presence will occur naturally. There is no need to ask for confirmation from outside because confirmation will arise confidently from within. This inseparable view of meditation and conduct is called "The River Flow Training of the Great Perfection."

3.20 Those with Pure Presence Are Labeled "Buddha," while the Ignorant Are "Sentient Beings"

The thick darkness of eons that enshroud the threefold world is illuminated by the sun of primal awareness in a second, and the naturally clear and self-abiding dharmakaya mind involuntarily arises. This gives us deep confidence in the difference between buddha and sentient beings. Repeating that well-known line from Longchenpa's *The Treasury of the Dharmadhatu*, "Simple recognition of the nature of being is called 'Buddha.'" Recognition of the nature of mind is buddha; in the absence of that recognition, we remain deluded "sentient beings." That is how we distinguish between buddha and sentient beings. The cause of all delusion is attachment, and the secret key of all the sutras and tantras is nonattachment, although the ways in which sutra and tantra deal with attachment are as far apart as the earth is from the sky. Further, Dzogchen goes beyond the arena of meritless people with small minds. As it is said in the tantra *Recitation of the Names of Manjushri*,

> Instantaneous alienation,
> But also instantaneous buddha!

Once the profound view is accomplished, we may attain buddha, like king Indrabhuti. If on this path we fail to fully attain buddha in this life, we will certainly have happiness while we live, and we will be certain to attain buddha in the next. This path is the source of happiness in this and in every life, so it should be everyone's path! The attainment of buddha is ultimate happiness.

In *The Dakini's Heart-Essence*, Longchenpa says,

> The difference between buddhas and sentient beings is the difference between happiness and suffering. The bliss that arises in the dharmakaya is called "buddha." Not recognizing the bliss and being stuck in the delusion of grasping at materiality is called "suffering." He who knows the joy and happiness of body, speech, and mind and the empty bliss of the dharmakaya is called "buddha." If anguished suffering and austerity is regarded as buddha, then hungry ghosts and the devils of hell are buddha. It is certain that those who are not free from suffering and are not happy are not buddha. This is an essential point.

So long as there is intellectual mind, we are caught in dualistic perception; when with no-mind we are free of that inner dualism, there is intrinsic awareness.

3.21 Three special features of intrinsic awareness

In *The Most Secret Essence of the Dakini*, Longchenpa lists:

> The secret precept not received in transmission;
> The buddha not originating in the mind;
> The result not generated by a cause.

The primordial dharmakaya Buddha Samantabhadra, who cannot be found in either samsara or nirvana, is reflexively released in self-recognition of basic pure presence beyond any need of the intervention of an external guide. The pure presence that was not known previously is not a function of the lama or the Buddha's prediction but rather it arises afresh with intrinsic awareness. Thus it is the oral instruction that is not received by transmission.

All the buddhas of the past, present, and future are primordially free of the labeling function of the intellectual mind, and, since they are free of the eight types of consciousness, they never experience delusory samsara. They recognize pure presence through reflexive release and thus they are the buddhas not originating in mind.

All experience of the external universal container and the internal lives of sentient beings depends upon negative causes and conditions derived from the habitual tendencies inherent in nominal delusion, and so, in reality, this experience is not as it appears. On the other hand, intrinsic awareness is the essence of the dharmakaya, forever untouched by the habitual tendencies emanating from nominal delusion. It does not depend as much as a hair's breadth upon the meritorious two accumulations and traversing the path of liberation. In the knowledge of basic natural perfection, pure presence is reflexively released and thus is a result not generated from a cause.

3.22 Discursive thought necessarily dissolves into basic pure presence

Until we realize that intrinsic awareness is already present, we must understand that striving to generate that awareness is a wrong path. If we wonder how effortless self-arising awareness is practiced, look at this: during formal and informal contemplation, no matter what outer object of the five senses arises and no matter what afflictive inner thought arises, at the moment of its arising sustain that space without modification, and it will release itself as it arises, just like a drawing on water. What is self-arising and self-releasing will not abide for a second moment, but will just disappear like a line drawn in water or a snake's coil unwinding. There is no need of any antidote to the dualistic perception because it releases into the dharmakaya, just as it is. In *The Three Incisive Precepts*, Patrul Rinpoche says,

> Spontaneous arising and release are incessant;
> Whatever occurs nourishes naked empty presence;
> Whatever moves is the creativity of sovereign pure being.
> It is traceless natural purity—amazing!

When thought arises, if we recognize its arising without following it, that itself is the crux of liberation, and the thought will not touch the meditation but rather intensify it. As it is said, "The more thoughts, the more dharmakaya."

In the sutra *The Pile of Jewels*, it is said,

> Kashyap, it is like this: just as the one who is protected by mantra and medicine cannot be harmed by poison, so the bodhisattva who possesses wisdom and skillful means cannot be harmed even by the poisons of emotional affliction. Poison can do no harm to those people who recite mantra, and bodhisattvas who possess wisdom cannot be deceived by emotivity. Kashyap, it is like this: The excrement of the big city is valuable for sugarcane fields and grape fields, and, Kashyap, the fertilizer of the bodhisattva's emotional affliction benefits buddha-dharma. Just as the excretion of the big city is useful as fertilizer in sugarcane fields, so the emotional afflictions of the bodhisattvas are beneficial to Buddha's teaching.

In luminous mind, emotion can be taken as an enhancement, and with the Dzogchen view, there is no need to speak more. In the tantra *The Lamp of the Three Modes*, it is said,

> In one single clear meaning, no ignorance;
> Many skillful means, no difficulty;
> With the power of a sharp mind,
> The path of tantra is best!

In that way thought helps rather than harms the yogin. As the rigzin Garab Dorje says, as quoted by Longchenpa in *The Heart-Essence of Vimalamitra*,

> In pure timeless spaciousness,
> Momentary attention to adventitious pure presence,
> Like a jewel recovered from the ocean depths,
> The dharmakaya is not created or modified by anyone.

This crux of "thought released upon its arising" is the main Cutting Through training of view and meditation combined.

3.23 Detachment from samsara, nirvana, and the path between them is the crux

The famous Indian king Ashoka ruled almost one third of India, and there has never been another like him. One day he invited his Hindu priests to the palace and asked them how he could become even more powerful and famous. The priests advised him that he had accomplished most of the things that needed to be done, but if he yearned for still greater fame, he should build ten thousand stupas and sacrifice human beings at each. The king, agreeing to this plan, went to the borders of his empire and ordered the construction of a beautiful temple. He then appointed a priest to take care of the temple, ordering him to kill any person who might visit. The priest began his duty of sacrificing the devotees who came to visit the temple, and when the number of sacrificial victims had reached five thousand, a monk, a disciple of the arhat Kriti, who had reached the stage of the path of training, happened to present himself there. The priest caught him and was about to kill him, but the monk, surprised by the priest's intention, asked him why he wanted to kill him. The priest then told him the story of the temple. After hearing this, the monk begged the priest for a week's reprieve while he stayed at the temple, and after a week, he could kill him or not, as he wished. So the priest let him go free for a week.

The monk was about to attain arhatship, and for a week, constantly absorbed in single-pointed samadhi, he did not sleep. On the morning of the last day of that week, he attained arhatship, with foreknowledge and the power of creating miracles, and he awaited the priest, who indeed came to fetch him to take him to the sacrifice. The monk submitted, offering his breast to the sword, and the priest tried hard to kill him, but the sword would not penetrate the monk's body. The sword having failed, the priest tried fire and boiling oil, but to no avail. By the end, the monk had become even more imposing than before, and the priest went off to report to the king.

King Ashoka with his many ministers came to see the monk, and the arhat showed great miracles, awakening deep devotion in all toward him. That is how king Ashoka came to embrace buddha-dharma. The arhat gave the king deep teaching, and told him particularly of the immorality of human sacrifice. The king felt remorse and asked how he should confess his misdeeds. The arhat told him that he could not tell him how to atone for his sins, but that he should visit his own teacher, the arhat Kriti, who surely knew the method.

The king went to see the arhat Kriti and told him the whole story about the temple, and, feeling deep remorse for his misdeeds, he told Kriti he wanted to make confession. Arhat Kriti told him to dig up two kilos of buddha relics from Rajgriha, build a stupa, and fill it with them.

Ashoka did as the arhat Kriti suggested. When he dug out the relics, he found a copper plate with an inscription prophesying that a poor person would be the one to dig them up and, having dug them up, would dig further. The king thought that since he was wealthy it was not his place to dig up more relics, and he went to confer with the arhat Kriti. Arhat Kriti told him that it was indeed Ashoka himself who was indicated in the inscription. To deflate the pride of such a king, a copper plate had been engraved with the mention of a poor king on it. The arhat taught him, saying, "O king! Even a huge mountain can be washed into the sea, what then of your little kingdom? So he went again to that spot and dug up more relics until he possessed a treasure trove of forty kilos, which included innumerable precious stones. Seeing those enormous riches, the king's pride diminished, and he took the relics and ordered many stupas to be constructed around his kingdom. Some historians say he built ten million stupas, but generally it is believed that he built eighty-four thousand. He also served millions of Buddhist monks, and because of his great service to buddha-dharma, it prevailed for three more centuries in India. Later, with the Hindu resurgence and the Muslim conquest of India, buddha-dharma gradually declined.

Supreme virtue is that untouched by any reference to act, agent, or object. Take the example of generosity: the act of giving can lead to nirvana and buddha only if performed without attachment to the action of giving, without attachment to the recipient, and without attachment to the gift itself. Likewise, in order to live a moral lifestyle, we should practice morality untouched by any reference to act, agent, or object. This is the root of buddha-dharma. If engaged in morality with attachment, even an otherwise pure monk cannot attain nirvana and buddha. In *Entering the Way of the Bodhisattva*, Shantideva says,

> The root of buddha-dharma is the monk,
> But the path of the monk is very difficult;
> And because of mental fixation,
> Nirvana is very difficult to attain.

If we have attachment to samsaric activity, of course we cannot attain anything, but if we have attachment to the conduct of the six perfections, which is a certain path to nirvana, we will lose our way. Due to the propensity to become attached to samsara, nirvana, and the path between them, such instruction is said to be on a lower level than the provision of sutras and tantras that teach the definitive truth, and, particularly, these lesser instructions are inferior to Dzogchen. The tendency to establish samsara as what must be rejected and nirvana as what must be attained, and to follow this, considering it a true path, is a point of temptation to be avoided on the effortless Dzogchen path. Samsara, nirvana, the path, or any reference point whatsoever, cannot help but vanish into itself, reflexively released, like a magician's illusion. This is the special Dzogchen teaching.

3.24 "Hand-holding" instruction, in short

The following is extracted from Longchenpa's *The Most Secret Essence of the Lama*:

> To sustain informal contemplation experience, first, in formal contemplation, hang loosely, relaxed, with open, natural clarity, without labeling and without any attachment to the primal awareness of naked empty presence. Without reifying the form

in the eye, the sound in the ear, the taste on the tongue, the sensation in the body, or the hosts of positive or negative thoughts in the mind—the six kinds of phenomena—with open cognition, know pure presence. Without following or running after the object, in translucence, experiencing forms that are without hope or fear, without modification or adulteration, without rejecting appearance, they are released by themselves. The mind that apprehends apparent objects is in this way reflexively released, and there is nonduality of subject and object.

The purified eye is a god's eye, without obscuration, so that, for example, walls, fences, mountains, and so on, appear transparent. The ears can hear the voices of the gods and the nagas, for instance, regardless of whether they shout or whisper. The nose has a vast range of smell, larger than the human range. The tongue without eating can taste the hundreds of tastes of concentrated absorption. The body can feel the heat of clarity and bliss and primal awareness. The mind can remember our own many lives and see those of others, and is clairvoyant. That is our conduct when all is completely undefiled.

No matter what appears in informal contemplation, the gap between meditation sessions should be understood to be like one of the eight metaphors of magical illusion; and thereby we are released from desire, hatred, and all emotional affliction. When positive or negative mental display arises, convinced that it is without root or base, neither fixate upon it nor reject it.

While the ego still has not dissolved into its inner spaciousness, meditate according to the profound instruction, abide by the law of karma, and through devotion and pure vision, do not let the notion of sin or error stain the mind. Stay alone in solitude, keeping the sutric commitments and vows. Without distraction and frivolity, depend upon renunciation. Without desire, without forming attachments, walk the path of selflessness. Keep death in mind and keep the fires of exertion burning. Day and night, consumed by meritorious activities, abandon the concerns of this life. Serve the rigzin-lama and pray devotedly to him. Remain without any ambition or goal and stay in nonac-

> tion. Abandon the distinction between oneself and others and eradicate fear and hope. Take misfortune as the path and visualize all appearances as the lama. Understanding that all experience is one's own envisionment, get rid of egoistic clinging. Since everything is without substance, sustain the joke of the absurd. Understanding primordial emptiness and adventitious emptiness, everything always arises as one's own envisionment. Through such conduct, by such means, practice day and night.
>
> So long as mental conditions allow, optimize the creativity of pure presence. Stay in a place of solitude. As long as we still make judgments and hold to them adamantly, as long as virtue and vice are still distinguishable, we must familiarize ourselves with nonduality. When there is apparent conflict, turn the argument upside down and look at inherent pure presence. When there is fear of birth and death, we familiarize ourselves with the meaning of birthlessness. In that manner all internal and external phenomena arise as dharmakaya, and we reside in the yoga of nonmeditation that is like the flow of a river.

In both sutra and tantra what needs to be abandoned are the shackles of concepts and the shackles of attachment. But their manner of doing so is different, as explained above. Some will run away from the poisonous tree, some will try to cut it at its root, and some will take its fruit as medicine. The method of Dzogchen yogins and yoginis is to allow every emotional affliction at the moment of its arising to dissolve into its own natural state of being. There is no attempt to turn the affliction into something positive or to neutralize it by application of antidotes. Over time, through familiarization with the methods of Dzogchen, whatever thought a yogin might have arises as the meditation; but from outside, from the point of view of ordinary beings, the appearance of the fear of suffering and the hope for happiness seems no different. Unlike Dzogchen yogins, ordinary people turn these into solid entities, cultivating them or rejecting them, thus accumulating karma. For the yogin or yogini, whatever appears is released in the very moment of its appearing, so there is never any opportunity to become attached to it. At first, simply by knowing the thought, it is released, just like meeting a long lost friend. In the middle, the thought releases itself, just like a snake unwinding its coil. At the end, the thought releases without help or harm, just like a thief entering an empty house. To comprehend the manner of release is crucial. If we understand the manner of release, we will be free of the bonds of a dualistic mind.

When we venture into the kingdom of gold, we will find nothing but golden stones; just so, no matter what emotionally adulterated thoughts arise, they are all just objects of meditation. Even if we look for some substantial delusions or material objects, we will not find them. At all times and in all situations the sole practice is the reflexive release of whatever arises, and, as the main practice, it is imperative to scrutinize whatever appears. The person who has such a practice is certain to be released in the bardo of this birth, the bardo of the death process, the bardo of reality, or the bardo of rebirth. And besides, we can live in harmony with our friends, relatives, parents, and all living creatures. As Dudjom Rinpoche says in *Calling the Lama from Afar*, “Whoever is friendly and happy, he is a heart-son of Padmasambhava.”

On the basis of such practice of formal contemplation and informal contemplation, the great rigzin Garab Dorje and the other seven great rigzin, the eighty great siddhas of India, Padmasambhava and the twenty-five, king and subjects, and the eighty great drubtop of Yerpa attained buddha.

4. The Attainment

4.1 The spontaneous manifestation of buddha-potential in basic pure presence

Properly establishing the view of natural perfection on the path of the natural great perfection, we rest—we hang loosely—in all-embracing primordial alpha-purity. By attesting the key point of the practice—that through reflexive release of whatever arises in informal contemplation we arrive at the one taste of formal and informal contemplation—the propensity toward dualistic appearance and its most subtle tendencies dissolve, and intrinsic awareness is revealed as timeless buddha. It is not that through engaging in the practice of meditation as the path that the nature of pure being and primal awareness of buddha, not present previously, are suddenly newly created and thereafter recreated in every moment. Rather, the adventitious obscuring concepts of mind and mental events arising with dualistic perception in the presence of naturally abiding primal awareness dissolve in their own spaciousness. At that time, the buddha-potential of basic pure presence shines forth spontaneously, and it is irrelevant whether "the nature of mind is revealed as 'buddha'" or "buddha-nature manifests in sentient beings."

In *The Treasury of the Dharmadhatu*, Longchenpa says,

> If we gain familiarity with the luminous essence,
> The luminous spontaneity of things,
> Through the key precept of nonstriving and effortlessness
> Another buddha awakens in the timeless buddha
> And that is the actuality of the peerless vajra-heart.

In the spontaneity of intrinsic awareness, arise the five dimensions of being, the five modes of primal awareness, and the rest of the twenty-five aspects of buddha-potential in fruition, manifesting naturally. Thereby, like the reflection of the moon appearing in limitless buckets of water, limitless compassion arises as the display of all beings of the six realms of the ten directions. So long as samsara exists, buddha activity fulfills the requirements of all beings according to their needs and continuously and precisely shows profound and broad physical, energetic, and mental dynamism—the movement of manifest buddha-potential. The reason for such activities is mentioned by Ju Mipham in *Beacon of Certainty*:

> This body of form, the apparent aspect,
> Protects all beings
> With its potential for happiness:
> Thus ultimately its nature is compassion.

Out of the natural uncrystallizing radiance of intrinsic awareness, the apparent aspect (the sambhogakaya and so forth, arising as the rupakaya with its major and minor marks) is itself compassionate in nature; thus through effortless spontaneity, all sentient beings gain benefit of both temporal boons and ultimate happiness so long as the world exists. As to this luminous aspect of the rupakaya: all its unbounded activities lead to the great fruition of spontaneity and impartially and continuously protect all beings, pure and impure, from all the troubles and crises of samsara.

If we speak from the perspective of the dimension of being that is the outer container and the inner awareness therein contained, those dimensions of being are classified as the dharmakaya, sambhogakaya, nirmanakaya, unchangeable vajrakaya, and the bodhikaya of manifest enlightenment. The modes of primal awareness that they contain are the awareness of spaciousness, mirrorlike awareness, awareness of equality, discriminating awareness, and all-accomplishing awareness. These many tabulations have been mentioned briefly in the section on view above. Please look at it!

In the tantra *The Supreme Source* it is said,

> All buddhas of the past
> Taught only what our own mind is;
> Keeping it just as it is, without alteration,

No discursive thought in samadhi,
A silent mind is the accomplishment.
Present and future buddhas will establish the same—
Thought-free sameness.

According to this approach, the nature of mind itself is great reflexive release right from the beginning, and the recognition of it is called "pure presence." By sustaining that recognition, with a strong impetus, we will attain buddha much faster than on other paths.

With intrinsic awareness as the ground and the four modes of freely resting [*chokzhak*] in Cutting Through as the path, if we attain constancy in confident self-expression, buddha is realized. If we take the sitting postures and fixed gazes of Direct Crossing as the path, accomplishing the four visions is the budha mode. In *The Golden Letters*, Longchenpa says

Through the manifest vision of reality,
The intellectual view dissolves;
Just as the intensity of the vision increases,
Primordial bardo awareness manifests;
As the vision of pure presence reaches optimal measure,
The sambhogakaya matures;
When the reality of appearances is consummate,
The fruition of action-free Dzogchen is attained.
If we gain perfection in the ground like that,
There is no need to look elsewhere for nirvana.

4.2 Knowing the Great Perfection: Buddha in One Lifetime!

In *The Three Incisive Precepts*, Patrul Rinpoche says,

Vision is Longchen Rabjam, the All-Pervasive Matrix;
Meditation is Khyentse Wozer, Radiance of Wisdom and Love;
Action is Gyelwai Nyugu, the Aspiring Buddha.
In the experience of such vision, meditation, and action,
Without stress or strain, we attain buddha in this lifetime.

Possessing the keys of view, meditation, and conduct, it is certain that if we do not attain buddha within this lifetime, at the worst we will attain buddha within three or seven more incarnations.

In the past, the great rigzin Garab Dorje, his disciple Jampel Shenyen, his disciple Sri Singha, his disciples Padmasambhava, Yeshe Tsogyel, and others have attained the rainbow body in Tibet, while many hundreds like Pang Mipham Gonpo, Nyelam Jangchub Gyeltsen, Nyangben Tingdzin Zangpo, and others have attained ordinary buddha. From those days until now, Direct Crossing in the great perfection has produced a rainbow body and Cutting Through has vaporized the body into invisible atoms. These manifestations have been seen in the past, will be seen in the future, and are being seen in actuality in the present on the path of the Heart-Essence of the Great Perfection.

In the tantra *The Mirror of the Heart of Vajrasattva*, it is said, "There are two kinds of nirvana: immaculate buddha and manifest immaculate buddha." Immaculate buddha is the attainment of a body of light or a rainbow body without leaving any trace. With the attainment of a manifest immaculate buddha, phenomena of light, sound, relics, body, or earth tremor occur. The great and famous Chetsun Senge Wangchuk, who gained the rainbow body, is an example of the former, and the omniscient Longchen Rabjampa, whose death was attended by many and various miraculous phenomena, is an example of the latter.

Let me speak briefly about the attainment of manifest immaculate buddha by Longchenpa: one day, after having reached the age of fifty-six without a day of sickness, while Gyelse Zopa was writing down whatever he spoke, Longchenpa made a paper tube and spoke through it into Gyelse Zopa's ear, saying, "Now I, Pema Ledrel Tsel, will stay no longer. I will go to the place of great bliss and deathlessness. The strength of my prayers, my life, and my karma is exhausted." In such a manner, he foresaw his own death. Then, in the twelfth month of that year, at Samye Chimpu, he asked Acharya Kunga Pel and others first to make a great offering of desirable objects to the triple gem and then to wait outside the room. They begged him to let them stay inside, to which he acquiesced. "I am now abandoning this apparitional body," he told them. "You all sit in silent and fearless meditation." In the tantra *The Union of Sun and Moon*, it is said, "At that time obey the instructions of the lama." Like that, Longchenpa, while sitting with the fixed gaze of the dharmakaya, was gathered into the matrix of alpha-purity and spaciousness. At that time, just as with the passing away of Shakyamuni Buddha, the virtuous gods could not bear their grief and shook the earth, and Longchenpa's body moved in accordance with the shaking of the earth, and a great cry of sorrow was heard. As for the offerings to him, a rain of flowers showered down, and tents of rainbows appeared, and furthermore there appeared many amazing signs of rainbow light and light-spots in the sky. As it is said in the tantra *The Blazing Relics*,

> There are three types of lights: first, an encircling light in the environs indicates that no matter where he has come from, he will certainly attain fruition in the first bardo; second, if the light rises straight upward, he will not go into the bardo at all but in a moment will attain buddha; third, if the light appears from his body at a tangent, he will attain enlightenment in the final bardo.

Furthermore, the sign that the internal light had been captured was that the body, surrounded and suffused by the fragrances of camphor, saffron, and sandal remained for twenty-five days without losing its radiance. A sign that his mind was released into reality was an irregularity of the four seasons and random manifestations of the elements: in the coldness of the twelfth and first months of the year, the ice melted, and leaves grew on the sewa bush. Such signs indicated that he had attained the goal of the supreme path of atiyoga: dissolution into the matrix of the Vase Body of Eternal Youth, the consummation of Dzogchen.

Four lamas, with the four tantric karmas of pacification, enrichment, control, and destruction, performed his cremation. The sign that his heart, tongue, and eyes were transformed into the *ringsel* relics of the five buddha-families was that the sounds *shariram, bariram, churiram, pancaram, nyariram* were heard just as an uncountable number of relics of the five colors as large as mustard seeds appeared. As "multiplying relics," each of them increased many times through time, as anyone can see these days, and they became the basis for accumulation of merit.

If the questions arise, "Why did the great Longchenpa not attain a body of light after he attained buddha? Why did he leave his corpse behind?" The answer is that he left his body behind so that his disciples of that lifetime—and also disciples of the future—could receive the great benefit of the "four chances of liberation." These occur first by eating the relics of the body which remain; second, by eating the salt used to pack the body after death; third, by hearing the crackle of the cremation pyre; and fourth, by voluntarily allowing the smoke of the cremation pyre to enter the nose. Read Longchenpa's biography, *Doorway of Threefold Faith*, for more details.

4.3 Contemporary stories of physical dissolution and liberation in a rainbow body

Stories such as that of Longchenpa are not found only in the distant past. Recently, on August 29, 1998, at Dome Khamngak in Azi Rong in Tibet, Khenpo Choying Rangdrol, commonly known as Khenpo Acho, eighty years of age, attained physical dissolution. Khenpo Acho was a reincarnation of Drokben Kheuchung Lotsawa, as prophesied by the spiritual head of the Nyingma school, Dudjom Jigdral Yeshe Dorje, and he was the holder of the teaching of *Vajrakilaya: The Razor Slash*. One day at noon, lying in bed, without having suffered any recent illness, while in the posture of a sleeping lion and reciting the six-syllable mantra, he attained buddha in the primordial basic matrix of alpha-purity, his heart of clear light reality perfected beyond the intellect. As his body dissolved into light, his wrinkles vanishing, he seemed like an eight-year-old child with a beautiful complexion. After a week had passed, when people came to know of his death, they performed his death puja secretly in order to deceive the authorities, and at that time, rainbows appeared inside and outside, and a pleasant aroma pervaded the place. His body gradually diminished in size, and at the end, he attained buddha; not even his nails and hair were left behind. It was just like a bird flying off from a rock—people nearby have no idea where it might have gone.

As the tantra has it, quoted in Jigme Lingpa's *Chariot of Omniscience*,

> The yogin freed, like the sun rising at dawn,
> The dharmakaya appears. Wah! Wah!

There have been many such occurrences, like that of Nyang Sherab Jungne at Pukmoche in Lhari, whose body dissolved into its subtle composite particles, like mist vanishing in the morning. Such stories are so common that it is impossible to write them all down. Through the phases of Dzogchen—the alpha-purity of Cutting Through and the spontaneity of Direct Crossing—buddha is accomplished not without cause or condition. If we train properly on this path from this time forward, we too can attain dissolution of the body into its most subtle particles, or indeed, even the rainbow body. Such assertions do not in any way denigrate buddha-dharma and do not negate common sense or inferential logic as valid means of cognition, just as scientific assertions regarding motive power, for example, do not damage actual physical traction.

Around 1960 in Derge Yelung, Mani Gaygo, Yelungpa Sonam Dorje passed away in a rainbow body, testimony about which we can still hear from some of the elders in that place. When I was residing in Kham, I went to see the house where Sonam Dorje had attained the rainbow body. I even had the opportunity of staying there for a few days. At first hand I heard from his niece and nephew how he achieved the rainbow body, and I was utterly convinced.

On the path of the alpha-purity of Cutting Through, Khenpo Acho's body dissolved into subtle particles, and on the path of the spontaneity of Direct Crossing, Yelungpa Sonam Dorje attained the rainbow body. These two are perhaps the most recent manifestations of their respective attainments. Countless rainbow bodies have appeared in India and Tibet since those of the twenty-five close disciples of Guru Rinpoche, the king Trisong Deutsen, and his twenty-four subjects. These stories can be read in *History of the Nyingma School* by either Guru Tashi or Dudjom Rinpoche.

Further, just as scientists can predict the precise course of the planets, so masters of Dzogchen can predict the time it takes to attain buddha. For example, when American scientists at NASA launched a rocket to the planet Mars, they needed to allow for the change in Mars' location during the rocket's course. It was as if the rocket were launched to the south when Mars was located in the east. Yet the scientists predicted exactly where Mars would be when the approaching rocket was ready to land upon it. They predicted to the second the exact speed of Mars—an extraordinary feat. Likewise, we can predict how long it will take on the path of Dzogchen for those of high, middling, and low acumen to attain buddha (six months, three years, and a lifetime, respectively,) and what signs will occur. Learned and accomplished masters of the past including Khenpo Acho have given us evidence of this.

5. The Four Bardos

5.1 For those of middling acumen: instruction about liberation in the bardo

If we are unable to learn through extensive study of the scriptural tradition that holds the precepts of the Dzogchen view, meditation, and action, there are simple secret Dzogchen precepts consistent with our varying constitution and powers. Such profound instruction, which is unknown in the lower tantra vehicles, can be manifested by a person who attains buddha in a single lifetime. We can read innumerable simple precepts in Omniscient Longchenpa's *The Heart-Essence of Vimalamitra*, for example. About this special Dzogchen teaching, which of course is not found in other prosaic sources, Mipham Rinpoche in his *Beacon of Certainty* says,

> It goes without saying that the special Dzogchen teaching,
> The practice of simple direct Dzogchen precepts,
> The extraordinary superior crux, broad and deep,
> Categorized as mind, space, and secret precept,
> This Dzogchen with its origin in tantra,
> Cannot be found in any other scripture.

Introducing the nature of mind in accordance with the aspiration of the individual, the way to practice with body, speech, and mind is then shown. This method is unlike ordinary tantra in which the body is visualized as a deity, speech is transformed into mantra, and mind is a samadhi, and neither is it the method of cutting attachment of body, speech, and mind directly as in outer, inner, and secret liberating *rushen* practices . Rather, it comprises the sundry precepts concerning substances, consorts, and dark retreat, for instance, which can give us buddha in one lifetime. Consider the case of the eighty-year-old Mipham Gompo to whom Bairotsana introduced pure presence over a cup of tea, providing him with a meditation belt and a chin rest, and who then attained a rainbow body and buddha.

So those who hunger for the scriptures containing the precepts of the immediate "here and now" Dzogchen but are unable to study deeply or extensively should roll over into the various secret precepts that facilitate liberation, such as those relating to the bardos.

Conventionally there are six bardos. But in the uncommon supreme Dzogchen root tantra *Beyond the Sound*, four bardos are named: the bardo of life, the bardo of the death process, the bardo of reality, and the bardo of becoming.

5.2 The bardo of life

First, if we fail to recognize the appearances of this life as they emerge from the ground of being as our own primal awareness, it is the fault of "innate ignorance." When we fail to recognize those appearances as our own envisionment due to the perception of them as "other," it is the fault of "conditioned ignorance," "the ignorance of imputation." Conditioned by the objective fields of form, sound, smell, taste, and touch, we are lost in gross concepts. Through attachment to the five aggregates (name and form, feeling, thoughts, karmic tendencies, and consciousness), we are conditioned by the verbal forms "I" and "mine," and the notions of "my son," "my parents," "my country," and so on, arise. This produces attachment to one's own side, hatred toward the other side, and a neutral feeling toward those in the middle. Such gross delusion cascades like a waterfall over a cliff face, and from beginningless samsara until now, we wander in the six realms of being. If we do not now follow the profound Dzogchen path, it is certain that we will wander continuously in this samsara. So we need to understand this bardo of life, search for a rigzin-lama as a spiritual friend, and excel in the common creative and fulfillment stages of vajrayana tantra and in the view of uncommon Dzogchen. Just as it is foolish to venture onto the island of gold without returning with gold, so having met a rigzin-lama, a rare occurrence, it would be foolish to leave him without first securing the real message of Dzogchen that can give us buddha in a single lifetime. Likewise, having attained this so-difficult-to-obtain human body with its six fortunate qualities, it is foolish not to cultivate the aspiration to use it in some meaningful way.

Furthermore, to eradicate skepticism, cynicism, or conditioned prejudice against the Dzogchen view, meditation, and conduct in this bardo of life, consider the swallow: among birds she is the most excellent nest-maker, building in the most sheltered spot where no danger from people or other animals threatens. Only when she is free of all uncertainty and doubt does the bird nestle down. Take this instruction to heart and resolve any skepticism you may feel regarding the lama's advice.

We should have the conviction of a Shenga Rinpoche as narrated in the story of his encounter with Guru Rinpoche in the section on view. Here is a similar story. There was once a yogin called "Khangkhung Lama Sampa" who, three years into his retreat, contracted a serious disease. It gave him no pain, but one day, because of his weak health, he could not move. He sent his wife to fetch his dharma friend Lama Pema. When his old friend arrived, Lama Sampa told his wife to go outside the house and asked Lama Pema to recite the prayer known as "Calling to the Lama from Afar," adding that there was no way that he could stay in his body any longer. Lama Pema began to recite the prayer melodiously and Lama Sampa raised himself a little off the pillow. Halfway through the prayer, he had his spine straight, and his hands placed in the gesture of samadhi. When the prayer was finished, Lama Sampa was dead, but his body had begun to shine, and by his expression, it seemed that he was about to speak. Lama Pema went outside to tell the wife that her husband had passed on, but she did not believe it until, at just that moment, a mass of rainbow light appeared near the doorpost. Many people saw the rainbow light, and it became a matter of common discussion. Lama Pema is still alive and continues to relate this incident.

These days science creates disturbing doubt and skeptical thought. If we have any bias regarding the natural perfection of our basic view, it is very important to eliminate it the moment it arises. There is a Tibetan saying that one wish cannot be accomplished by two minds, and another that says that there can be no stitching with a two-pointed needle. Whatever training we engage in, we must complete and perfect it. This perfection should not be assumed, as in the inferred view of the common Approach with Signs, but rather it should be perfected through our own experience. Consummate experience depends upon an authentic rigzin-lama, so we need to search for such a lama, regardless of hardship. If the lama has no realization of the nature of mind, whatever guidance he gives will be misleading, so be careful in your search for him.

Beings of the six realms are deluded in six different ways. Water, for example, is perceived as nectar by the gods, as water for drinking and cleansing by men, as a thirst-quencher by animals, as pus and blood by hungry ghosts, and as blazing fire by the devils of hell. Since it can be seen differently by different beings, we say that it has no objective substantial existence. In *Entering the Way of the Bodhisattva*, Shantideva said,

> Who creates the fields of blazing iron?
> From where do those blazing fires emerge?
> According to the Buddha,
> They are created by, and in, sinful minds.

When intrinsic presence is enveloped by dualistic perception, each class of being of the six realms sees things differently, just as a patient with jaundice might see a white-colored object, such as a conch, as yellow. In the human realm, envisionment of a life span from birth until the inevitable disease of death should be understood as a vast lying delusion. If we have some experience in Dzogchen through oral instructions given by a lama, however, then in the bardo of life, we can hold firmly to pure presence and gain release. This is of vital importance.

5.3 The Bardo of the Process of Dying

Acharya Aryadeva is quoted in *The Words of My Perfect Teacher* as saying,

> The conditions for death are very many;
> The conditions for life are very few:
> Life becomes the condition for death.

And so in this present age—to some extent due to climate change—the natural catastrophes of fire, flood, storm, and earthquake occur more than ever before. Thousands of people die at once in events that seem to occur daily.

In 1992, fifteen minutes before it was due to land at Tribhuvan airport in Kathmandu, flight TG 218 crashed into Mt. Bhatidhara. All three hundred people aboard were killed; there were no survivors. None of those three hundred passengers were aware, previously, that he or she was going to die that day. Moreover, the parents and relatives who were at the airport to meet them were left bewildered and incredulous at the news of the crash on the mountain. The remains of the plane are still there. The bodies could not be found, gone like the track of a bird vanishing in the sky. This present body cannot be trusted to continue in its existence indefinitely!

Science may have made it easier for us to travel and to live longer, but it has also created more ways to die. Such circumstances, for example, machines contrived from the four elements, have been created by the developed countries—or rather by greedy people in those countries—for short-term benefits, Through their manufacture, there is great danger that, by the end of this century, this world will have become uninhabitable by humans and animals. If we come to such a grave pass, the ways to die will be even more numerous.

Furthermore, because of subtle chemical reactions, new diseases now kill people irrespective of their gender, social status, or location on the planet. Rather than dying of natural karmic causes, people are facing death by these new diseases, weapons of war, and so on, that every day kill on a large scale. People who die in these ways are not without parents, relatives, spouse, and friends, but like us they love and are beloved, and they leave unfinished work behind them.

The time of death is uncertain; death waits for no one. It will not look to see whether the child can yet stand on its own two feet. Death comes all of sudden, like a clap of thunder in the sky above our heads. At that time, only our training can help; wealth, children, fame, and so forth, will be of no avail. All of that must be left behind. So start now and remember death and the need to engage in training of the mind. We must know about the nature of death so that in the bardo of the death process, we can successfully engage in the modes of liberation.

5.4 The actual practice in the bardo of the death process

The bardo of the death process starts when the pain of death attacks us and finishes with the cessation of our breathing. Its duration is variable.

The best of us, trusting in pure presence, will think to ourselves, "Now is the time of my certain death, and I pass into nirvana, into the matrix of simplicity," and, exhaling long and deeply, we rest in consciousness without any focus. That is the swiftest way of death, and we should practice the long and deep exhalation again and again.

When death comes to us during that last exhalation of air, yet release does not occur, if we have practiced repeatedly beforehand, we visualize pure presence as a white "A" in the heart center that shoots out from the fontanel, opening out into space. Articulating twenty-one white "A" syllables one after the other as they shoot from the heart center up and out of the crown of the head, we rest in unfocussed pure presence and gain release.

Those who possess such a key instruction as given above need not depend upon the certain and gradual threefold dissolution of the sense faculties of the body-mind and the vision of pure presence. They attain nirvana by means of the bodhisattva's method of breath transference.

Those who, when death comes to them, do not have much confidence in such instruction should know the stages and process of the threefold dissolution. But first let us consider the process of generation: during the sexual union of our father and mother, the father's white seed and the mother's red blood commingle, and, driven by the wind of karma, consciousness enters the embryo. At the outset, the elements' materiality-producing tendencies of energy, moisture, heat, and air coalesce, creating a body that emerges out of the five elements; then, by stages, the gross sensory organs—the eyes and so forth—appear.

At the end, at the time of dissolution, it is the five senses that dissolve first. Then the body separates into the five elements, and each of the five elements dissolves first into itself and then into oneself. That unity separates into its white and red elements, consciousness separates from them, and the three stages of dissolution, the three visions, occur: the effulgent light of vision, an increasing intensity of the effulgence, and the penultimate stage of dissolution.

Let us first look at the sequence of dissolution of the senses. At the time of our death, if there are lamas, monks, relatives, spouse, or friends close by, and if, when we try to hear their recitation of texts or their talk, we find them inaudible, this indicates cessation of our auditory sense. Or, perhaps, whatever is spoken cannot be heard because it seems to us as if the words come from very far away. Even though we hear some sound, we cannot make out the words. Likewise, when we look at things, we no longer see them properly, indicating cessation of our visual sense. In like fashion, our olfactory, gustatory, and tactile senses cease. This is the sequence of the loss of the external senses.

Once when I was at Yelhung, I observed the death process of a woman. She said, "What is happening? I cannot see properly." Then, she said, "Please raise the pillow a little higher," when she was trying to rise up from under the sense of a weight of earth pressing her down. I was witnessing the sequence of the dissolution of the senses and the four elements. At that time, if there is a guide available, then it is the right time for him to start. If there is someone to perform the consciousness sublimation, then it is also time for that.

In *The Superrefined Oral Instruction*, Pema Lingpa says,

> As the element earth dissolves into the water element, we feel heavy and cannot stand; as water dissolves into fire, the nose and mouth dry up; as fire dissolves into air, heat is lost; as air dissolves into consciousness, inhalation ceases but exhalation is smooth, and we will feel as if pressed down by a huge weight, engulfed in darkness, or as if thrown from a cloud: all visions approach with the sound of the whistling wind.

When our flesh dissolves into the element earth, and the element earth into the element water, we feel heavy, as if cast into a pit or pressed down by a mountain, and some people will say, "Please pull me up!" or "Raise my pillow!" When blood dissolves into the element water, and the element water into the element fire, saliva dribbles from mouth and nose. When heat is absorbed into the element fire, and the element fire into the element air, our mouth and nose dry up, and the body loses its warmth. Some people's fontanel opening leaks a dribble of liquid at that time, which indicates loss of heat. When breath dissolves into the element air, and the element air into consciousness, all subtle and gross breath is collected into the breath of life, and inhalation is difficult. The air is sent from lungs to throat and gathers there. All the blood of the body gathers in the main artery that supports life, and three drops of blood strike the heart center, and after three long exhalations, gulped inhalation ceases.

At that time the white drop received from our father runs down from the crown chakra to the heart. The sign of death is like the sky turning the color of the full moon, while internally consciousness is quite clear, and the thirty-three thoughts of aversion all cease. That is called "the effulgence of vision." Then the red drop received from the mother runs upward from the navel chakra. The sign of death is a reddish sky as if the sun is setting, while internally consciousness is blissed out, and the forty thoughts of desire cease. That is called "the optimal, or increasingly intense, effulgence of vision." Then consciousness separates from the center of the red and white drops. The sign of death is a clear reddish sky covered by darkness, while internally consciousness is thought-free, and the seven concepts of delusion cease. At that moment we are blind, and we faint away. That is called "penultimate attainment."

Then as we regain some consciousness, the clear light of basic time (which arises at the moment of conception and then again when dying), which is free from the three stages of dissolution that disturb space, is recognized, and as we rest in meditative absorption, consciousness is transferred to the supreme dharmakaya, and in buddha, one is beyond all bardos.

In actuality, when the breath stops and the father's white seed from the head and the mother's red seed from the navel mingle in the heart chakra, consciousness leaves the body simultaneously. If we lack knowledge and familiarity with this process, consciousness will faint away for a long time. Therefore, during the period of unconsciousness, tradition provides forty-nine days of the well-known rituals.

For those who have had good training, unconsciousness lasts for only a short time, and then consciousness is absorbed into space. Space is absorbed into clear light or, rather, it claims the citadel of basic pure presence, where it is released. When our breathing stops, good previous training results first in the complete sequence of effulgence of vision, optimal effulgence, and penultimate attainment, and then, with recognition of the clear light of the sameness of the ground abiding naturally in itself, we gain liberation.

If we can accomplish the view of the unmodified natural great perfection, starting from this moment to become familiar with it, by the time of death, with mastery we will pass confidently along on the swift path of Cutting Through, where pure presence and spaciousness, neither separated nor united, provide liberation into the dharmakaya of simplicity. That is what contemporary existential yogins call "*tukdam*," or the experience of clear light at the moment of death.

The following anecdote illustrates the key point of tukdam. In July 2005, at Mt. Pukmoche in Nepal, there was a great yogin known as Me Me Gyeltsen, who had stayed in retreat all his life. For several months he had had some minor sickness; then one day he asked his friends to invite Tulku Degyel Rinpoche to visit him while he was still able to greet him. They did so, and when Me Me Gyeltsen met Rinpoche, he told him that he had completed his life's work and requested him to perform the consciousness sublimation. Rinpoche reminded him that he had trained in tantra for his whole life and had met many authentic rigzin-lamas during that time, so that he did not need anyone to perform consciousness sublimation for him. "Just pray to those rigzin-lamas," he told him. "And at the time of death, don't forget to continue the yoga in the same way that you have always done in the past and that will help you." "Yes, I can induce consciousness sublimation myself," Me Me replied. The next day at around 10 o' clock a monk called "Gendun" came to visit him and talk for awhile and to make some hot porridge for him. While he was making the porridge, he heard the explosive sound of the syllable PHAT repeated thrice, and upon going inside, he saw Me Me Gyeltsen seated with a straight spine, cross-legged, repeating the syllable again four times but in a small voice. This was during the time of the Maoist insurgency in Nepal, and the Maobadi kept watch even over death ceremonies. In our neighboring villages of Yangar and Yolwang, they would come to witness a lama's death, and this time they were surprised to see the lama seated upright in cross-legged position. They gained some faith in buddha-dharma and praised the yogins who could sit cross-legged in death.

In 1959 at Golok Serta in Tibet, Dorje Dadul, the lineage-bearing heart-son of Dudjom Lingpa, sat cross-legged in the middle of the market square, stared at the sky, loudly articulated the syllable PHAT, and died. The incident was seen by many people. Tukdam, or experience of the clear light at death, is occasioned by the mingling of the clear light of mother and son. By virtue of capturing the citadel of the primordial ground of being, by virtue of attaining unchangeability on the path of the creative and fulfillment stages, and by gaining freedom from the delusions of the bardo of the death process, the immaculate sign is to be able to remain in the experience of unfabricated body-mind.

Moreover, at the instant before death, it is necessary to scrutinize the precepts as carefully as a dancer examining herself in a mirror, clarifying uncertainties. A lovely lady dressing for a party first puts on her clothes and ornaments flawlessly, then puts on her makeup, and only after checking herself in the mirror and feeling completely satisfied does she confidently leave for the party. Likewise, when we learn consciousness sublimation, first we must practice it until we are fully confident, making sure the inner and outer signs manifest accordingly. Later, when death comes to us, we apply the practice, in actuality transferring consciousness to a pure realm. Those who have confidence in consciousness sublimation are not afraid of death but rather welcome it. The mahayogin Milarepa sang,

> What we call death,
> That is a small thing for a buddha-yogin.

Born into a supreme pure-land and training in what of Dzogchen remains to be practiced, they attain perfect buddha.

5.5 Consciousness sublimation is among the five nonmeditation methods of attaining buddha

Just before the time of death, we should clarify anything still unclear regarding consciousness sublimation, like a dancing girl looking in the mirror. There are four types of consciousness sublimation: dharmakaya, sambhogakaya, and nirmanakaya consciousness sublimation, and ordinary consciousness sublimation comprising the three perceptions.

The ordinary consciousness sublimation comprising the three perceptions is to regard the central channel as the path, consciousness as the guest who moves on, and the supreme buddha-field of Sukhavati as the destination. We need to train in these three perceptions until inner and outer accomplishments manifest. When death comes, if we have been able to make our practice a part of our karma, and we are able to transfer our consciousness, we are released from the suffering of samsara and take birth in Sukhavati or some similar place in the supreme realm of nirmanakaya. The precise details of consciousness sublimation practice can be learned from Pema Lhungtok Gyatso's commentary on the *Cutting Instruction* of Dudjom Lingpa.

If we are an ordinary person with no experience of the practice of consciousness sublimation, at the time of death, we should learn the names of the eight successive buddhas (Vipasyin, Sikhin, Vishvabhu, Krakuchanda, Kanakamuni, Kasyapa, Shakyamuni, and Maitreya), the names of the eight sugatas who are the medicine buddhas, and the names of the eight bodhisattvas who were the closest heart-sons of the Buddha (Manjushri, Avalokiteshvara, Vajrapani, Kshitigarbha, Nirvaranaviskambin, Akashagarbha, Maitreya, and Samantabhadra). Simply by hearing their names during the bardo of the death process, we shall be freed from the suffering of the lower realms.

There is a story that once Sariputra recited the names of the buddhas and their mantras into the ear of a dying ox. By the power of mantra, the ox took rebirth as a Brahmin and was later ordained and received teaching from Shakyamuni Buddha himself before finally attaining arhatship. Likewise, if dharanis, mantras, and the name of a person's root lama are recited at the deathbed of a person, the dying person will obtain great benefit. This should be understood by all.

With the sequential dissolution of the senses, the four elements, and then the effulgence of vision, optimal effulgence, and penultimate attainment, we die in perfect equanimity. The mind faints away, and with consciousness regained, but purified, the light of the ground arises, and its reality is sustained. When the clear light known as "the reality of the natural creativity of pure presence" dissolves, upon its disappearance, the bardo of reality gradually dawns.

5.6 The Bardo of Reality

The present gross body that contains the ego, produced from our parents' sperm and blood, is abandoned, and the clear light of the universal visionary display arises in basic pure presence. During this bardo of reality, just as a baby totally trusts its mother while in her lap, so we should trust the instruction that our experience has not the slightest substantial existence and is in reality the envisionment of clear light. Just as a small child, unable to talk and lost in a big crowd, when later reunited with its mother, climbs confidently and unhesitatingly onto her lap, due to the closeness of their relationship, so the son clear light, which was revealed by the nonmeditation praxis introduced to us by the lama, merges with the mother clear light of unconditioned, intrinsic, basic pure presence. These two, the mother clear light that is the essence and the son clear light that is the natural creativity of envisionment in the bardo of reality, are one, like the sun and its light rays, and with that certainty, we are like the son climbing onto his mother's lap. In that instant, the propensities of the twin veils induced by dualistic perception from beginningless time are instantly purified, and we attain buddha without any bardo.

If we ask why the basic clear light arises at that time, consider that we have just become free from the corpse of gross flesh and blood, and that the eighty concepts relating to visionary effulgence, optimal effulgence, and penultimate attainment have ceased to arise. At that juncture, therefore, we are free from attachment to the mystical experiences of bliss, clarity, and no-thought. Then recollection through memory and the generator of memory that is the ground consciousness itself seem to dissolve into space, and intrinsic basic presence is utterly without limit. Here is freedom from all bias and partiality, and empty clarity, free from veiling obscuration, is now recognized as such. Resting loosely in the natural state without fabrication, we are powerfully released into the vast inner spaciousness of alpha-purity as the magnificent reality of the spontaneity of the primordially released ground of being.

If we are not released at the moment of cessation of inhalation and exhalation, when external objects normally perceptible to our senses become invisible, including our own corpse body, we must recognize the clarity of our body of light. Our field of perception consists of rainbow light rays; visionary appearances change timelessly so that the animate and inanimate objects such as earth, stone, rock, trees, forest, sun, moon, and so forth, vanish, and wherever we look, we see rainbows—all appearance dazzles with a shimmering radiance. At that time, our degree of training on the Dzogchen paths of Cutting Through and Direct Crossing determines whether or not we see those light-forms as a liberating catalyst to pure presence. Those who do not have previous experience will see it only for a moment, just like a flash of lightning. If we can sustain the visions, knowing that everything is self-envisionment, in the first moment we have trust in the insubstantiality of that envisionment; in the second, we are released as we stand; and in the third, we have seized the citadel of release. After this, there are no appearances whatsoever.

When the clear light becomes part of unitary reality, envisionment naturally dawns as the buddha-dimension of form, as forms of pure being. Peaceful deities arise from the heart center, and "wrathful deities," a dynamic dimension of envisionment, appear out of the conch-house (the cranium). Spreading into the world of bardo, their size will be unpredictable, large or small. If we do not recognize these visions as self-envisionment, then the light creates fear and the light rays and sounds create panic. If we did not understand the point of the guru's instruction, then failing to recognize the light, light rays, and the sounds, we will wander in samsara.

Furthermore, the clusters of male and female deities in union of the five buddha-families appear in direct proportion to our training on the paths of Cutting Through and Direct Crossing, and according to the length of time we can remain in concentrated absorption. The mandala assemblies of the deities of the five buddha-families appear from the first day to the fifth day. If we are unable to sustain those visions, then the visions of the four aspects of primal awareness, Vajrasattva's secret caverns, will arise.

Those who are not familiar with the Dzogchen path will be unable to recognize those visions of the bardo of reality arising out of the ground and sinking into the ground and suddenly disappearing, like the sun setting over a mountain pass. Those who have familiarity with Dzogchen may remain in that space awhile, and deep faith and devotion to the lama arising, they may evoke him. The lama may appear as the teacher of the self-envisionment that is to be recognized and thus assuaged, and may in this way show us the path of liberation and the attainment of liberation.

5.7 The Bardo of Becoming

Consciousness is moved only by wind; it is impeded only by the unchangeable alpha-purity of the vajra-seat and also by the mother's womb. We cannot be obstructed by earth, rock, mountain, tree trunks, or any other solid object—we can move through everything without hindrance. In this bardo we have a mental body that is inimical to fleshly forms or material bodies. Appearances are like dream, existing merely as labels. Through karma we can take part in incongruous and miraculous events. We can see only those various beings of the bardo similar to ourselves and other samsaric beings; and, possessing the divine eye, we know the likes and dislikes in the streams of consciousness of still-living beings on the other side.

We may hear our parents or children talking or monks reciting texts, but when we try to speak to those on the other side, they cannot hear our voices, and they do not respond. We may then think that everyone hates us, and aversion to them arises. When we are among them at the dining table, for example, no one serves us food. Neither the sun nor any other light casts our shadow. We leave no footprint in the sand and no imprint of wet feet. Gradually the realization emerges that we are dead, and deep fear and pain engulf us.

We may go to seek refuge among lamas and monks, but we discover that they are performing false rituals, their samaya vows have been broken and not repaired, and they ignore creative and fulfillment stage training. Especially when we see their avarice, we feel that they are fooling us and are the agents of the lower realms, and that we will generate only wrong views by association with them. The desire to take rebirth soon grows strong, and we search everywhere for an entrance to a womb. But until the karma of life in the bardo of becoming is exhausted, there is no possibility of finding that womb.

The vision of our death recurs every seven days, and due to the recurrence of the intense suffering of that event for the dead, the tradition insists on performing death ceremonies every week for seven weeks. At that time, we hear the four fearful sounds—rumbling landslide, billowing ocean, blazing fire, and cyclonic storm. The three poisons (hatred, desire, and jealousy) appear as an abyss of embodiment, and we feel intolerable panic at the prospect of falling into it. Feelings toward the embodiment of consciousness, with its impulsions, conceptualization, and name and form are all felt to be of the nature of intense suffering. Existence blown by the winds of karma, without an earth, is like a feather blown by the breeze.

Consciousness, fickle and misty, is seven times clearer and more alert than before, so that the seven weeks of the bardo seem very long. During the first three weeks, our previous bodily form is sustained, and we behave in much the same way as before, but even that is unpredictable. When we are sitting down, we suddenly feel as if we must move, and when we are happy, sudden panic attacks may afflict us, or we may have other such unpredictable experiences.

After the third week, we experience the particular behavior of beings in the realm in which we are going to take rebirth. If we are to be reborn as a pigeon, for example, we feel the beak, wings, and talons of the pigeon. Sometimes we feel we have half the previous life's body and half of the next life's body.

The signs of rebirth in each of the six realms are as follows: if we are going to take birth as a god or a man, we will hold our heads high and gaze upward; if we are going to take birth as a demon or animal, we feel an inclination to look sideways or to the side; if we are going to take birth as a hell-being or hungry ghost, then we cast our eyes downward.

The color signs are as follows: inclining toward hell, we see black light and a burnt tree stump; toward the hungry ghost realm, we see wafting black wool; toward the animal realm, we see an ocean of blood; toward the human realm, we see white light; toward the demonic realm, green light; and toward the god realm, white light about a meter in length. We should recognize these signs immediately for what they are and understand our destiny, and without suppressing this knowledge, and recognizing the place of our putative rebirth, the dharmakaya is revealed as the pure presence that abides in the ground of being. With our confidence in pure presence, the basic clear light and the primordial alpha-purity of the dharmakaya appear to us again, and through these indications, which are like the material for repairing a broken irrigation ditch so that the water flows smoothly, we gain liberation.

Just as in the miracle of instantly reaching a place by the mere thought of going there, those who can see the door of the Dzogchen view will understand the bardo consciousness and will recollect the pure fields of nirmanakaya emanation of the ten directions. With a strong aspiration to be in those fields, the tendency to remain in the bardo existence dissolves, and as we enter the flow of blessings of true reality, the pressure to reincarnate is released, and taking birth in a pure-land, we attain buddha.

The rituals of the Perfect Completion of Life [*gongdzok*] to be performed each week after the death are highly efficacious and must be done regularly and punctually. The wise men of ancient days made the bardo of becoming a special method of benefiting sentient beings by inviting a rigzin-lama trained in the creation and completion yogas to create the mandala of wrathful and peaceful deities. He calls the consciousness of the deceased into a name card and burns it, and then bestowing empowerment, providing an introduction to the nature of mind, and indicating the path, he impels consciousness toward a pure-land. This is of great benefit to the deceased. Just as we can lead a wild horse into a cul-de-sac ravine by the reins, in the same way, when devoted disciples who have kept their commitments are in the bardo, a rigzin-lama can confidently lead them to safety. In the story of Dzogchen Mingyur Namkha Dorje, merely by guiding his disciple Nyak Kepon Shar by means of the wrathful and peaceful deities, he released him from the lower realms into the human realm. If within the fourth day, we can release consciousness from its place, it is of vital benefit to the deceased.

If the lama performs the *sur* offering ritual along with the *tsok* feast offerings and butter lamp offering, the deceased will obtain food, drink, and clothing in the bardo and again benefit will ensue. Consider the example of the beneficial effects of a single sur offering rite. Once a group of Yilung men ventured out on a trading expedition to Golok, and, after a protracted period, their families heard that they had been robbed and killed by Golok bandits on the road. They invited Gyarong Pontrul Rinpoche to perform the prayers for the deceased, and Rinpoche performed a sur rite. One person in the group of traders, however, had escaped the fate of his friends and was returning home despite the many difficulties of hunger, thirst, and bitter cold. When he reached the high Changtang plateau, all of a sudden he smelled burned sweet tsampa, and instantly he lost all his hunger and thirst. When he reached home, he saw Rinpoche and his monks performing the sur rite, and he realized where the smell of tsampa had come from. His family was amazed at the effectiveness of Rinpoche's ritual.

Moreover, the power of visualization and recitation of mantra by a lama generates the compassionate attitude and a special samadhi for the deceased, and the deceased will thus be released from the illusion of fear in the bardo and will take rebirth in the nirmanakaya buddha-fields of Great Bliss (Sukhavati), in the buddha-field of the Copper-Colored Mountain, or somewhere like that. Even if the deceased is unaffected in that way, he or she will temporarily take birth in a higher realm and finally attain nirvana or super-nirvana. So it is essential to perform the seven weekly sur rites after the death of our mother or father, along with protection and offering rites, as much as we can.

The stages of instruction about the four bardos are now completed. The purpose of explaining the four bardos after the detailed explanation of the main Dzogchen praxis of view, meditation, conduct, and fruition is clarified by Longchenpa in *The Treasury of the Dharmadhatu*,

> These modes of being defy goal-directed endeavor;
> They shine only while freely resting in the spontaneity of the now.
> This supreme secret is disclosing itself in this moment,
> And since we shall not be lured away from it, even in the bardo,
> This apex approach of the vajra-heart
> Towers, exalted, above all progressive, graduated approaches.

This explanation of the stages of the four bardos in this fifth chapter is an addendum to the main practice of Cutting Through to alpha-purity in Dzogchen. Its stages accord with the various intellectual needs of those who cannot gain immediate or direct release on the path. This step-by-step instruction on the four bardos benefits the student—Dzogchen has many powerful, efficacious, skillful means of instruction.

If we fully assimilate this Dzogchen teaching, for the best of us, all subjective envisionment in this life will vanish into the matrix of reality, and we will accomplish the dimension of great transference and the rainbow body as did the rigzin Garab Dorje and Guru Tsokye Dorje. For those of lesser acumen, it is vital that, at the time of death in the bardo, we should recognize the three lights—effulgence, optimal effulgence, and penultimate attainment. Then, practicing consciousness sublimation, we can take birth in the pure-lands of the trikaya. In the bardo of reality, we should not be afraid of the sound, lights, and rays of the assembly of wrathful and peaceful deities, but directly recognize our naked self-envisionment as the natural creativity of pure presence. Like a child nestling into its mother's lap, the clear light that we have recognized through the lama's introduction unites with the basic clear light, and we are released into the ground of being. If we have not been able to use any of these three opportunities to gain release, finally, when we enter the bardo of becoming, if we can be sure that whatever appears is delusion and if we remember our present root guru, Amitabha, and the others, then, by the power of a single-pointed devotional prayer to be sublimated to the nirmanakaya pure-lands, we can overcome all the sufferings of that bardo of becoming. This advice is of crucial importance, so keep it in mind.

Furthermore, in order that we should not waste this precious human body, first, we should accumulate merit by practicing the four discursive meditations that turn the intellect back upon itself: meditations upon the precious human body, the impermanence of life, karmic cause and effect, and inexorable karmic retribution. Then, through the preliminary practices of the five "hundred-thousand" exercises and the graduated practice of the unique tantric teaching, we should obtain buddha in this lifetime, relying on the same supreme practice as the great masters of the past.

If people who have great interest in buddha-dharma in general and in Dzogchen in particular would exert a little effort right now, not only might they take rebirth in a pure-land in the next life, but they might attain buddha in this very lifetime. Just look at the condition of people in the world today! The stress of competition day and night among people with wealth, fame, and power, like the roaring of thunder and lightning in a thick cloud, seems to preclude the possibility of happiness and peace of mind. This body-mind has limited capacity, and if we go beyond that limit, then bodily pain, stress, and tension inevitably arise, and modern illnesses such as depression and so forth, leading to insanity and even death can result. Depending upon Dzogchen, to the contrary, the body remains relaxed, and all emotional stress is immediately resolved. Dzogchen praxis is like the universal panacea that solves everything that we consider to be a problem and takes the sting out of every vicious event, so that the essence of happiness is pure pleasure and harmony among family, friends, partners, and the community. Nothing is better than a life spent happily in harmony with all. If only for that reason, I urge you all to practice the dharma.

Author's Colophon

I HAVE WRITTEN THIS book after repeated requests from my two Taiwanese disciples, Shen Yee-Yun (Yeshe Dolma) and Lui Shenli. Great benefit would accrue, they assured me, if I would publish a book that contains everything that I have taught them. My Singaporean disciple, Hui Sheun, added his request to theirs. I have composed it at Pal Dagmar Namkha Kyungdzong monastery, in Nepal, far from the madding crowd but close to Mount Kailash, the Palace of Chakrasamvara, the chief power place in Tibet.

To repay my mother for enduring the suffering of pregnancy
I could not but make good use of my time in this world;
So seeking also to repay the lifelong offerings of others,
I offer this book now to all the peoples of the world.

Remembering the gratitude I owe to my glorious lamas,
So that their precious instruction should not be wasted,
Through the merit acquired by this work,
May it become a necklace adorning youth,
May Buddhism flourish, and may all beings benefit.

Selected Glossary

English equivalents of technical Dzogchen Tibetan terms:

alpha-purity	ka dag
basic pure presence	gzhi rig
buddha	sangs rgyas (pa)
buddha-potential	yon tan
calm-abiding meditation	zhi gnas (Skt. shamata)
carefree, free of convention	bya bral
certain, predictable, unequivocal	nges pa
creativity	rtsal
display	rol pa
emotional affliction	nyon mongs
envisionment	rang snang
Great Perfection	Dzogchen
insight meditation	lhag mthong (Skt. vipasyana)
intrinsic awareness	rang byung ye shes
intrinsic creativity, self-expression	rang rtsal
intrinsic creativity of pure presence	rig rtsal
intrinsic presence	rang rig
luminous mind	byang chub sems (Skt. bodhichitta)
matrix	klong

ornamentation	rgyan
primal awareness	ye shes
pure being and primal awareness	sku dang ye shes
pure presence	rig pa
space (existential)	ngang
spontaneity	lhun grub
trikaya, the three dimensions of being	sku gsum
truly existing, substantial existence	grub
unpredictable, uncertain, equivocal	ma nges pa

Works Cited

Sutras

The Amitabha Sutra
'Od mdo
Amitabha-sutra

Ananda's Sutra
Kun dga' bo'i mdo

Avatamsaka Sutra
Mdo sde phal po che

Awareness of the Moment of Death
'Phags pa 'da' ga ye she kyi mdo
Atajnananama-sutra

The Explanatory Sutra of Interdependent Origination
Rten cing 'brel bar byung 'ba'i don bshad pa'i mdo
Pratityasamutpada-sutra

Gandavyuha Sutra
Sdong po bskod pa'i mdo

The Great Matrix Perfection of Wisdom Sutra in One Hundred Thousand Verses
Yum chen mo stong phrag brgya pa
Aryaprajnaparamita-sanchayagata-sutra

The Heart Sutra
Shes rab snying po'i mdo
Prajnaparamita-hrdaya-sutra

The Inexhaustible Mind
Blo gros mi zad pa'i mdo
Aksayamati-nirdesa-sutra

The King of Samadhi Sutra
Ting nge 'dzin gyi rgyal po'i mdo
Samadhiraja-sutra

Lankavatara Sutra
Lang kar gshegs pa'i mdo

The Medium Matrix Perfection of Wisdom Sutra in Eight Thousand Verses
Yum bar ma brgyad stong pa
Astasahasrika-prajnaparamita-sutra

The Pile of Jewels
Dkon mchog brtsegs pa'i mdo
Ratnakuta-sutra

The Sutra of Individual Liberation
So sor thar pa'i mdo
Pratimoksa-sutra

The Teaching of the Noble Youth "Incredible Light"
Phags pa Khye'u snang ba bsam gyi mi khyab pa bstan pa'i mdo
Sanskrit title unlocated

Vinaya
'Dul ba lung

Tantras

Tantras in the Kangyur

Hevajra Tantra
Rgyud rtags gnyis

Recitation of the Names of Manjushri
Manjusrinamasangiti
'Jam dpal mtshan brjod

Nyingma Gyubum Tantras

Beyond the Sound
Sgra thal gyur rgyud

The Blazing Relics
Sku gdung ’bar ba’i rgyud

The Compendium of Pure Presence
Kun ’dus rig pa’i rgyud

The Discourse of the General Assembly
Mdo dgongs pa ’dus pa, ’Dus pa’i mdo

The Essential Heruka Tantra
Heruka gal po’i rgyud

The Lamp of Immaculate View
Lta ba yang dag sgron me’i rgyud

The Lamp of the Three Modes
Tshul gsum sgron me’i rgyud

Magnificent Unelaborated Clear Meaning
Spros bral don gsal chen mo’i rgyud

Meditation upon the Luminous Mind
Byang chub sems kyi sgom pa

The Mirror of the Heart of Vajrasattva
Rdo rje sems dpa’ snying gi me long gi rgyud

The Rampant Lion
Sen ge rtsal rdzogs kyi chen po’i rgyud

The Secret Core
Rgyud gsang ba snying po’i rgyud
Guhyagarbha-tantra

The Secret Core: Illusory Display
Sgyu ’phrul gsang snying

The Source of Sacred Samadhi
Ting ’dzin dam pa’i le’u

The Supreme Source
Kun byed rgyal po'i rgyud

The Tantra of Perfect Creativity
Rtsal rdzogs pa'i rgyud

The Union of Sun and Moon
Nyi zla kha sbyor rgyud

Sanskrit Treatises and Commentaries

Asanga
The Thirty Stanzas
Sum cu pa
Trimsika-karika

Atisha
The Lamp of the Path
Lam gyi sgron ma
Bodhipatapradipam

Chandrakirti
Entry into the Middle Way
Dbu ma la 'jug pa
Madhyamakavatara

Maitreya
The Supreme Tantra
Rgyud bla ma bstan bcos
Uttaratantra

Nagarjuna
In Praise of the Dharmadhatu
Chos dbying bstod pa
Dharmadhatustapa

The Root Stanzas of the Middle Way
Dbu ma rtsa ba'i shes rab
Prajna-mulamadhyamaka-karikas

Padmasambhava
In Union with Buddha
Sangs rgyas mnyam byor

Saraha
Dohakosa

Shantarakshita
Ornament of the Middle Way
Dbu ma rgyan
Madhyamakalamkara-karika

Shantideva
Entering the Way of the Bodhisattva
Spyod 'jug
Bodhicaryavatara

Tibetan Treatises

Sba gsal snang
The Samye Chronicles
Sba bshed

Botrul Dongak Tenpai Nyima (Bod sprul mdo sngag bstan pa'i nyi ma)
Analysis of View and Doctrine
Lta grub shan 'byed

Dilgo Khyentse Rinpoche (Dil go mkhyen brtse)
Oral commentary on Garab Dorje's *The Three Incisive Precepts*

Drubchen Pema Dewai Gyelpo (Grub chen pad ma bde ba'i gyal po)
The Rampant Lion
Sen ge rtsal rdzogs

Dudjom Lingpa (Bdud 'joms gling pa)
Cutting Instruction
Gcod pa'i khrid

Dudjom Rinpoche (Bdud 'joms 'jig bral ye she rdo rje)
Aspiration on the Gradual Path of the Wrathful Dakini
Khro ma'i lam rim smon lam

Calling the Lama from Afar: Spontaneously Calling to the Lama from Afar in Song
Bla ma rgyang 'bod gnyug ma'i thol glu

The Dakini's Heart-Essence: A Manual
Mkha' 'gro thugs thig khrid yig

Heart-Essence of the Dakini
Mkha' 'gro thugs thig

History of the Nyingma School
Chos byung lha dbang gyul rgyal

The Intrinsic Nature of Being
Gnas lugs rang byung

Lifeblood of the Mountain Retreat
Ri chos dmar khrid

Vajrakilaya: The Razor Slash
Phur ba spu gri reg phung

Gendun Chophel (Dge 'dun chos 'phel)
A Collection of Elegant Verses
Snyan rtsom 'thor bu

An Ornament of Nagarjuna's Mind
Klu sgrub dgongs rgyan

Guru Tashi (Gu ru bkra shis)
History of the Nyingma School
Chos byung ngo mtshar gtam gyi rol mtsho

Jigme Lingpa ('Jigs med gling pa)
Autobiography
Legs byas yongs 'du'i snye ma

The Chariot of Omniscience
Rnam mkhyen shing rta

Ju Mipham ('Ju Mi pham)
The Aspiration of Ground, Path, and Fruit
Gzhi lam 'bras bu smon lam

Beacon of Certainty
Nges shes gron me

Ketaka Commentary (upon the ninth chapter of the *Bodhicaryavatara*)
Sher grel ke ta ka

Reply to Refutation
Brgal len nyid byed snang ba

Traditional Shastra
Lugs kyi bstan bcos

Voice of Vajra Awareness
'Jam dpal rdzogs pa chen po'i smon lam

Karma Lingpa (Karma gling pa)
Liberation by Hearing in the Bardo
(*The Tibetan Book of the Dead*)
Bar do thos grol

Lakla Chodrup (Glag bla chos grub)
Doorway of Threefold Faith
Rnam thar dad pa gsum kyi 'jug ngogs

Longchen Rabjampa (Klong chen rab 'byams pa)
Collected Fragments
Gsung thor bu

The Dakini's Heart-Essence
Mkha' 'gro snying thig

Finding Comfort and Ease in Meditation
Bsam gtan ngal so

The Golden Letters
Gser yig can

The Heart-Essence of Vimalamitra
Bi ma snying thig

The Most Secret Essence of the Dakini
Mkha' 'gro yang thig

The Most Secret Essence of the Lama
Bla ma yang thig

The Treasury of Natural Perfection
Gnas lugs mdzod

The Treasury of the Dharmadhatu
Chos dbyings mdzod

The Treasury of the Supreme Approach
Theg mchog mdzod

The Wish-Fulfilling Treasury
Yid bzhin mdzod

Milarepa (Jetsun Mi la ras pa)
Songbook
Mgur 'bum

Ngari Panchen (Nga ri Pandita Pema dbyang kyi rgyal po)
Ascertaining the Three Vows
Sdom sgum rnam nges

Ngulchu Tokme (Dngul chu thog med)
The Thirty-Seven Practices of the Bodhisattva
Rgyal sras lag len so bdun ma

Orgyen Lingpa ('O rgyan gling pa)
The Chronicles of Padmasambhava
Pad ma bka' thang

Patrul Rinpoche (Dpal sprul rin po che)
Collected Fragments
Gsung thor bu

Exhortation to Read the Seven Treasuries
Mdzod bdun blta bar bskul ba

The Three Incisive Precepts
Tshig gsum gnad brdegs

The Words of My Perfect Teacher
Kun bzang bla ma'i shal lung

Pema Lhungtok Gyatso (Padma lung rtogs rgya mtsho)
Commentary on "The Cutting Instruction"
Gcod khrid grel ba

Pema Lingpa (Padma gling pa)
The Superrefined Oral Instruction
Gdam ngag mar gyi yang shun

Rongzompa Mahapandita (Je Rong zom chos kyi bzang po)
Applying the Mahayana Method
Theg chen tshul 'jug pa

Great Memorandum of View
Lta ba'i brjed byang chen mo

Sakya Pandita
Elegant Sayings of Sakya Pandita
Sa skya legs bshad

Sakya Zangpo (Sa skya bzang po)
The Legend of the Great Stupa of Boudhanath
Bya rung kha shor lo rgyus

Shabkhar Lama (Shabs dkar bla ma tshogs drug rang grol)
Flight of the Garuda
Mkha' lding shogs bslabs

Totshun Drubje (Mtho tshun grub rje)
Extraordinary Exalted Praise
Khyad par 'phags bstod